a *good*
life

And we are put on earth

A little space

That we may learn

To bear the beams of love.

William Blake

The strategies offered in this book are provided for the general guidance and benefit of the reader. This book provides information. It does not provide legal advice.

The information contained in the book is accurate at the date of publishing. However, we recommend that readers contact their own professional advisor or consultant when planning to implement any strategies. This will ensure the latest available information is taken into consideration and matched with the individual's or family's circumstances.

PLAN – Planned Lifetime Advocacy Network
101B – 3790 Canada Way
Burnaby, BC V5G 1G4
Phone 604.439.9566   *Fax* 604.439.7001
Web site http://www.plan.ca   *E-mail* planned_lifetime@telus.net

This book uses the term "disability" to refer to those challenges, conditions, circumstances, handicaps, and impairments that limit the functional ability of people. As is common in most publications of this kind, the person is the focus, the disability secondary.

Canadian Cataloguing in Publication Data

Etmanski, Al, 1947 –
A good life

ISBN 0-9680462-1-5

1. Handicapped–Family relationships. 2. Handicapped–Social networks.
3. Estate planning.   I. Title.
HV1568.E85 2000   362.4'043   C00-910104-7

Design and production by Working Design

Printed in Canada

a good life

For you
and your relative
with a disability

Al Etmanski

PLANNED LIFETIME ADVOCACY NETWORK (PLAN)

To my parents, Walter and Margaret Etmanski,
who endowed me with a good life
and to my wife Vickie and children
Catherine, Elizabeth, Lina, Theressa, and Joel,
who continue to bless it.

Acknowledgments

I thought about and wrote this book while continuing my responsibilities as Executive Director of Planned Lifetime Advocacy Network. I thank David Cohen, Sharon DiSanto, Jacinta Eni, Brian Follett, Ken Gordon, Gerry Hodgson, Clarke Jackson, Ed Kaufman, Ted Kuntz, Joan Lawrence, Arthur Mudry, Madeleine Nelson, Caroline Nickel, Alexis Pidlisecky, Pat Richards, Ruth Sherk, Pat Tesan, Ryver Tupper, and Chuck and Gordon Walker for their encouragement and the pleasure of their company.

In particular I thank Peter Bogardus, Vickie Cammack, Jack Collins, Theressa Etmanski, Mary Hamilton, Bonnie Sherr Klein, Richard Steckel, Joanne Taylor, Doug Walls, and Dave Wetherow for contributing, reviewing, and significantly improving the manuscript.

Kris Klaasen's gifted design undoubtedly attracted you to the cover and encouraged you to dwell on the presentation inside. The skillful editing of the unflappable Gayla Reid ensured clarity and continuity. Together they treat you to an effect beyond comparison with my original material.

The people who inhabit this book are the source for its personality and the motivation for writing it. I pray I got it right.

This book could not have been written without the moral and financial support of Katharine Pearson and Tim Brodhead of the J.W. McConnell Family Foundation, Bob Williams, VanCity Credit Union, Dave Driscoll of the VanCity Community Foundation, and Richard Mulcaster and Valerie Hunter of the Vancouver Foundation.

A special thank you to Erica and Cindy Frostad whose image on the cover personifies the joy and vibrancy of our work at PLAN.

Finally, Vickie Cammack and Jack Collins continue to inspire me. As co-founders of PLAN we operate as a trinity – everything I have learned can be attributed to our free rein and our connection. I just happened to be the one with the word processor this time. Our work at PLAN can only be described as an act of love and this book is the latest manifestation.

PLAN™
for a good life

contents

preface

Dear reader

The world is like a
big round ball.
What bounces
the world?
LIZ ETMANSKI

this is not your typical book about people with disabilities. Rather it is a gentle nudge into a new way of thinking. *A Good Life* offers a very different perspective about what is truly important when contemplating the future of people with disabilities. *A Good Life* catapults over the traditional supports and services available to most people with disabilities and suggests another approach.

Trying to write about a good life is as elusive as trying to live it. Our own experience is far from complete and our maturing has been anything but smooth. The mystery of what constitutes a good life has provoked and stimulated people for centuries. We enter the discussion without pretense and without prescription, but with a strong faith that families and friends can begin a new conversation about what will provide for the well being, safety and security of our loved ones who have a disability. This is a conversation that looks beyond contemporary social and rehabilitation services and programs to support our family members.

In many ways this is not even a book about disability. It is a book about discovering a good life for ourselves. One of the gifts of having a relative with a disability is the gift of insight about the true meaning of life – our life. More and more families across North America view their worry and concern about the future of their relatives with a disability as both a practical challenge and a metaphor. A metaphor for coming to terms with matters of life and death for themselves.

We write as parents who have a family member with a disability. We also write as founders of a unique civic organization that has struck a resonant chord with families everywhere.

We must cultivate our garden.
VOLTAIRE

Planned Lifetime Advocacy Network (PLAN) is nestled in a community near the beautiful city of Vancouver on the northwest coast of North America. We have been struggling for over twelve years with the challenges of creating a safe and secure future for our own sons and daughters with disabilities when we die. That perspective and those experiences shape this book. We want to liberate you from the misplaced faith contemporary society places in the social service system. We offer our stories in the hope they stimulate your imagination and change your dreams.

We are not interested in reforming the social service system and its institutions. Instead, we want to create a different approach – an approach that relegates the social service system to the background. In the decisions you and your relative make as you create a safe and secure future with them, you will likely find that the social service system and its institutions play a supplementary role.

We want to create a new team – a team that places your relative, their friends, neighbors and family at the heart of the solution. We want to create a new question. Instead of, "What variety of services and programs will my relative need?" the question becomes, "What is a good life?"

Some readers will be familiar with our earlier work, *Safe and Secure – Six Steps to Creating a Personal Future Plan for People with Disabilities*. You will recognize *A Good Life* as a larger, expanded and more mature version of our first book. The themes have been enhanced and the steps expanded. The stories represent the harvest of the past dozen years. We are proud of their splendor and variety.

We realize and expect you will apply what we have to say

with modification, reservation, and qualification. We have adapted and adjusted our work with families in response to a myriad of influences. We pass our stories on to you expecting they will be continued in the same manner.

A good life may be a mystery but it is a delicious mystery. It's not the kind of mystery that can't be solved, but a mystery that must be approached with the heart and soul, not just the head. It is a mystery best approached with curiosity and openness, not logic and certainty. In the approach we will merge with fellow travelers who are there for a variety of reasons but with the same motivation. And we will most certainly encounter a path, well worn and ancient. The path of pilgrims. The way home.

Yours sincerely

Al Etmanski

Love is not enough

Our purpose

1. To inspire you to develop a Personal Future Plan with your loved one.

2. To guide you through the process.

3. To offer practical tips and technical advice.

4. To connect you with other families.

5. To improve the present.

there are at least two emotions that inspired you to pick up this book. The first is love. The second is fear. We know this because we experience them too, as do the hundreds of parents of children with disabilities we have met over the years. You are definitely not alone.

Like everyone else, you want to die with your affairs in order. You want to leave a clear blueprint of your wishes for your relative. You know that your death will be a time of great emotional stress – you want to minimize the trauma. You also want to provide a secure future for those who survive you, especially your son or daughter with a disability.

That's the voice of love speaking.

Nevertheless, over 50 per cent of North Americans die without a will. Most of the other 50 per cent of us haven't reviewed and updated our will in the last five years.

That's the voice of fear speaking.

So let's get right down to it. In matters of future planning, love is not enough. That's one of the main reasons this book has been written.

We want to do five things:

1 We want to motivate, inspire, and challenge you:

- to begin and complete the future planning process with your relative, and in so doing
- to replace fear of the future with faith in the future.

2 We want to guide you through the process of creating a "Personal Future Plan" for your relative with a disability. We want to expand your vision of the possibilities and to help you make them realities.

3 We want to shed light on the legal, financial, and technical solutions available to assist you to carry out your wishes, and to share practical tips on how to apply these solutions to your unique circumstances.

4 We want to introduce you to families who have the same doubts and difficulties as you have. They yearn for peace of mind about the future of their relative with

Warning: Lives in Progress

This book is written from the parent perspective because that is who we are. The corollary is obvious. We are not writing from the perspective of an individual with a disability. Our membership in the parent group will occasionally collide with membership in our sons' and daughters' group. This sometimes causes conflict with individual and human rights advocates and with service providers. We are not attempting to diminish individual rights and self-determination for people with disabilities, particularly for our loved ones. These issues get much fuzzier, however, when you are a parent.

A Good Life is a book about the future of your loved one whose life has been shaped by their disability. People do have disabilities. Unfortunately, the disability tends to define their lives out of proportion to who they are or could be. Yet we have written a book about

disability. We recognize the contradiction. We hope you recognize our ambivalence as you encounter the term in this book.

We realize that words by themselves cannot create a good life. The phrase, "a good life," is one that has been used in a myriad of ways. We know that a good life is not the equivalent of "the lives of the rich and famous." A good life is more subjective than that; it is more of an attitude. To us it has a lot to do with appreciating who one already is and what one already has. On a good day we do experience some clarity about a good life. On the bad days we are at least as bewildered as anyone else.

Those are all the major warnings we can think of. We offer the rest of these pages in the hope that enough light has filtered through.

a disability and they have formed an organization (Planned Lifetime Advocacy Network) to help each other and other interested families. They do not have all the answers. They continue to learn. But they are passionate and committed to new ways of thinking and acting on their hopes and fears.

5 We want to show you that planning for the future is one of the best ways to improve the present.

What we believe

An act of courage

Planning for the future when you have a son or daughter with a disability means planning to let go.

Pay off is now

Planning for the future is one of the best ways to improve your relative's life in the present.

We believe that planning for the future of your son or daughter is a courageous act because in effect you are planning to let go of your child. Forget all the studies about what distinguishes families who have relatives with disabilities. The single defining distinction is that we must plan to let them go. Parents of typical children don't have to – their children do it for them.

That's what makes it so hard.

We believe in families. We believe in your initiative, your dedication, your creativity, your tenacity, and your commitment. We believe that your wishes, dreams, and desires for your relative can shape the future. We believe in a world of possibilities. We believe in the capacity of communities. We believe that if you are willing to commit to the process of future planning outlined in this book, then the chances are increased that that will be the future your relative will have.

This book allows you to look over the shoulders of families like yours. In this book you will meet people who are breathing life into their dreams right now. They are giving shape to a brighter future for themselves and their relatives with disabilities. While the details of their plans may be different, the issues they are confronting are remarkably similar to yours.

Another belief of ours is that this book can help. Its contents have already helped thousands of families.

A Good Life will provide you with an overview of a whole

complete planning process for your relative. There are no single answers, no single solutions, and no miracles. In fact, some of the solutions will never look perfect. Do not worry about the term Personal Future Plan. We had to call it something. In fact it is more a process than a plan. We apologize for its redundancy, and while we are at it, we apologize to the stockbrokers. Besides, it is just a mixture of old-fashioned common sense, commitment, hard work, and a dash of bravado.

So enjoy, cry, laugh, create.

It is like solving a mystery

Ring the bells
that still can ring
Forget your
perfect offering
There's a crack
in everything
That's how the
light gets in.
LEONARD COHEN

The French theologian and philosopher Gabriel Marcel makes a distinction between mystery and problem. He suggests that a mystery is a problem in which you are involved. A problem, on the other hand, is a mystery reduced to something objective – once that happens, someone else can solve it and you don't even have to be part of the solution.

Developing a plan for the future welfare of your relative with a disability is like solving a mystery – one of your life's mysteries. It is not a problem for someone else to resolve, nor is it something to attack with a boilerplate solution. It is your mystery. It is your relative's mystery. It is your family's mystery.

Many of us never really take the time to sit down and discuss what our future intentions are for our relative with a disability. Nevertheless it does come up. Maybe it surfaces when you are driving home from a family gathering. Maybe one of your children mentions something in passing, but the topic quickly changes. Maybe you wake up in the middle of the night and decide that this time you're going to talk about it in the morning. Then you don't.

So many thoughts, ideas, and worries go rolling around in your head. You can hardly remember them all. How could you expect someone else to? There are so many confusing messages and so many complications. The need for resolution lurks just beneath the surface, emerging at the most unexpected times.

Sound familiar? That's our experience, too. We have all felt overwhelmed by the seemingly endless bits and pieces of advice about what we must do to prepare for our child's future.

However, PLAN's work with families over the past twelve years has shown us that the process is not as complicated as it first appears. We have found that it is in fact a simple mystery.

A Personal Future Plan is like a labyrinth

Almost every tradition has some form of walking meditation associated with a labyrinth. In the medieval Christian tradition, labyrinths were laid in stone inside many of the great churches, including the cathedral at Chartres. After a hiatus of hundreds of years, Grace Cathedral in San Francisco and St. Paul's Church in Vancouver have reintroduced the labyrinth for prayer and meditation.

One of the great gifts of the labyrinth is that you don't have to follow it in any particular way. There is only one path but there are many ways to walk it.

The Rev. Dr. Lauren Artress, creator of the labyrinth project at Grace Cathedral, speaks of walking the labyrinth in a manner that reflects the experience of families who follow the seven steps of our future planning process:

"Walking the labyrinth is a spiritual discipline that invites us to trust the path, to surrender to the many turns our lives take, and to walk through the confusion, the fear, the anger, and the grief that we cannot avoid. . . . We can ask for guidance and pray for ourselves and our loved ones. It calms the confused mind, the chaotic, fearful heart. It allows us to release all that is in our way of relating to the Divine: our hard-heartedness, our judgments, and our impatience. While walking the labyrinth, the healing power of gratitude often visits the heart."

A Personal Future Plan
Seven steps to a safe and secure future

We are convinced that there are only a few key elements you need to focus on. We have combined these elements into what we call a Personal Future Plan. That is what this book is about. It is what we advise you to develop with your relative.

A Personal Future Plan is a seven-step process that families follow to create a safe and secure future for their family members with disabilities. It includes the best of your experiences, your dreams, your wishes for the future, and your knowledge and expertise. It combines all of these with the active involvement of your relative with a disability, other members of your family, and a few knowledgeable professionals.

It is a plan that you create, control, and direct. It is focused on the here and now. It is also geared to a time when you will no longer be around.

Our seven steps are as follows:

STEP ONE	**Sharing Your Vision**
STEP TWO	**Building Relationships**
STEP THREE	Creating a Home
STEP FOUR	Making a Contribution
STEP FIVE	Ensuring Choices
STEP SIX	Developing Your Will and Estate Plan
STEP SEVEN	Securing Your Plan

How to use this book

After you have read Step One: Sharing Your Vision, we suggest you skim through this book until you come to a section you'd like to work on. Once you've decided to focus on one section, answer all the questions and complete all the worksheets. You'll be surprised how the questions in one section will lead directly into the concerns of another section. Each one informs and guides the other. Before you know it, your planning will be complete and you'll have a record of your intentions—all contained in this book.

This book will allow you to be an informed consumer of the professional services that are available in the "future planning industry." We define this industry as those firms, financial institutions, non-profits and government departments that offer advice, products, programs and services intent on taking uncertainty and worry out of the future. By following the steps presented here, you will be better prepared, use fewer professional services, and save yourself time and money. Most importantly, you will have peace of mind.

We invite you to customize this book to your needs. Add your own personal data, photos, records, medical information, etc. Keep this book in a safe place. You should never underestimate how valuable this information will be to your survivors. Think of it as your manuscript to the future.

One last reminder: things go better with families. What you will read in these pages has been mined from the insights, wisdom, and experience of literally thousands of

This book is for you if:

- You have concerns about the future of your relative with a disability.
- You do not have a will.
- Your will has not been updated in the past three years.
- You think there is something more to life than social service programs.
- Your relative is lonely, bored, and isolated.
- Your relative needs help making decisions.
- You wonder what will happen when you are gone.
- You would like to be inspired.
- You would like to have peace of mind.
- You would like to improve your relative's life right now.

families we have met and worked with over the past twelve years. We could never have written this book without them. They could never have written their Personal Future Plan without each other. That is a simple fact. It is also the beauty and the strength of the family-based disability movement. We are an association of families who are both good problem-solvers and good shareholders. We have much to learn from each other and much to share.

As you begin to work on a unique plan for your relative's future, we encourage you to seek out other families and problem-solve together. PLAN is a splendid testimony to the fact that things do go better with families.

sharing *your* vision

When I dare to be powerful –
to use my strength in the service of
my vision, then it becomes less and
less important whether I am afraid.

Audre Lorde

Rick's chances were down to one

George Hall's life is a paradox. Like that popular movie of the 80's, George has gone "back to the future."

"My wife and I always felt we should deal with Rick's future ourselves," says George. "Yet seven months before she died my wife said, 'We still haven't done anything about Rick.' She worried about it to the day she died."

George's story is a familiar one to parents raising children with disabilities just after the Second World War.

"After Rick's birth, my wife and I – well, mainly my wife – focused our time and energies on raising Rick. There wasn't an infant development program then, you know. A bunch of us parents got together. We helped each other. We started a school for Rick and others like him in the basement of one of the local churches. Nothing fancy, mind you. And we raised the money to hire the teachers and buy the supplies. Eventually we got the government to take the school over.

"I was involved in the local association from 1961 to 1971. For a time I was on the provincial board as well.

"I remember back in the seventies, someone proposed a Lifetime Friendship Plan to the provincial association. The idea was to pay for friends to look in on the disabled person after their parents died. You see, parents have always been concerned about their child's future. We used to talk about it all the time. What would happen if one or both of us were run over by a car? I used to phone the provincial association periodically to see if there were any new developments. There never were.

"Then my wife took ill and matters really came to a head. We did have our will prepared during that time and we arranged with a trust company to manage the money we left in Rick's trust.

"Still my wife kept saying, 'Isn't there something else we can do?'"

After George's wife died, he was devastated. "As you can imagine it was a terribly painful time. Normally I'm a pretty optimistic person but I confess there were days when my dreams for Rick turned into nightmares.

"I knew I had to do something. Somehow the plans my wife and I had put in place didn't seem adequate now that she was gone. I figured Rick's chances were down to one."

continued on page 16

step one
Sharing your vision

Our convictions

There is a future.

Whatever you decide
can be changed.

You will proceed faster by
starting than by stalling.

An imperfect plan is better
than no plan at all.

Family and friends are the heart
of the matter.

Money, trusts, and wills
are simply tools.

Safety and happiness for your
relative is the goal.

You won't run out of gas.

You will get through it.

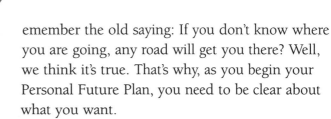

remember the old saying: If you don't know where you are going, any road will get you there? Well, we think it's true. That's why, as you begin your Personal Future Plan, you need to be clear about what you want.

What are you trying to achieve for your child or relative? What are your goals? What do you want to preserve? To prevent? What do you want people to know when they gather around to discuss your wishes after you have gone?

Without clear answers to these questions, the rest of your planning will be cloudy and incomplete. Knowing what you want to achieve is the first step to creating a Personal Future Plan.

We have found that families embarking on this process think they should first be paying attention to the technical solutions. In reality, ninety per cent of the planning time should be spent identifying what you are trying to achieve, thinking through your goals and objectives, and clarifying your vision. It's like the preparation you must do before you begin to paint. Once your vision is clear, you will be in a better position to evaluate the various options available. Then the technical solutions, such as increasing the value of your estate, choosing your trustee, and finding the precise legal clauses, will follow. Then, and only then, should you seek the advice of professionals.

Think of your last plane ride. Did you ask the pilot where you should go? Of course not. You made that decision first.

GEORGE'S STORY
continued from page 14

This haunted George. Finally in March 1988 he made one of his periodic calls to the provincial association. This time they had an answer. They mentioned an ad hoc committee called the Senior Parents Network and suggested he might want to look into it. The Senior Parents Network was simply a group of parents in similar situations. Their common bond was their willingness to search for an answer to this question: "If we were to die tomorrow, what would happen to our mentally handicapped child?"

George found an instant solidarity with these parents. Their worries were the same as his. Their questions were no different from the ones on his mind.

George liked their honesty. He enjoyed their candor and humor. They were in league together. Parents helping parents.

That motivation led this group of senior parents to mount an international search to discover how parents elsewhere were confronting the challenge of creating a secure future for people with disabilities. They collected material from Canada, United States, Australia, New Zealand, and England.

They discovered that conditions for people with disabilities were universal. Institutions were closing. Government financial support for services was either in decline or threatened. Health care was being rationed in some areas. Formal monitoring was non-existent in most places. Services and programs had their limitations. They didn't provide much opportunity for friendship. Many people with disabilities remained lonely and isolated.

In response, parents elsewhere had begun to create new organizations, which they called advocacy trusts or continuity foundations. These were usually non-profit organizations, family financed and directed. They were dedicated to protecting the quality of life of people with disabilities after their parents became infirm or died. George and the others took the best of what existed elsewhere and spent the next five years developing the Planned Lifetime Advocacy Network (PLAN) organization.

George was so impressed by the thoroughness of the review that he became a founding board member of PLAN. He agreed with their philosophy – family control, self-sufficiency through member contributions, entrepreneurial fund raising, and independence from government. As parents who had been promised many miracles during the life of their child with

continued on page 18

Worksheets

Four worksheets are located at the end of this chapter, starting on page 34. Take a look at them now, and plan to fill them out when you're ready to begin developing a Personal Future Plan.

WORKSHEET 1 **After You're Gone: Sharing Your Vision** provides you with a list of questions you can use to create your vision.

WORKSHEET 2 **A Family Portrait** provides an important record of your relative's family experiences.

WORKSHEET 3 **A Letter to the Future** should contain your wishes and worries – your direction, in as much as that's possible, for the future. If writing isn't your cup of tea, get out a tape recorder or videotape and dictate your letter to the future.

WORKSHEET 4 **Parent Contract** This contract with yourself commits you to the process of developing a Personal Future Plan.

> The first duty of love is to listen.
> PAUL TILLICH

Then you examined the options available to you around scheduling, service, price, and so on. That's the most effective way to utilize the services of professionals in the future planning business. The good ones will give you the same advice; they don't want to be making the decisions for you. Knowing what you want saves them time and you money.

What is a vision?

Visions are creations of the heart as well as of the head. Angeles Arrien, a cross-cultural anthropologist from California, says that visionaries make the truth visible. Visions are about embracing the unknown, your nightmares as well as your lofty aspirations, without embarrassment or self-consciousness. Therefore visions are not about editing, withholding, or pleasing others. They are about authenticity and truthfulness. They are about diving deep and surfacing.

> All cultures respect the importance of vision and its capacity to magnetize, or open up, the creative spirit.
> ANGELES ARRIEN

The enemy of vision is denial. Denial means we see things only as we or others want to see them rather than accepting them as they really are. Denial means avoiding issues, people, or circumstances. Denial means hoping not to disturb the status quo and trying to maintain harmony. Denial means

GEORGE'S STORY
continued from page 16

a disability, they were careful not to promise any.

   They had two assets. One was their wisdom. They liked to joke that their past
mistakes had created enough scar tissue
to make them clever. It had given them
good instincts. Now they could smell the
mistakes coming a mile away. Their second asset was the interest and enthusiasm of a younger generation of parents
who had joined forces with them. By this
time the Senior Parents Personal Network
had become a fully fledged society, PLAN,
open to parents of all ages. The generation gap that has the potential to divide
had been bridged.

   As George said, "I had always felt a bit
uncomfortable with the younger parents I
met. They seemed so naive. I felt they
were in for the same big surprise we
experienced when our kids got older. Most
people think kids are cute and want to
help, but they fall by the wayside when
our kids become adults. And I suppose
they saw me as an old fuddy-duddy. I
realize now, we have so much in common.
PLAN has given us the opportunity to
work together. With their energy and our
wisdom, no one can stop us now."

cutting weeds off at the stem, knowing full well that the tenacious roots are still there.

A vision is your description of a desired future for your child or relative. A vision is about passion – your passion for the future safety, security, and well being of your relative. That's why it's so important to address the dreams as well as the nightmares. Both are keys to unlocked passion. It is the tension between them that forms the boundaries of the vision you are creating. A vision is not only a photograph or moving picture of what you want. It is also a picture of what you don't want.

A clear statement of your vision will help focus your attention. Since a vision reflects your values, your traditions, and your family history, it creates a personality for the other components of a good life you and others are creating with your relative.

I've dreamt in my life dreams that have stayed with me ever after, and changed my ideas; they've gone through and through me, like wine through water, and altered the color of my mind.
EMILY BRONTË

Sharing your vision – from best to good

What will happen to our sons and daughters when we die? What's best for them? Those two questions started it all. In fact, we formed an organization to pursue the answers. And that search led us to another question, What is a good life?

Clarifying and sharing your vision:

- makes you involve your relative
- helps you see your relative in a different light
- encourages you to involve other members of your family
- allows others who become involved with your relative to better understand what's at stake
- helps you discriminate between preferred and undesirable results
- suggests new opportunities
- paves a pathway for moving forward
- provides a basis for people (including other family members) to work together
- reduces anxiety
- shares the challenge
- creates results

Vision Quest

The great French philosopher and mystic Simone Weil defined prayer as "absolute attention." This holds true for vision. Developing a vision requires focus. It is about reviving and reviewing your dreams. It is about realignment. It is about taking stock. This is not typical work or practice and requires a special focus.

Families report that the following are helpful in their quest for a vision:

- Spend quiet time each day. Expand into the silence.

- Go for a walk on a regular basis.

- Try to set aside an extended period of time each year for solitude.

- Keep a journal.

- Draw inspiration from nature.

- Practice some form of meditation and contemplation.

- Listen to music, sing, and dance.

- Reserve time to simply enjoy your family.

- Savor a good bottle of wine.

I have spread my dreams under your feet; Tread softly because you tread on my dreams.
WILLIAM BUTLER YEATS

When we focus on the answer to what is best for our relative, it may be hard to disentangle our views from those of the professionals, service providers, and advocates we are associated with. Their thinking has become our thinking and vice versa. We may think the answer involves only programs and services. We are all products of the limited view that has gained momentum world-wide since the Second World War – that professional intervention through services and advocacy is the most effective way to deliver support and caring.

However, the answer changes radically when we ask, What is a good life for our son or daughter with a disability, and indeed for ourselves? Changing the context invites the spiritual, poetic, and philosophical. Our hopes might include such phrases as "a life of meaning," or "a life of passion and contribution."

We think this is a better place to start than asking, "What services and programs will our relative need?"

Naturally the meaning of these terms will manifest themselves differently for each person. As parents, we quickly learn our job is not to dictate what they will mean, but simply to provide a nurturing framework for a unique and individualized process of development.

We think the search for a good life provides a nurturing framework for discovering what is best for people with disabilities. In fact, what's best for our relative with a disability should be what's best for each of us.

"Oh great," you say. "At least the disability experienced by my relative gave me a place to start. Now I must try to understand the unfolding of the universe."

Well, why not?

We're convinced that unless we ask new questions we are in danger of slipping into old answers. A new way of thinking about our sons and daughters with disabilities must embrace the questions, What gives meaning to life? What *is* a good life?

As we have explored new ways of supporting our relatives with disabilities, we have concluded that the following elements are the basic building blocks to creating a safe, secure and enriched life not only for our relatives with disabilities but also for ourselves. They are not guarantees of a good life, but they are certainly pre-requisites. The elements are:

- Caring and loving relationships (Fellowship)
- A place of one's own (Home)
- Making a contribution (Meaning)
- Directing your own life (Choice)
- Basic financial security (Wealth)

Take the test yourself. In the autumn of your life would you want these five elements to be present? Would you want any of them to be taken away from you? What would happen if any one of them were missing?

Dreams shape reality.
JUDITH SNOW

Just because a thing is inconceivable doesn't mean it's impossible.
LEWIS CARROLL

It wasn't raining when Noah built the ark.
HOWARD RUFF

So what are we afraid of?

Before we go any further, we need to discuss why so many people don't prepare adequately for the future. What keeps so many of us from formalizing our future wishes for our survivors? What causes our paralysis? Why don't we act?

Fear.

Fear is an intriguing emotion. Fear distorts our perception and confuses us about what is going on and about what is possible. When, for example, we use words such as "cannot," "ought to," "if only," and "impossible," we are under the influence of fear. Fear draws a dark and cold curtain between our intentions and our actions. Like any school-yard bully, its appearance is deceiving. It's more imposing in our minds than in reality.

In our own personal struggles with the issues of future planning and in our work with families, we can identify five "school-yard bullies" that everyone must summon the courage to confront. We offer them here because we believe that where there is clarity, there is comfort. Where there is understanding, denial ends and change occurs.

Fear of change

Vision shapes reality when it is:

- Based on dreams.
- Shared with others.
- Made concrete.

It has become popular to claim we live in an era of change unrivaled by any other period of history. People in fourteenth century Europe had to deal with the 100 Years War, the Black Plague, and the shift from feudalism to the tentative beginnings of the nation state, not to mention the competing claimants to the papacy and marauding bands of mercenaries in between several crusades. In other words, change is a natural albeit stressful fact of life, regardless of era.

Change, any change, shakes our world up. It disturbs the status quo and can be threatening. Whether we view change with fear and dread or with excitement and anticipation, we know deep down we cannot go back. Many of us try. We have a few hiding places ourselves. As my mom used to say,

> It is better to act yourself into a new way of thinking than to think yourself into a new way of acting.
>
> HENRY EMERSON FOSDICK

Keys to a good life

- Fellowship
- Home
- Contribution
- Choice
- Wealth

Creating a vision requires

- tolerating confusion and ambivalence
- living with chaos
- keeping your sense of humor
- nurturing your intuition
- reserving time to visualize
- confronting your fears
- harnessing your passion

change is welcomed only by babies with wet diapers.

There is certainly a lot of change going on right now. A little greeting card that plays "Happy Birthday" carries more computer power than room-sized computers of the early 60s. That is bound to have an impact comparable to the transition from horse and buggy to automobile. And in the midst of our culture's raft trip on the rapids of change, we have our own special whirlpool of turbulence in the life of our family: to begin planning, we have to change; and the process of change in turn precipitates even more change.

Our encounters with change require us to be open-hearted and clear-sighted, to trust our competency and to understand the future is ours to direct, not control.

Fear of dreaming

Creating a vision requires a conscious type of dreaming which may reconnect us with painful events and experiences. The first realization that our child has a disability may twist our stomach, squeeze our heart, and paralyze our dreams. It rebounds for decades. The shards of pain, confusion, and terror infiltrate our flesh, our senses, and our spirit. More damage is done to our softness and innocence than we realize.

The dreams we had, once suspended, are not easily recalled and certainly not without sadness. Over time we may stop dreaming them.

Creating a vision means confronting the dream of the elusive "perfect child" that was snatched from us, and replacing it with a new dream. It means seeing the possible, seeing the good hidden away in the disappointment, setbacks, aches and longings. It means rekindling hope, faith, and innocence.

We had to do the same for our other children. They did not follow the script as we first imagined either.

At the same time, let us not forget our relative with a disability, who may be struggling with the challenge of dreaming for the first time. Too often we have met people with the handicap of never having dreamed. Imagine that. All their lives others have spoken for them and determined what they were thinking and feeling. There was no space for dreams, no encouragement. So none were cultivated.

As we begin this process, let us remember that our friends and family members with a disability may be dealing with the anxiety of a new experience, of dreaming for the first time.

Fear of opening up

Sharing your future plan means discussing intensely personal and private matters with others. Sharing your vision is sharing something sacred.

This is unfamiliar territory for many of us – opening up with family members, friends or acquaintances, and professionals. We may need to contact people we think are not interested in our relative. Or we may not know which professionals to turn to or trust.

We've grown up in a culture that promotes self-sufficiency. We've taken our obligations seriously. We've done the best we can. We've tried all our lives to make sure others wouldn't have to shoulder our responsibilities. Now we have to break that mold and conduct our lives in an unaccustomed fashion.

Opening up also means courting rejection. Sharing one's

> A vision needs spiritual energy compatible with the scale of the vision in order to sustain the vision through to action.
> JACQUES DUFRESNE

Qualities of an Olympic athlete: Not just physical ability

The success of a great athlete is dependent not just on physical ability. In fact many people with superior athletic ability fail to achieve success. Successful athletes must also have qualities that we all need:

Vision The ability to see, taste and feel themselves making the jump, kicking past other racers in the final lap, imagining themselves on the podium, head bent to receive a medal. . .

Tenacity The first to arrive, the last to leave practice. Steadfastness and determination.

Social support Support and nurturing from friends and family (more about this in Step Two).

Look on each day as
if it were your last
And each unlooked for
hour will seem a boon.
HORACE

private and intensely personal hopes and fears is risky business. It is possible we may be ignored or worse, rejected and ridiculed. We may be put in a very vulnerable position. We may be turned down. People may not tread softly.

With future planning we have to share our hopes, our dreams, our fears and anxieties with others.

We are obliged:

- to ask others to help us with our planning.

- to ask others to carry out our wishes after we are gone.

- to trust others to believe in the possibilities for the future of our children.

Memento mori

At PLAN I am often called upon to describe our work. Over the years I've written hundreds of variations on the theme of supporting families to prepare a safe and secure future for their relative. Certain patterns develop and an outsider would be hard pressed to time date my comments. Until recently, that is.

Preparing yet another proposal, I began with my usual narration. To my astonishment, the writing continued, "and we assist parents prepare for their own deaths."

An unknown hand had taken over momentarily. A bold unfamiliar hand. One that seemed arrogant and pretentious.

That was my immediate reaction.

I think differently now.

The Tibetan Book of Living and Dying observes: "There is no greater gift of charity you can give than helping a person to die well." It took me years to acknowledge it, but that's what we do at PLAN. Our gift involves helping people embrace the mystery of faith in other human beings. "Letting go" in this way is a prerequisite for setting up a personal future plan. We have found that the accompanying peace of mind can give people the freedom to live well and to die well.

During the seventeenth century, artists would often finish their paintings with a miniature skull in one corner. The image was called a "memento mori," which means, "remember, you must die." The intention was to remind the viewer of the transitory nature of life.

Stephen Levine's popular book *You Have Twelve Months to Live* attempts to do the same. It shows how a close call with death or a terminal diagnosis may give us the freedom to live more intensely, to appreciate the precious nature of each moment.

In a less dramatic way, PLAN plays a role in helping people prepare for their own deaths. You won't see a tiny Baroque skull on our literature. But you might see the occasional reference to "memento mori." In other words, "remember you must die."

To do this, we need to reach out. After all, what good are your plans if no one else knows about them? We need to know whom we can rely on. Sure, they could read about your wishes in your will. But will the readers get the complete picture? Will they know what you really want? What if they have questions? How can you be sure you will be understood? Will they understand your passion? Wouldn't it be better to involve them now?

Fear of death

Death is not a popular topic in our society. Even a cursory look at the popular media suggests that our culture is obsessed with youth, living forever, and avoiding sickness and infirmity. Articles appear regularly in the mainstream media. One New Age guru even claims proper body/mind discipline will enable us to live forever. An illusion is offered: you can cheat death. While it may not be stated, the implicit message is that diet, exercise, and medical intervention will keep us "forever young" or "forever alive." As Margaret Mead said, "When people are born we rejoice, and when they're married we celebrate, but when they die we try to pretend nothing has happened."

We may believe that others have fewer anxieties about death than we do. Rest assured the fear is there for all of us. It lurks just beneath the surface, never deep enough to be quite ignored. Perhaps it presents as anxiety, perhaps as an awful sense of impermanence, perhaps as loneliness. For younger parents in particular, thinking about death can seem a kind of perversity.

However, death is a natural part of life which we all have to face sooner or later, and which we cannot overcome. We believe that with effort, the mind can convert death into something useful. The Dalai Lama says there are two ways we can choose to deal with the prospect of our death: we can ignore it or we can confront it. By confronting it, we can bring consolation to others and grow in wisdom ourselves.

Those who lose
dreaming are lost.
AUSTRALIAN ABORIGINAL PROVERB

He who has learned how
to die has unlearned
how to be a slave.
MICHEL DE MONTAIGNE

Fear of not being perfect

Now here's an irony for you. In thinking about the future, many of us feel we need to create the perfect plan. We are afraid that we haven't covered all the bases. Somehow we think we can control the future even though we struggle to negotiate the day-to-day.

According to financial and estate planners, lawyers, and everyone else involved in the future planning business, the most common excuse for not making a will is the fear of not getting it right. Indecision can paralyze those with the best intentions. Perfection equals postponement. In trying to make perfect decisions, we risk indefinite delay.

Passion makes progress

The willingness to confront our fears is important to creating a vision. If you accept that fear is a basic ingredient of passion, then confronting our fears is a way to tap into our passion. Fear ignored is paralysis. Fear then becomes the great plug to the imagination, preventing progress. On the other hand, fear acknowledged and confronted opens the door to another companion – love. Love and fear are really two sides of the same coin, the coin called passion. The Greek and Latin roots of the word passion meant suffering.

Passion will provide the fuel for your journey, the yeast for the bread to rise, and the energy to create a plan for your friend or family member with a disability. Passion sustains us over the rough spots, pricks our lethargy, and sparks our creativity. Passion is one of the defining factors that helps us to see with new eyes and motivates us to action. According to Gunilla Norris, author of *Home – The Making of Sanctuary*, it takes 21 days to start a habit, 40 to make it your own and 90 to become it.

Passion will get us through that crucial time.

A good vision is like an elastic band

Morley Callaghan, one of Canada's best short story writers, said that a good vision is like an elastic band. It has to have tension and it has to be stretched. Here are two tips about developing and maintaining clear vision.

1 Check your views with your relative.

Creating a vision of a good life for your son/daughter with a disability means just that – a vision for their life. The vision you are developing is for someone else's life, not yours. Make sure you check your views with your son or daughter.

Do not forget to:

- include them in the process.

- share your wishes with members of the network who will "steer" the vision.

- be prepared for a few surprises.

One aunt we met in New Jersey highlighted the danger. Her niece, who had lived with her for nearly a decade, had always wanted a German Shepherd. The aunt was allergic to animals. Her vision for her niece did not include a dog. Not surprisingly, her niece's vision did. Guess whose vision needed to be adjusted?

2 Acknowledge that bringing dreams to reality can be tough.

Brightness brings both clarity and shadow. So it is with your vision. The shadow side of vision is getting stuck. There are four reasons for this. One, the dream can be so expansive and so ambitious that you feel exhausted just thinking about how to bring it into action. Two, parents can be immobilized by guilt that they haven't acted before. Three, people can forget or think they should ignore the good things they are already doing. Four, the vision has no tension or challenge in it.

We have learned to ask people to describe both their

dreams and their nightmares. Staying in a dreamy airy state without your feet on the ground means you have no roots. Staying with the nightmare can paralyze. Together, dreams and nightmares create enough tension and energy to propel you into action. Both are necessary. They complement each other and provide the energy to act.

Plans evolve

It takes time for anyone's dreams to evolve, including your relative's. When they do, you need to update and revise your future plan. In fact, you should expect to make changes as life carries on, as your relative's circumstances change and as you pick up tips here and there. Who among us can predict the future? Can we anticipate all eventualities?

Here's a simple exercise: Place yourself twenty years in the past. Who would have predicted the breakup of the Soviet Union? The destruction of the Berlin Wall? The release of Nelson Mandela? The death of Princess Diana? The careers

> Perhaps all the
> dragons of our lives
> are princesses who
> are only waiting to
> see us once,
> beautiful and brave
> RAINER MARIA RILKE

Top ten reasons for not preparing for the future

1 The future is uncertain. Better eat dessert first.
SARAH LEE

2 Why should I care about posterity? What's posterity ever done for me?
GROUCHO MARX

3 I'm afraid that if I make a will, I will die.
JOE AVERAGE

4 I'll get to it as soon as I finish this one little chore.
GOLIATH, PHILISTINE GIANT, 1013 B.C.

5 I don't see any dark clouds on the horizon. There's nothing to worry about.
GENERAL CUSTER, U.S. CAVALRY

6 I've developed a new philosophy—I only dread one day at a time.
CHARLES M. SCHULZ, PEANUTS

7 Dying is a very dull and dreary affair. I intend to have nothing to do with it.
SOMERSET MAUGHAM

8 Eternity is a terrible thought. I mean, where is it going to end?
TOM STOPPARD

9 I never think of the future. It comes soon enough.   ALBERT EINSTEIN

10 Making predictions is really difficult... particularly about the future.   YOGI BERRA

of your children? The amount of your savings?

The truth is that we often have to proceed as best we can without all the answers. Hindsight is the only guarantee of perfect vision.

We invite you to enter into the spirit of developing a vision. A clear vision becomes a beacon, a light to head towards. However, it is not the roadmap. The path to implementation will be cluttered with dead ends and detours as well as the discovery of new lands.

We trust the remaining steps in this book may help. You will see, for example, how Personal Networks help people to dream and keep the dream alive. You will see your friend or family member grow in confidence as they learn to dream and express themselves within the security of a network.

If you are like us, you'll find your vision undergoing constant change, driven by the events in your relative's life. We believe this is called re-vision! Enjoy the discovery.

On the one hand . . .

- We're not in crisis yet. We've still got lots of time.
- The process is too costly.
- I don't know who to turn to.
- I'm worn out from fighting too many battles.
- We're still young.
- The future is too hard to contemplate.
- I'm a procrastinator. What more can I say?

On the other hand . . .

- It's fair to other family members.
- That's a load off my shoulders.
- My worries about government interference are gone.
- I'm better prepared to face the unknown.
- I've done the best I can.
- I've left a legacy of love.
- I'm at peace.

Gloria

**"This is the only death
I'll ever have."**

I am attracted to courageous people. Like Gloria, for instance. Gloria knew she was dying when she came to PLAN. She had good reason to be concerned. She was 83 and had been diagnosed with inoperable cancer. When she died Michael would be all alone. Her life was coming to an end but she had a pressing matter to take care of.

She was focused and determined when we met. Sell the house; divide the proceeds; establish a trust for Michael; point me in the direction of a good lawyer; build Michael a Personal Network. No waiting, no thinking it over, no hesitating.

Despite her weakened state she embraced change as a friend. There was no sentimentality, just the motivation of pure love.

"I've been a fool for too long," she confessed, "hoping for a miracle. Pushing it all to the back of my mind. What foolishness. As if I could live forever."

Her blue eyes held me in their gaze.

"This is the only death I'll ever have and I want to be ready for it. You know I'm afraid, not for me but for Michael. I'm afraid for his loneliness. I'm afraid for the derision, for the pity, for the misunderstanding, for his loss. Sometimes I think he'd be better off going first."

She choked as she remembered things past. My throat swelled in sympathy.

The memory of Gloria's beautiful clear intention reminds me of the importance of dying well. Sowing the seeds of a safe and secure future for our relative can be a metaphor for coming to terms with our own mortality. Gloria understood this. So do most of the parents, young and old, who cross our path.

Louise

"My self-sufficiency was going to be the death of me."

Louise made very few mistakes. As a widow with four children, she couldn't afford to.

Janice, her youngest, was living in a rented townhouse with two other people. They received support from the local service provider to help prepare supper and get organized for the morning. The rest of the time they were on their own.

Louise had been a social worker so she knew the ropes. Forty years of advocacy for Janice and the equivalent involvement in the local association made her a formidable authority.

In preparation for a cruise to Alaska, her first extended vacation in decades, she phoned her children to make sure they knew Janice's schedule. They were more than willing to look in on Janice but the conversations alarmed Louise.

She discovered that her children knew nothing, absolutely nothing, about Janice's medical condition and her medical history.

Louise had assumed that her other children would be well versed simply because they had lived in the same house. They, on the other hand, had been too busy being kids! Besides, Louise had handled everything so well on her own there was no reason for anyone else to get involved.

It was time for a family meeting. Louise put as much as she could remember on paper, made sure they knew all the ways to contact her, and left feeling slightly better. She was relieved the cruise was only five days. Besides, she was able to phone every evening just to check in.

During the cruise Louise resolved to change. "I realized that my self-sufficiency was going to be the death of me."

The next time Louise went away everyone, including Louise, was better prepared. Before leaving on a European vacation, she called a meeting of the entire family, including all the in-laws.

Janice had a mild stroke when her mother was away. Louise's eldest daughter, after consultation with the rest of the family, decided not to spoil her mom's trip and did not contact her. Instead, the daughter stayed in touch with the specialists and the rest of the family rallied around Janice.

On her return Louise surprised herself by reacting calmly to the news. As she explained later, Janice was in loving hands. What more could a mom hope for? Besides, she had a few more trips planned!

Richard and Celia

The gardener didn't cut it

We were meeting to begin creating a plan for Richard and Celia's 45-year-old son, Ken. My question was innocent enough, "Who will watch over Ken when you're not around?"

Celia's answer was alarming: "We don't really know, I guess the lady who comes to do the garden and lawn every two weeks could do it. She's nice to Ken, always has a smile."

"Is she a family friend?" I asked.

"Well, kind of. She came over from Sweden nearly two years ago. Ken likes her; she always has a kind word to say to him."

Over the next few months it became clear that the gardener was living in the area on a temporary basis and intended to move to the United States as soon as she could. She was completely unaware of the family's expectations.

Fortunately we were able to connect with a nephew in Calgary and the nephew's daughter, a second cousin of Ken's, who lives in a small town near Vancouver.

And just in time. We weren't able to develop a Personal Network but we were able to create a small team who could assist with executor and trustee functions.

Shortly after the will was completed, Celia died. Richard developed diabetes and lost most of his vision along with his lifeline to the outside world – his driver's license.

Richard is particularly reliant on his nephew's daughter. She, in turn, is much clearer about Richard's wishes for his son. As she gets to know Ken, our hope is they will now recognize the value of establishing an expanded network of support for Ken.

By the way, the gardener has moved to Seattle and is no longer in touch with the family.

Worksheet 1

AFTER YOU'RE GONE SHARING YOUR VISION

It's one year after your death. What would be the best possible day in the life of your relative? _____

_____

_____

Can you describe the sounds, the smells they would experience?_____

_____

_____

What kind of music would be on the stereo? _____

_____

_____

Who would they be living with? _____

_____

_____

What would be going on? _____

_____

_____

What would the plans for the evening be? _____

_____

_____

What would breakfast be like? Supper? _____

_____

_____

What would the day look like in your worst nightmare? _____

_____

_____

What would their place look like? _____

_____

_____

What would they be doing during the day? _____

_____

_____

What would they be wearing? _____

_____

How would your relative answer the first two questions? _____

_____

_____

How would other family members answer the first two questions? _____

_____

_____

What stands in the way of turning your vision into reality? _____

_____

_____

Who or what can you count on to achieve your vision? _____

_____

_____

List some key words to sum up a typical day for your relative, in the best of all possible worlds. _____

_____

_____

List some key words to sum up your worst nightmare for your relative after you're gone. _____

_____

_____

What is the most important message you want to leave your relative? _____

_____

_____

_____

What is your most urgent concern? _____

_____

_____

_____

What do you want your other surviving family members to help with after you've gone? _____

_____

_____

_____

When your executors/trustees meet, what do you want them to do first?

_____

_____

_____

What are the three priorities you want future caregivers to remember about your relative?

    1. _____

    2. _____

    3. _____

What are the important arrangements to ensure quality of life for your relative that others need to know about? _____

_____

_____

_____

_____

_____

Worksheet 2

A FAMILY PORTRAIT

Use this worksheet to develop a portrait of your relative. It will be an important record to pass on to your survivors. This is a lengthy worksheet; we suggest you complete it in your own time. You may wish to complete it after you have reflected on all the steps contained in *A Good Life*.

Health

List names of current doctors, specialists, and health practitioners. _____

_____

_____

List current health concerns. _____

_____

_____

_____

List current health treatments. _____

_____

_____

_____

List current health precautions and alternatives. _____

_____

_____

_____

_____

Briefly describe key features of medical history. _____

_____

_____

_____

_____

Do you have a Supported Decision-Making Agreement for health care?

(see Step Five) _____

_____

_____

_____

Education and Work

List your relative's current educational and/or work activity. _____

_____

_____

What are your future dreams in this area? What other possibilities would you and

your relative like to see explored? _____

_____

_____

_____

_____

_____

What are some highlights from your relative's school experience? What did your relative like about it? What didn't they like about it? _____

_____

_____

_____

Who are the people from childhood that your relative had or still has a close connection with? _____

_____

What are some highlights of your relative's work experience? What did they like about it? What didn't they like about it? _____

_____

_____

_____

_____

Housing

Describe current living arrangements. _____

_____

_____

_____

What are some future housing options/possibilities for your relative? _____

_____

_____

_____

Summarize briefly previous living arrangements. _____

_____

_____

What did your relative like about them? Dislike about them? _____

_____

_____

Who are the people who had a significant relationship with your relative in these

previous living arrangements? _____

_____

_____

_____

Leisure and Recreation

List current social, recreational, cultural, artistic and athletic activities. _____

_____

_____

_____

What are your relative's interests and preferred activities in these areas? _____

_____

_____

_____

What are some future possibilities in the area of leisure and recreation? _____

_____

_____

_____

What does your relative most like to do? _____

_____

_____

_____

Personal

How would you describe your family's beliefs and values? _____

_____

_____

_____

What customs and traditions are important in your family? _____

_____

_____

Is spiritual and religious worship important for your relative? Is this an area that

could be explored further? _____

_____

_____

What are the significant events, markers, or milestones in your relative's life?

_____

_____

What brings comfort and peace to your relative? _____

_____

_____

When were they most happy? _____

_____

_____

_____

What has been their greatest source of emotional support? _____

_____

_____

_____

What does your relative derive the most pleasure from? _____

_____

_____

_____

Who are the most significant people in their life? _____

_____

_____

_____

What are your relative's favorite possessions? _____

_____

_____

What are their passions and gifts? _____

_____

_____

_____

Worksheet 3

A LETTER TO THE FUTURE

The last wishes of parents for their children are honored and respected in our society. A letter to the future is your opportunity to tell your survivors how you would like to be remembered, and how you would like your relative with a disability to be loved and cared for.

This is not an easy letter to write. Think of it as the letter you might write in the middle of the night when you can't sleep. Be frank about your hopes and fears. Tell those who will survive you what's most important to you.

Dear _____

_____

_____

_____

_____

_____

_____

_____

_____

_____

_____

_____

With love,

Worksheet 4

PARENT CONTRACT

I, _____, commit myself to creating a plan for the safety,

security and well being of _____ by _____ (date). I commit to

developing a clear vision with _____ and sharing this vision with the

following people:

_____   _____

_____   _____

    Further I commit to drafting and signing my will by _____ (date) and

reviewing it every two years.

    I understand it is impossible to predict or foresee the future and that the great-

est gift I can give to myself and to _____ is the gift of a net-

work, a team of caring friends, family members and professionals who love, respect

and understand how to support _____. I trust them to confront

the challenges that will surface in _____'s life after I am gone.

    I further understand that following the seven-step process may be emotional,

disturbing, and frightening. I also understand that others have encountered the

same challenges and that committing to the completion of _____'s

future plan will bring relief and peace of mind. During this period I promise to take

good care of myself – getting enough sleep, eating well, walking or exercising

regularly, and enjoying daily the beauty of the world around me.

I realize feelings of guilt may surface from time to time and that these are fueled by my fears. However, my love is stronger and by committing to the seven-step process I am doing my absolute best.

_____

Signature

_____

Date

building
relationships

For one human being to love another; that
is perhaps the most difficult task
of all. . . the work for which all other work
is but preparation. It is a high inducement
to the individual to ripen...
a great exacting claim upon us,
something that chooses us out and
calls us to vast things.

Rainer Maria Rilke

A web of support for Rick

"I used to work in government, you know. In government they come up with all kinds of programs. Many of them are baloney – no matter how thin you slice it! At one of these senior parent meetings, this young woman came around and started talking about networks – Personal Networks. I have to admit I thought it was one of those baloney stories. How could this possibly work?

"It was too theoretical. It looked good on paper but it would never work. I thought it was all gobbledygook.

"But they turned the tables on me. They said they wanted a 'guinea pig' for one of those Personal Network things. I guess they figured if they could convince me they could convince anyone. Several of the other parents were prepared to take the risk. So I took a chance. Remembering what my wife had asked I said to myself, 'What have I got to lose?'

"Now, at the time Rick knew only a couple of people. He had a very narrow social life. He bowled once a week and he played hockey for Special Olympics. That was it. He wasn't working or in any kind of a day program at the time."

When George came home to talk to Rick about the network, he got a chilly reception. Rick was emphatic. He wouldn't have anything to do with the network.

"Dad, you can have what you want. Just don't include me!" said Rick.

Not a great start.

George explains Rick's disinterest simply. "Rick had been to many meetings over the years and attended lots of classes and nothing ever changed for him. I guess I really couldn't blame him. Besides if truth were told, I didn't really know what I was talking about. I'm sure Rick picked that up."

Despite his own ambivalence, George persevered. To this day he doesn't really know why. Perhaps it was the memory of his wife's insistence that they do more. Perhaps it was his apprehension about the future – he was ready to try anything. Perhaps it was the assurance he felt from the other families who also were stepping into the unknown by forming personal networks.

There were lots of reasons why George could have been as firm as Rick in refusing to explore the "network idea," as he still calls it. He and his wife had never discussed their concerns about Rick's future with any of their relatives. It was a private matter. It was their responsibility

continued on page 50

Building relationships

a good life is a human life. A human life is a social life. The essence of human nature is to be in the company of others – companionship, fellowship, and connection to others are essential to our well being. We embark from birth on a journey of the heart. The fuel for this journey is love, in all its manifestations. Love is the most pervasive and persistent aspect of our nature. It is an unquenchable thirst and a fountain of nourishment.

Some of our oldest literature attests to the importance of friendship in our lives. The Old Testament draws its lessons from tales about people and their relationships. We are, above all else, social beings. Friendship is a necessity for all of us, as important and essential to life as food and drink. Aristotle, a Greek philosopher and major influence on Western thought, put it succinctly: "For without friends no one would choose to live, though he had all other goods."

Perhaps it's because friendship is so fundamental to our existence that we take it for granted, or we aren't conscious of its importance until it is brought to our attention. A recent political leader's comment on his recovery from a life-threatening illness underscores this point. During recuperation he spent much of his time counting the blessings of friendship. In particular, he recalled those friendships that had lapsed or been fractured, and determined to repair them. Most of us, when asked to boil

GEORGE'S STORY
continued from page 48

and theirs alone. Who would be at all interested? Wouldn't they be too busy? Did they even like Rick?

George didn't know it at the time, but this is the hardest part for most families – asking family and friends for help.

"It was the awkward part," he admits. "You feel so exposed. You're brought up to take care of your own. Asking for help was just not in our vocabulary."

Finally he hit upon a solution. PLAN had developed a short questionnaire on examining the relationships in the life of a person with a disability. George found the questions thought-provoking. He decided to mail the questions out to his relatives. His reasoning was simple. "I told them I was thinking about starting something like this for Rick. I figured this might be a way to test who might be receptive to the idea of a network. If anybody showed any interest in Rick as a result of this, I would invite them to a meeting."

George also talked to a neighbor across the street who had always been friendly towards Rick. He invited this neighbor to the first meeting. He also invited a former staff person from the local association who would occasionally drop by to visit Rick.

"There were eight of us at the first meeting. Rick was in the other room, but his name kept coming up. I guess he was straining to listen. Pretty soon he was standing at the entrance to the living room. Before you knew it he was sitting down with the rest of us and joining in the conversation. That was a turning point for Rick and me. Neither of us could believe that people were actually interested in him that way.

"After the network formed, Rick went through a change. He had always been very quiet – a bit of a loner. Either keeping to himself or doing things just with me. Never one to initiate a conversation. Never one to pick up the phone. Soon he found there were people he could talk to. And they would phone him. And they'd go for coffee or something. And he was phoning them!

"You know, it all adds up. Rick gets all kinds of help now, beyond our wildest imagination. In fact, I couldn't have imagined any of this five years ago."

For George that has been the greatest benefit of the network. He can sit back and watch a web of support being spun for Rick before his eyes. It's like watching a movie about the future from the comfort of your easy chair.

our life down to its basics, would likely have similar comments.

We are interdependent, not independent, creatures. The impact of this recognition is far greater than our contemporary society acknowledges. Understanding this interdependence is critical to our health, our quality of life, our sense of belonging, our peace of mind, and our security. And it is profoundly important to the future security of our sons and daughters with disabilities.

The essence of their future security is not the size of the estate we leave for them or how thorough the legal arrangements are. Yes, those are important factors in building a successful future plan for our relatives with disabilities. However, what completes the planning and makes it all worthwhile are social supports and relationships.

No one will ever be able to look after your child with the same love, persistence, interest, and determination as you do as a parent. That's a fact. However, unless you've tapped into the fountain of youth, you won't be around forever. That's also a fact. So what's the next best thing?

The answer is obvious: Replacements!

Step Two will focus on how to expand, enhance and nurture relationships for people who are isolated and lonely, for people who may need a little push, nudge, or welcome back into the heart of community life. We realize this can be a painful process for many parents. It has been for us. We have witnessed the rejection and isolation of our children first-hand. It may not be easy to shed your cynicism. However, if you are willing to suspend painful memories, we may offer comfort and encouragement. Step Two includes a practical discussion on building a network of support for your relative.

In our experience there is no disability that precludes relationship. This is so important we will write it again. There is no disability that precludes relationship. At PLAN, we have seen it with our own eyes.

> We are not human beings in search of a spiritual life, but spiritual beings in search of a human life.
> TIELHARD DE CHARDIN

There is a critical reason for viewing relationships this way.

The best guarantee of a safe and secure future for a person with a disability is the number of caring, committed friends, family members, acquaintances and supporters actively involved in his or her life. Caring, loving people like you. It's as simple as that.

The real strength of these relationships will come not just in their connection to the person with a disability but in their connections with each other. Imagine a spider's web. The strands extend from the center of the web to the edge. Imagine if there was nothing else holding them together. They would flap in the wind. Their functional value would be minimal. They need to be linked with each other to form the web. Otherwise spiders would starve! The strength of the web comes when all the components are interconnected.

It's the same for people. The focus of support for people with disabilities must be not only on their individual relationships but also on the relationships among their friends and supporters. A Personal Network is a team of people who have come together for one single purpose: to befriend, support, and advocate for your relative. It is their "job" to worry, to oversee, and to plan in advance, to anticipate, to "be on top of." A healthy Personal Network is one where all members of the network are in touch with each other. They coordinate their support. They assign responsibility among themselves.

All the functions you as a parent provide now will one day be divided among this group of people. Their interconnections will create a web of support that can approximate the thoroughness with which families care for each other.

Nobody sees a flower, really. It is so small it takes time. We haven't time, and to see takes time, like having a friend takes time.
GEORGIA O'KEEFE

Worksheets

Two worksheets are located at the end of this chapter, starting on page 100. Take a look at them now, and plan to fill them out when you've finished this chapter.

WORKSHEET 5 The Web of Friendship

We've provided a sample web and a web for you to work with. To fill out your own web, follow the instructions on page 100.

The web will help you examine the current relationships in your relative's life and to explore ways of strengthening the Personal Network.

WORKSHEET 6 Personal Resource Map

We all have connections. Good facilitators of Personal Networks know and use their connections. Good facilitators also encourage others to appreciate the density of their own connections and to use them.

We've provided a sample personal resource map.

The role of friendship in our lives

The Beatles sang the contradiction in its simplest form. On the one hand, "All you need is love." On the other, "Can't buy me love."

To be isolated is an enormous tragedy for any human being. Yet we cannot force someone to love us, to be our friend. We cannot claim it as a right. Government cannot provide it. Money cannot buy it. To be in relationship comes from somewhere else. It is part of our deepest nature. It is integral to the history of our species. It is the history of our species.

Humans require love, respect, belonging, dignity, fellowship, and solidarity to flourish.

This is where many of us have gotten stuck. We have put our efforts into developing and guaranteeing the apparent "basics" of life for our relatives with disability. We should pay as much attention to the most fundamental of all human needs – our yearning for love and for relationships.

Relationships without love or caring are relationships devoid of respect, honor, and dignity. Without caring, the

> We need a path, not to go from here to there, but from here to here.
>
> JAKUSHO KWONG

provision of food, clothing and shelter will be no different than the treatment of political prisoners, food slopped into bowls and passed through bars without comment or recognition.

Friendships, ranging from acquaintances to intimate relationships, are formed by choice. They are freely given connections based on mutual interests. Friendships are reciprocal, a two-way exchange. They are not one-sided. The reasons for our connections with one another are varied. Similarly, there are a variety of ways to describe the functions of friendship. However, friendship usually involves:

- doing things with another person;
- doing things for another person; and
- sharing feelings or emotions.

The result of these exchanges is to create and reinforce the belief that we are valued. With social support, we become more secure in our interdependence. The sense of being cared about by others reduces our loneliness, keeps us safe, enhances the quality of our life, and builds our sense of self-esteem.

A genuine friend is one who is faithful, devoted, and true. We don't change ourselves to be with friends. Our gifts and our frailties are accepted as part of who we are. Our friends are not expected to fix us. They are just there. Friendships are naturally enjoyable.

The good feelings that arise from feeling connected to others are an obvious benefit of friendship. There is now a mass of evidence to indicate that being cared for may be one of the critical factors that distinguish those who remain healthy from those who fall ill. A review of the medical and health literature clearly indicates that social support is necessary for the maintenance of good health.

The research indicates:
- People with supportive social ties are less likely to become ill or die.

The only disability is having no relationship.
JUDITH SNOW

Men who have real friends are less easy to manage or "get at," harder for good authorities to control or for bad authorities to corrupt.
C.S. LEWIS

- Social contact reduces the likelihood of mental illness.
- Social supports contribute to the successful adjustment and well being of the individual.
- Social supports affect our sense of control over our well being and improve our ability to stick with healthy behavior patterns.
- There is no label or attribute that prevents committed relationships from forming.
- Friendship aids the workings of the immune system.

Relationships – a source of support

To be isolated is the greatest tragedy for a human being and the most generic form of stress.
JOAN BORYSENKO

Think of our own lives. When our parents die, we are not alone. We are still surrounded by a circle of loved ones and friends. We want to create the same supportive experience for our child or relative with a disability. Reinforcing and building friendship is an attractive alternative for families worried about who will replace them when they are gone. The warmth, concern, and caring that our friendships embody create a social environment of safety and security. And that spells comfort for moms and dads.

Since our relatives are vulnerable to government cutbacks and service decline, the presence of friends and supporters becomes critical. Individuals who lack supportive ties are vulnerable to a wide variety of negative consequences. They may be at risk of abuse, neglect, and exploitation. An individual's needs may be jeopardized by the system's needs unless there are people around who care about the individual and who are prepared to act as advocates.

Let's be specific. Investing in an extended Personal Network of friends and family for our son or daughter provides both short-term and long-term returns.

Networks of personal support can serve as:
- safeguards for the security and well being of our family member, particularly after parents are gone

- the arms and legs of our personal future plan
- monitors for the formal programs and services our relative receives
- companions
- advocates
- executor and trustee(s)
- advisors to executors and trustees
- guardians if our children are under 19
- friendly support from a trusted source
- links to others in the community
- connections to community resources
- a safety net
- continuity for the family's hopes and wishes

The art of making friends

Did you know that over 50 per cent of the first attempts that young children make to join in a group with other children are rejected? They must keep trying and trying before they are accepted by their peers.

In other words, the first step in meeting another person is a learned skill that comes with practice and persistence. This is a skill that most of us take for granted and which we had to start developing at a very early age. A Seattle psychologist, Dr. Michael Guralnick, has observed that children with disabilities often do not experience this trial-and-error process.

He has suggested that there are three skills that very young children develop while playing with each other:

1 Learning how to initiate contact with our peers.

2 Maintaining play. These are the skills we learn to keep the interaction or relationship going.

3 Conflict resolution. Inevitably in any relationship we have to learn to negotiate, to share, and to compromise.

If you want something
different to happen,
you must do
something different.

SHARON DI SANTO

People who are lonely and isolated may have distinctive traits and histories that make it difficult for them to form and maintain relationships. As family members we recognize and know what most of them are. However we may have become so comfortable in our accommodation and adjustment they have slipped from our consciousness. Over time we may have forgotten many of them.

We encourage you to approach these traits with eyes open, not to discourage you from starting to create a Personal Network, but to ensure they do not work against your friend or relative's acceptance into relationships. We do not recommend trying to "fix" these traits or offering life skills training. Many of our friends and family members have had hundreds of hours of such training to no impact. Personal Networks are about acceptance, not repair.

Gord – Don't call me; I'll call you

When we first met Gord he had the dubious distinction of having endured the most hours of life skills training in the Greater Vancouver area. Life skills were a pre-condition to entering the job market, the community, and relationship.

Gord had flunked course after course. He lived in a cluttered apartment. His mother, much to her distress, was his only companion. Her goals for the Personal Network were purely functional: Get Gord out of the house and teach him to clean his apartment.

"Oh yes," she advised, "I should warn you, don't expect Gord to call you. He never calls anyone, not even me."

Gord disagreed about her priorities, particularly the housekeeping. (Eventually he "banned" his mom from his apartment, but that's another story.) As we set about the business of connecting Gord with people who shared his interest in model airplanes, war memorabilia and self-advocacy, we had one caveat.

We took mom's advice just a step further. "Don't expect Gord to call you. You should call him." And they did.

Today Gord has one of our oldest and strongest networks. For a number of years the standing good-bye with Gord went something like, "Don't call me; I'll call you."

No one can quite remember when the transition happened, but it did. Gord reached a level of comfort and he started calling people. Now he has call waiting, call alert, a message center and a beeper. He keeps in touch.

If the network ever folds, its members might want to try their hand at the life skills business.

From our experience at PLAN, none of the following characteristics have prevented the facilitation and fostering of relationships. In fact, as the individual basks in the support of their Personal Network, many of these traits eventually fall by the wayside. It was usually necessary, however, to make some accommodation at the start.

To prove that these traits do not preclude relationship, you might recognize traits of your friends, acquaintances, co-workers, or even yourself in this list.

People who are isolated may

- be extremely shy and painfully self-conscious
- find it difficult to introduce themselves
- experience discomfort in crowds
- not enjoy parties and social gatherings
- have a hard time making phone calls
- feel awkward in extending invitations
- be slow to respond, perhaps giving the impression they have not heard or are not interested
- tend to stray off topic or change the subject more frequently
- be inclined to talk more about themselves and show little or no interest in the other person
- rarely express a preference or propose an alternative
- be quite stubborn and single-minded
- be set in their ways and resistant to change
- be armored from disappointment and risk
- dress in non-traditional ways
- have limited appreciation of personal hygiene

Friendships rarely develop by chance. We need to cultivate them as carefully as we nurture a job or a family, a talent or a hobby. Some of us may think that friendships happen naturally and if they don't occur there is nothing we can do about

Michael – Birth of a precise ladies' man

One of the delights of working in our offices is our regular phone calls from Michael.

At 53, Michael is curious, enthusiastic, and positive about every new experience. And there have been many in the last four or five years. Just ask Alexis, our office manager. Michael has an appointment to call her twice a week. These calls serve as a window on an inquiring mind and delightful character.

A call from Michael used to be one-sided in his favor: a blast of enthusiastic reporting, a precise litany of facts and an abrupt good-bye. That was it.

Nowadays he is engaging both conversationally and emotionally. A recent telephone exchange between Alexis and Michael went something like this.

"I, who am about to get a real job, would like your advice. What do you think I should wear my first day on the job?"

"Well Michael, do you have a suit?"

"Yes, I have a suit, a very good one. My mother and I bought it on September 23, 1979, at Dunn's." Michael is very precise with dates and numbers. "It's a very good suit. That's a good suggestion. I'll wear my suit."

"And how about a clean shirt?"

"A clean shirt? I never thought of that. Yes I have a clean shirt, I'll wear a clean shirt."

"And Michael, I think you might want to have a shower first."

"A shower! Hmmm. Yes, a shower. Yes, that's a very good idea. I'll have a shower as soon as I get up in the morning."

"And a tie," adds Alexis.

"A tie! So I'll look like a real businessperson? I'm going to look real sharp aren't I? I see what you're doing. You really want me to impress them don't you?"

Michael, they aren't the only ones who are impressed. According to Alexis, your shell is gone. You have allowed yourself to be exposed to the charms of the world. Now you take the time to listen. You are interested in what others have to say. And your thirst for knowledge continues. Good luck with your new goal – learning, as you put it, "to socialize with the opposite sex." Something you are, "really looking forward to learning a lot more about."

Precisely!

it. However, there appears to be a certain discipline associated with initiating and developing our acquaintances and friendships.

This discipline may never have begun for people with disabilities. They may have had limited opportunities to be with other people their own age. They may have lived most of their life in a segregated environment. They may have been overprotected. They may have tried to make friends, been unsuccessful – as we all have – and have either given up or not been encouraged to try again. Most importantly, there may never have been the expectation that anyone would care to be their friend or that they would be able to contribute anything to a friendship.

For a variety of reasons, it may be necessary to approach the development of relationships for people with disability in a deliberate manner.

Pushing hands

Ever helped a child learn to ride a bike? You're running down the driveway holding onto the back seat of a bicycle, with the training wheels hanging marginally higher than the back tire. You're simultaneously pushing and restraining. Ready to tear ahead to catch a tottering bike and falling child, and at the same time willing to provide forward energy and propulsion. Eventually the fits and starts subside and you let go, either because you cannot keep up, or the actual driver begins to steer and propel herself.

Inevitably our triumphant child asserts with all the innocent daring in the world, "See, that was easy."

Not so fast, we think. Riding a bike is easy; the hard part is letting go.

But our children do not understand. They are fortunately oblivious to the laws of gravity.

And so it goes, another leap forward on the trail of freedom for our children. Each achievement provides a glimpse of an accelerating horizon and more confidence to chase it. Why? It's in their script.

We, on the other hand, must learn a higher law, "to let go." That doesn't appear to be in our script.

It's great advice, but who wants it? Another paradox of parenting.

We are expected to be freeing agents but would prefer not to be. Whether we like it or not, the paradox eventually dissolves. Our children, as we come to appreciate, are expected to tear themselves away, and they usually do.

This normal movement toward the adult world is recognized in all cultures and by all religions. Ceremonies such as confirmation and the bar mitzvah mark the transition to adulthood – the separation of the child from the parent, the beginning of a new relationship. The psychologists call this natural process "differentiation."

We have noticed this great tug of war between parent and child does not occur as frequently when our children have a disability. There are a number of reasons for this. Some, like the functional limitations of their disability, are obvious. These limitations provide practical reasons why your child may not have learned the many lessons that come from stumbling, falling, and picking yourself back up again – lessons that instill the confidence to encounter the deeper mysteries of life.

Lack of friends is another reason the separation process may have halted prematurely in our children with disabilities. When our son learned to ride his bike, he ventured

> Some friendships are made by nature, some by contract, some by interest, and by souls.
>
> JEREMY TAYLOR

Is a Personal Network useful for my relative?

- Are there any non-paid people in my relative's life?

- Is there room for others to be involved?

- Am I anxious about the safety and well being of my son or daughter or relative?

- Do I believe others will care and contribute to his or her life?

- Am I prepared to take some risks and ask others to help?

farther and farther from the house, speeding down the big hill often with no hands on the handlebars – not at our suggestion, but at the urging of the other kids in the neighborhood. Friends pull you into their orbit, expose you to new worlds, and provide a framework for exploration. They assist in the pulling away. Without friends, this critical awakening to your place in the wider world might not occur.

We have found that the process of establishing a Personal Network provides an opportunity either to begin or resume the process of parent/child separation. However, we have also discovered it may need a boost or a push from you, the parent. Your role in introducing your child with a disability to the company of others may simply be one of gently freeing them from your orbit. Or it may require a firm push on occasion. Over the years your gravitational pull may have become too strong. There were no other orbiting bodies to offset your influence.

Psychologists tell us that human growth is a healthy mix of the familiar and unfamiliar, the reliable, and the unexpected. As parents we can help. It is definitely never too late. The Academy-Award winning documentary film, *Best Boy*, gives a glimpse of the director's cousin beginning this process in his 40's.

Building relationships requires our trust, our blessing, and our facilitation. You have already begun this process by becoming interested in establishing a Personal Network.

And let's admit it. Despite all the tension and conflict of kids pulling away, we're usually pushing at the same time,

> A child is a child. They get bigger, older, but grown? What's that supposed to mean? In my heart it don't mean a thing.
> TONI MORRISON

Getting started

- Are there people who would be willing to move into a closer relationship with my son/daughter?

- What am I currently doing for my relative that I would be willing to let someone else do?

aren't we? We understand our role intuitively, even though it's an "unnatural act." The tension and conflict isn't really over the pulling away, it's over the how. After all, that is what is required of all parents for all their children – gentle firm pushing hands for momentum and guidance. And for catching. Just in case.

How relationships challenge families

While many families recognize the importance of relationships in their loved one's life, they may feel ambivalent when it comes to actively seeking opportunities for relationships to form. From our experience, there are three challenges that families face in facilitating these relationships: asking, opening, and believing.

Asking

To ask is to make ourselves vulnerable. There is always the possibility of refusal. Yet reaching out and asking is integral to developing and deepening our relationships. Friendships often form because we ask others to participate in a shared activity. We invite acquaintances over for tea to get to know them better. We ask neighbors to help us with building a fence. We ask friends to give us a hand with setting up for a party. Each of these casual invitations presents an opportunity for the relationship to grow.

Nevertheless, asking for help is not easy or natural for many of us.

We grew up with the unwritten expectation not to complain and to solve our own problems. We are fiercely and justifiably proud of our self-sufficiency.

Reaching out and asking on behalf of our sons and daughters may not be any easier. We may feel that extending even casual invitations is risky. We worry that others will feel obliged, or worse, that they might be saying yes because they feel sorry for us or our loved one. This worry speaks to how deeply many of us have been hurt by our culture's devaluing of difference. It makes us forget what our sons and daughters have to offer. It makes us forget that others may care.

We need to remind ourselves of the contributions and richness our sons and daughters have added to our lives and the lives of those around them. There are many, many stories from ordinary people attesting to how their relationship with an isolated or labeled person has changed their life. They are often people who wanted to reach out but did not know how. Each invitation we offer is an opportunity for others to extend their community and broaden their relationships.

Opening

In order for others to come into our lives there needs to be a place for them. It is impossible to meet people or deepen a friendship if we have no time to spend with others. This is an issue for many people with disabilities. Virtually all areas of their lives may be programmed. To an outsider there is no apparent need for a friend. Friends and acquaintances may find it just too difficult to arrange any time together with your son or daughter. As parents, we may need to give up a program or change schedules to create a space for others to come in.

On a more subtle level, some of our own actions as parents might inhibit the involvement of others. Over the years we may have become used to doing many things for our son or daughter. The presence of an "outsider" changes our routines. Thinking about another person taking our son or daughter somewhere new might upset us. As we feel ourselves losing some control, we may resist the efforts of others to contribute. We may respond by saying we can do it ourselves. We need to ask ourselves honestly what we are willing to let go of in order to make room for others to become active and involved in our children's lives.

This letting go is our lifetime task as parents. We know it.

There is no harm in falling off a horse. The danger occurs if you do not get back up.
TRADITIONAL CHINESE PROVERB

One does not discover new lands without consenting to lose sight of the shore.
ANDRÉ GIDE

It is in the best interests of our sons and daughters to be able to manage without us. Friendships provide a catalyst for both of us to accomplish this task. Our sons and daughters grow richer from having experiences outside of the family. Our loved ones need friends to inspire them to take their own paths as they, too, grow into their own.

Believing

Of the three challenges, this may be the greatest. We remember there were no birthday parties or sleepover invitations when our children were young. We witness the lonely Saturday nights and every other night of the week as well. We notice yet again someone staring in the supermarket, or we receive a pitying look from a passer-by.

We feel hurt by these things and we ache for our son or daughter. Our overwhelming desire is to protect, and we cannot find it in ourselves to truly believe there is a caring community of people available to befriend our loved one. We do not need another bunch of romantic do-gooders. This lack of belief affects our ability to be open to others, and to trust in their integrity and their authenticity.

On the other hand, we live in caring communities with a growing understanding of our need to be responsible and care for one another. Self-help and support groups thrive in each community. Friends and neighbors are joining together to support a loved one to die at home. Whole neighborhoods form block watches to look out for one another's children. Rather than being sent off for professional care, people all around us are being supported to live and die in their communities. In spite of the negative view of an uncaring society sold to us every day by the media, people do honor their social obligations.

This has been PLAN's experience, as we create caring, non-paid, committed relationships for our relatives with disabilities. Our challenge as parents and as families has been to systematically approach the development of

Three challenges to families

- Asking
- Opening
- Believing

relationships while at the same time addressing our personal fears and biases.

PLAN's approach to building a Personal Network

A Personal Network is a group of men and women who voluntarily commit to support a person who is at risk of being isolated and vulnerable by reason of their disability, living arrangement, limited opportunities, or society's perception. A Personal Network is the bridge between living on the edge of community and active inclusion and participation. A Personal Network welcomes or connects people to the heart of community. Each member of the network has a relationship with the focus person and with every other member of the network. Through their relationship they offer support, advocacy, monitoring and companionship.

A Personal Network is the foundation of your future plan. While members contribute to the quality of your relative's life now, they are also preparing for their role after you are gone.

Members of a Personal Network can include other family members, particularly brothers and sisters, as well as neighbors, members of church congregations, services clubs and leisure and recreation groups, former service providers, teachers, and school friends. Virtually anyone can be a member of a Personal Network. Personal Networks are often called Circles of Friends, Support Circles or Circles of Support.

The process

PLAN hires a facilitator to develop and maintain the Personal Network. Their job is to do as much as necessary and as little as possible to develop a network. Most networks require at least eight months of facilitator involvement before they are established. Building a Personal Network is a three-stage process.

STAGE ONE exploration

This period is a time of exploration with the individual, their family, and the PLAN facilitator. Most of the time is spent getting to know the person – their current activities and relationships. It is a time when we focus on their passions, their gifts, their capacities, their challenges and their wishes for the future. It is a time when we focus on what is possible rather than on what cannot be done or what has gone wrong before.

At the same time we are looking for contacts and connections, people within the immediate and extended family circle, the neighborhood, and community who are potential network members. Finally it is the time when the individual, family and facilitator can assess their compatibility and PLAN's ability to meet family expectations.

During this period we will complete the web of friendship presented in Worksheet 5, and develop a profile similar to the one depicted in Worksheet 6. Usually these profiles are developed through a strategic planning session in the family living room.

At the end of this period the facilitator will provide a set of goals, a time line of activities to establish a network and a list of potential members.

> Facilitators do as much as necessary and as little as possible.
> VICKIE CAMMACK

STAGE TWO development

Now the work begins. This is the period when all the leads are followed up, contacts made and invitations extended, usually by the PLAN facilitator. This can be a nerve-wracking time for families, a time when they must confront the reality of letting go and of asking others (even if someone else asks on their behalf). Occasionally parents will cancel the process of developing a network at this point.

During this period the goal is to recruit network members and to introduce them to each other. The facilitator's community connections become another resource in the emerging and maturing life of the individual. Regular meetings are scheduled, at which time the individual's goals are discussed, reviewed, and revised as necessary. To achieve the goals, practical strategies are developed and a commitment to action is obtained from network members.

During this period the commitment and strength of the network is constantly being assessed. Many networks become self-sufficient at this point and require only ongoing "maintenance." Others require another round of recruitment. Regardless, at this point a second timeline is prepared outlining the next six months of activities. The family and their relative must give their approval before we proceed any further.

STAGE THREE maintenance

Once the Personal Network is developed, it settles in for the long haul. The facilitator can be useful in ensuring the network meets regularly and that network members follow through on their commitments. As new interests emerge, new connections may have to be made. Sometimes there may be a crisis and the network needs to rally for a concentrated period. Often networks will have formal celebrations around birthdays, Christmas, and other holidays. Occasionally they will have their own newsletter, photo album, web site or diary. The facilitator assists in this coordination.

Maintenance activities will vary from network to network but they are all determined by a regular written six-month plan that is approved in advance.

And in the end,
the love you take is
equal to the love
you make.
LENNON AND McCARTNEY

Common questions
about Personal Networks

What are the benefits to me of establishing a Personal Network for my son/daughter when I am still alive?

One of the most surprising and satisfying aspects of our work has been the present value both to families and the individual with a disability of having a Personal Network.

Developing a Personal Network now is important to parents for a number of reasons:

- it provides an opportunity to share your knowledge of the best interests of your son/daughter with the people you are counting on to support your child in the future

- it allows your relative to flourish socially and emotionally

- it helps prepare your relative for the changes that will occur when you are not around

- it enables you to see a healthy, functioning Personal Network while you are still here

---

The healing power of belonging

Some of the individuals we have developed Personal Networks for have suffered the trauma of physical and sexual abuse. Others have been or are engaged in very risky behavior or have made lifestyle choices that could affect their health or life. Personal Networks do not provide counseling or rehabilitation. Nor do they sermonize. Personal Networks are not moralistic in their approach.

Instead, Personal Networks start from the premise that belonging is a prerequisite to healing and to changing one's behavior. We believe that without the dedication and nurturing of supportive relationships, therapy, counseling, warnings and restrictions will not work. In fact, often these individuals have had years of professional intervention, with no success.

Personal Networks are a haven for healing to begin. They are a model of different behavior. Yet they are very careful not to cross the line into professional intervention.

That does not mean Personal Networks ignore risky behavior or past abuse. It does mean the individual knows they are cared about and supported, first and foremost.

- it enables an organization such as PLAN to have the detailed background and familiarity it needs to become an effective advocate and monitor
- it gives you security, relief, and peace of mind

How can Personal Networks help after I am gone?

Personal Networks are your eyes, ears, arms and legs after you are gone or when you are unable to be active in your son/daughter's life. After you die, Personal Networks and their members can:

- serve as an advisor and resource to the trustee(s) you select. Some members of Personal Networks are willing to assist parents by serving as executors and trustees (see Step Six)
- advocate on behalf of your relative
- monitor the services and programs your relative receives
- provide emotional support
- provide support during crises
- ease the grief and trauma associated with your death
- continue with all the other activities, support and advocacy they began when you were around

Where do you find people willing to participate in Personal Networks?

From all over. The key is invitation – asking people to assist our loved ones to overcome challenges, realize goals, or follow dreams. We start with the immediate and extended family, broadening to family friends and neighbors, and extending to people from every walk of life. We look for people who may have similar interests to your relative.

Do Personal Networks replace families?

No. Families are the foundation of a healthy network. They provide the bridge into the larger community. It is family ties which provide the vision, inspiration, and emotional fuel for new members of the network. Personal Networks cannot solve the isolation on their own. The blessing and cooperation of the family enables network members to make their contribution.

What are some tips for parents in building a Personal Network?

The primary requirement is a belief that relationships will develop. Network building can be an uncomfortable process for families. Challenges include paying for the service; listening to other people's ideas about our relative; and letting go even in a small way. Contact with parents who have gone through the same process can be very useful.

What experience and backgrounds do facilitators have?

At PLAN, we hire facilitators based on their knowledge and connections to the community and their compatibility with the individual with a disability. Previous experience with people with disability is a bonus but not a prerequisite. One of our most effective facilitators was the coordinator of emergency response in the rural community she lived in. She knew everyone.

   PLAN facilitators share PLAN's values. They range in age from their mid-twenties to their early seventies. Some are parents or relatives of people with a disability. Many have a background in community support and counseling. Several have university degrees. Most have at least two years of college. They all have a knack for seeing the person's contributions, and the enthusiasm to invite others to receive them.

... no land in human topography is less explored than love.
ORTEGA Y. GASSET

Do parents have to attend meetings of Personal Networks?

Many families do attend meetings of their relative's network, particularly at the beginning. They are kept informed by the facilitator, their relative, and summary reports of network meetings. They may decide not to attend once the network gets established and things are going well. Staying away from some meetings may allow your relative to grow in confidence and create opportunities for network members to step forward.

What are the limitations of Personal Networks?

Personal Networks do not work miracles. They will support your relative to pursue dreams and address immediate concerns. They will not guarantee all dreams will be realized and all concerns will disappear. As parents, we know the danger of assuming any new program, service or idea will cure all. The development of Personal Networks is hard work and requires perseverance and commitment from everyone involved.

No change happens overnight and this holds true for Personal Networks. A lifetime of isolation or loneliness cannot be overcome immediately. New contacts take months before they mature into relationships your relative can count on. The process can be slow and may at first seem as if nothing is happening. Even though results may take time, pleasant surprises occur frequently.

Do Personal Networks replace social services?

No. However, Personal Networks can sometimes minimize the isolating and impersonal aspects of human services. And they reduce reliance on paid service provision by involving the individuals in freely given relationships and connecting them to the community.

> You were alone, I got you to sing. You were quiet, I made you tell long stories. No one knew who you were, But they do now.
>
> RUMI

What happens if the Personal Network fails?

PLAN, or an organization like PLAN, can provide continuity for all Personal Networks. If for some reason network members leave and the network collapses, PLAN will dedicate staff resources to renew the network and provide personal support and backup until the network becomes healthy again.

How many hours does it take to develop and maintain a Personal Network?

On average 40 hours of facilitation are required over eight months to get started. Established networks average two to three hours of facilitation time a month.

The time for facilitating networks varies. Influencing factors include:

- how easy it is to get to know you and your relative
- connections you and your relative already have
- what your relative currently does and wants to do
- changes in your relative's circumstances
- change among network members
- how much involvement families want the facilitator to have

What makes a good facilitator or community connector?

The women (primarily) and men (wish we had more) described as facilitators in this book are people who often work off the beaten path, out of the spotlight and far from headlines and grand receptions (see the stories in The Gentle Art of Facilitation, beginning on page 94). Their conviction leads them to work outside the traditional social service delivery system. They may be disenchanted with their chosen profession of social work and relish the opportunity to practice in a way that got them into the profession in the first place.

They have chosen the path less traveled because they are guided by a vision of a better world for everyone. They jettison the certainty and predictability of the status quo approach to supporting people with disabilities and embrace ambiguity and flexibility. Their quiet activism reveals they do not think they have all the answers. They have been around forever, yet are re-emerging as artists from every walk of life. They resist claims they are part of an emerging profession because they know they must remain tied to the community.

You know you have a good facilitator or community connector if she:

- is comfortable asking
- realizes her first loyalty is to your relative
- is willing to seek out opportunities for your relative to make a contribution
- is willing to create opportunities for others to receive the contribution
- knows when to intervene and when to hold back
- does as much as necessary and as little as possible
- listens without judgment to dreams and desires but can act in the here and now
- is passionate
- resists parent/child dichotomies
- challenges, supports and inspires your relative
- helps people to open up
- knows when to be quiet
- is well connected in the community and neighborhood and is prepared to use her connections
- keeps secrets and confidences
- is accepting and does not try to fix your relative with a disability
- makes people feel relaxed

- sees beyond the boundaries of formal service
- understands that being in relationships is central to everything we do
- follows the iron rule: "Never do for others what they can do for themselves."
- accepts that the network defines the goals
- enhances the Personal Network's own values rather than imposing her own
- solidifies the experience of network members to care for each other
- is clear about the nature of her relationship with the focus person

The bird, a nest
The spider, a web
Man, friendship.
WILLIAM BLAKE

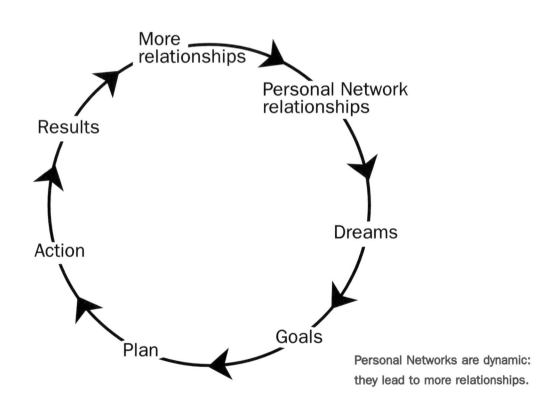

Personal Networks are dynamic:
they lead to more relationships.

That's what friends are for

There is something about being human that makes us long for the company of others, to be with and to be touched by our family and friends.

We have read accounts of prisoners of war who were able to endure physical torture, starvation, and privation but could not stand solitary confinement.

Viktor Frankl, the great European psychiatrist, in his marvelous book *Man's Search for Meaning* describes his refusal to take his name off a list of Auschwitz prisoners bound for the gas ovens. His reason was simple and profound. He would stay with his friends.

Isolation and solitude are devastating byproducts of having a disability. This solitude can be even more oppressive in a large or impersonal service delivery system. Especially when the only people in your life are paid to be there. Or when you are surrounded by people who seem to be secure in their life purpose and appear to have no time for you.

The only way to truly diminish this loneliness is through deep connections with others. Even though this may be challenging for our sons and daughters, it is critical for their health, security and well being now and in the future. The keys to creating these connections are first, our willingness to let them happen and secondly, the effort we are prepared to put into making them happen. All the riches of the world will not compensate for the security and pleasure of being in a loving and caring relationship.

The journey of love extends in ever-widening circles. It begins at home and is fostered, modeled, and nurtured by parents. It can radiate from its source to be shared with others, perhaps through the gift of a Personal Network. With time and opportunity and through the mystery of relationship it may lead to companionship, friendship, intimacy, and marriage – to what Rilke called "vast things," the love of one human being for another.

Love is a gift, not a debt. Parents know that. So do friends. Next to parents, that's what friends are for.

When your family is in crisis may not be a good time to start a Personal Network. It may, however, be a good time to reach out for help.
VICKIE CAMMACK

One's life has value as long as one attributes value to the life of others, by means of love, friendship, and compassion.
SIMONE DE BEAUVOIR

Who benefits from networks

- The person with a disability
- Families, especially parents, brothers, and sisters
- Members of the network
- Executors, trustees
- Social service workers

What we've learned about Personal Networks

- Brothers and sisters really like them.
- Connections among members of the network are as important as the relationship with the individual with a disability.
- Our communities and neighborhoods are inherently hospitable.
- Asking is the biggest and hardest step.
- Professionals should be seen only as advisors to the network.
- The feeling is mutual – circle members get as much as they give.
- Personal Networks are important for the future, but they make a difference right away.
- Parents with young children can form a Personal Network around themselves.
- The majority of network members stay together; they do not drift away. However, those who leave usually invite a replacement.
- The changes in your relative may challenge you. Your relative will grow in confidence and maturity.
- Expect to be pleasantly surprised by the changes in your own life.
- Relationship building takes time and patience, but the results are worth it. Like water filtering through stones, purity and clarity are the results.
- Networks develop identities. They have unique personalities and characteristics separate from the individuals in them.
- Without relationships there is no future plan.
- No disability precludes relationships.

Personal Networks: a Family Resource

An unexpected byproduct of Personal Networks is the role they play in the lives of family members. While the focus may be on their relative with a disability, the value and benefits are available to all who are touched by the hospitality of this process.

PARENTS

Gloria

A couple of years after a network was established for her son, Gloria's cancer returned and she entered hospital. Naturally Michael and his friends, members of his Personal Network, were regular visitors. It became clear that Gloria was not happy in hospital. She knew she would die soon and did not want to stay in the hospital. However, since she lived alone with Michael, everyone wondered how they would cope.

This bleak prospect was brought to the attention of Ken, Michael's facilitator. While it appeared to be outside the bounds of Ken's job description, his intuition suggested otherwise. A quick weekend call to Vickie confirmed his decision. Along with members of the network, he assembled a team of Gloria's friends and neighbors, arranged a visiting schedule, and established an emergency backup. As a result Gloria was able to return home, to familiar surroundings, to her cat and to Michael. She died peacefully three months later.

Louise

"I have no choice," she told Jack and Al. "My husband is dead and I have no other family members. Where do I sign? I need PLAN to look after the girls, when I'm gone."

The "girls" were Louise's two daughters, both in their early 40's.

Despite this, Louise was a tough sell. She vacillated. She was ambivalent about the PLAN approach. After six years as a Lifetime Member and hours of discussion with Jack, she still had not completed her will.

She went through three facilitators. Ignored is a better word.

She would forget to invite the facilitator to a meeting when an on-the-job crisis occurred for one of her daughters. She would call network members individually but essentially prevent them from getting together with her two children without her.

At meetings among PLAN families she would damn with faint praise. There was always some little thing wrong with the network or the facilitator. When asked for clarification or confronted by other families with the good things that were happening as a result of the network, she would go and make tea!

We knew our perseverance was worth it the day the current facilitator received a late evening call from Louise. She was in the hospital, an emergency journey by ambulance, and wondered if arrangements could be made to pack some toiletries, housecoat, and some pajamas. "Would you let my friends know? And by the way, keep your eye on the 'girls.' Please."

BROTHERS AND SISTERS
Jennifer

Her professional life was a breeze. Jennifer was an unflappable theater administrator capable of handling every imaginable personnel crisis. Yet she was in tears. She had a front-row seat to a real-life drama that was tearing her apart. A deep conflict with her sister was grinding the life out of her mother. The grooves of this conflict were clearly evident on her mother's face.

"I don't know how much more my mother can take. It's easier for my dad. He still goes downtown even though he's retired. My sister refuses to leave, but she must. My mother needs relief. She's exhausted."

Several previous attempts to find alternate accommodation had failed. Jennifer's sister would simply walk out of her new home, bus back to the family home and park herself on the bench across the street. And confidently wait to be invited back in. Eventually mom would relent, and the spiral continued.

With two young children of her own, there was little Jennifer could do. In desperation she bought the gift of a network for her family.

Jennifer's sister fought it. There's no other word for it. She would have nothing to do with the development of a Personal Network.

Barbra Streisand made the difference. Our facilitator found someone as passionate about Barbra as Jennifer's sister. They were introduced. They joined a fan club. "People who need people are the luckiest people in the world."

Another move is in the offing and tension is in the air. Jennifer and her family expect the old conflicts and pressures will return. This time they are prepared. Mom and dad have been convinced to go on a short vacation. Jennifer and the network will handle the heat. They are resolved. Jennifer knows it will work. She is no longer scripting alone.

Bob

"I hate it when he calls him Billy. He's 34 years old, for God's sake. The old martinet won't let go of the strings. We'll have to pry them out of his hands on the day he dies."

The martinet was Bob's father. Bill was Bob's brother.

These were private moments and Bob was letting off steam. Bob's father was a collector of imperfections and his children were his greatest trophies.

Bob couldn't establish a foothold toward the future care of his brother. Bob's dad dominated all discussions or, as Bob described them, "monologues." You could take the person out of the British army but you couldn't take the British army out of the person.

Take the discussion about "Billy's" eligibility for government benefits. It was agreed at the network meeting that Bob would visit the government office and straighten out an obvious oversight. Bob headed down the next morning. Too late. Dad had already been in and taken care of it.

It's hard to be objective in any parent/child dynamic. And maybe Bob overreacted on occasion. The facilitator recognized this. His main role for six months was listening to Bob and, as it turned out, the father's war stories.

Bob was encouraged to try one more time. His daily journey home took him past the local garden shop. A mound of topsoil left in the parking lot fertilized an inspiration. Bill needed something to do during the day. Why not a workout with a wheelbarrow? The owner, a family friend, was grateful for the offer. That was the easy part. Getting it past dad would be trickier. A network meeting was called. The proposal was made. The old martinet cleared his throat. The facilitator intercepted with a question. "Do you remember the story on the field of battle when the corps sergeant was hit and you had to step in because the second-in-command was unable to carry on? Do you remember how scared you felt? Wouldn't this be the perfect opportunity for your second-in-command to get a little practice?"

It worked. Nowadays the only clenched fists are handling a wheelbarrow.

DIVORCED

Anne and Doug

"Would you send a copy of the work plan and the bill to my ex-husband? Write him a letter and tell him I think it's time he made a contribution." That was Anne speaking.

"I keep getting this information about PLAN in the mail and my daughter keeps talking about a network. Can you tell me what it's all about?" That was her ex-husband Doug speaking.

Mother may I go out to swim?
Yes my darling daughter.
Hang your clothes on a hickory limb,
But don't go near the water.
TRADITIONAL NURSERY RHYME

They hadn't heard from each other in years, 17 to be exact. Anne had remarried. Doug lived alone. They were both over 60 and comfortably well off. Each had lengthy anecdotes about the other's faults.

PLAN's involvement originated with Anne. Could we interest Doug without losing Anne? Was there room for the two of them? The other siblings had not found a solution. Some had taken sides – the disadvantage of entanglement.

Their daughter Emily decided to host a family Thanksgiving at her new place. She had just moved in with two women who had previously been her caregivers. The network had introduced Emily to a cross-stitching club. Proverbs stitched on cushions were her specialty. Next came a night school course in cooking. That had led to a job in a bakery where she decorated cakes. She had a steady hand, an artistic eye, and imagination. Wedding cakes were another specialty.

She declared her dream in September, a Thanksgiving party for the whole family. The dream was detailed. She would cook and she would say grace. The network gulped and ventured into territory Emily's brother and two sisters wouldn't have dared enter.

Invitations were sent, menu prepared, RSVP's received, chairs borrowed, place settings personalized. Anne was asked to make the gravy and she did. Doug brought his grandparents' carving set and did justice to the bird. Network members and roommates were seated strategically.

Then Emily said grace – her proverb of choice uncanny in its accuracy: "Something old, something new, something borrowed, something blue!"

COUSINS
Paul

Paul had never been close to his brother. The rift in their relationship was never to be bridged. They had emigrated from England as adult men with wives and children, and had lived within fifty kilometers of each other. Yet Paul and his brother had no contact at all.

One day twenty years ago a neighbor of Paul's was in a bank lineup and noticed a man who bore such a striking resemblance to Paul that he asked if they were related. He was shocked to learn that he was talking to Paul's brother.

Paul's blank response to this chance encounter silenced any further discussions.

Until the first network meeting for Paul's daughter. They were filling out the Web of Friendship and the inevitable inquiry about relatives came up. The neighbor, a kind and wise friend if there ever was one, remembered he had met Paul's brother two decades before. On impulse he brought it up.

Perhaps it was Paul's desperation. His wife had died and he was alone with his daughter. Perhaps it was simply time to lay down past hurts and wrongs. Perhaps he had forgotten.

Paul gave his blessing to the facilitator to track down his brother.

On the road to developing a network for his daughter, Paul had to face the grim news his brother had died several years earlier. Too late to repair the pain and disappointment. But not too late to appreciate the power of family ties.

The facilitator's search led him to a nephew who lived nearby. A nephew honored to be invited into a relationship with his new-found cousin. A nephew honored to be chosen as executor and trustee for his Uncle Paul. A nephew manifest as an agent of forgiveness.

We are all angels with but one wing, and only by embracing each other can we fly.
LUCIANO DE CRESCENZO

Michael – The last word

Michael is a ham. He loves being the center of attention. These days he's a far cry from the abrupt, reticent, and withdrawn man of ten years ago. If only his mother could see him now. Her faith in the power of relationships would not be misplaced.

Tonight he is giving a workshop. The co-presenters and Michael meet beforehand. The topic is 'Personal Networks – Weaving the Ties That Bind.' They agree on a format. Vickie will assume the role of a television personality and interview Michael.

Michael is excited. A real television-style interview. No detail is too small. It must be authentic, for a man who is precise. It must be Oprah, not Rosie. There must be a microphone. There must be an elevated stage.

Everyone agrees. They go along with the illusion.

Seventy-five are in attendance. There is a camera crew from the local community college. The workshop is being taped for distribution.

The moment arrives and Vickie as Oprah turns to ask Michael her first question.

"Hold everything," shouts Michael. "Let's get rid of these extra chairs." The chairs are removed.

Then, nodding to the camera operator, he asks if they have enough light.

They do, but thank him for asking. Michael, clearly, is the one in control.

Next comes a sound check. You can never be too sure!

Vickie tries again. By now the audience is into the spirit of the occasion.

"Let's go, Rosie," they chant encouragingly.

"No no," interrupts Michael. " Not Rosie but Oprah. Oprah Winfrey."

"Yes," says Vickie, "Oprah would like to ask you a question."

"Wait a minute, " says Michael forgiving her indiscretion,

"You've got to start properly."

"Lights, camera, action," announces Vickie, clapping her hands to simulate take seven. "And now, here's Michael."

Everyone is finally satisfied, particularly Michael. The interview can begin.

He handles the preliminary questions with aplomb. Next comes a more personal question.

"Tell me Michael, what does your network do for you?"

"They give me hope, love and encouragement which I really need now that my mother is dead and gone up to heaven."

You could hear a pin drop.

It was worth the wait.

Peggie

A circle of friends

Peggie attended school for the first time at the age of nineteen.

She was brought to PLAN's attention by a local high school teacher who was concerned because Peggie was living in the extended care ward of a local hospital. Peggie shared her room with three other women who were in their early seventies. Peggie cannot speak and they did not appreciate the high-pitched sounds she made.

Peggie had lived in the hospital since the age of two. She had received a severe head injury as a result of a car accident and was immobile. Her family, unable to communicate with her, had eventually stopped visiting. Peggie had no other companions. Her only stimulation was a TV. Most of the time she lay on her back, unable to move or to communicate.

She was isolated, lonely, and bored.

PLAN agreed to create a Personal Network for Peggie. At the time, we were a new organization and had limited funds. Nevertheless, our Board of Directors was moved by Peggie's story and committed to improving the quality of her life.

We hired a facilitator who got to know Peggie. He found five others who expressed a willingness to spend time with her.

That was the easy part. Overcoming the objections of hospital personnel proved more difficult. They soon became defensive, threatened by questions, raised by Peggie's new friends, about her care.

Matters soon came to a head. PLAN received word that the hospital had recommended the removal of all Peggie's teeth. The hospital felt this would be more convenient for the staff who fed her. It took Peggie longer to chew her food and staff decided it would be easier to feed her puréed food if she had no teeth. Fortunately, PLAN's President and Executive Director, as respected advocates, were able to use their influence with the Ministry of Health to reverse this decision.

PLAN was also able to convince senior hospital officials to examine other living options for Peggie. With the active presence of friends and visitors, Peggie's life brightened. Contact was made with her family. Government agreed to consider Peggie for placement in a group home they were developing. The local school board agreed to extend Peggie's education for one year past the eligible age. Her eyes began to sparkle. She put on weight.

Peggie eventually moved to the group home. Although it is some distance from the hospital neighborhood, she has maintained contacts with the original members of her Personal Network. New friends continue to enter her life.

Peggie's one true love is music – lots of it. Music is her refuge and her joy. She becomes lost in its presence and truly "beams," revealing dimples and a huge smile. Our favorite picture of Peggie shows her dressed in a beautiful black dress with sheer black stockings outside a downtown Vancouver restaurant just prior to attending a Celine Dion concert!

A far cry from the ward of an extended care hospital.

Patrick

The leprechaun network

Patrick is a leprechaun. Short in stature, he glides a few centimeters off the ground as he walks. Twinkling eyes and twinkling toes. A charmer with the gift of the blarney. Dancing through life, he attracts people as naturally as he smiles.

At his first Personal Network meeting over twenty people were in attendance. And he had invited them all! In fact our facilitator wondered what she could possibly contribute.

Alas, as we soon found out, if another meeting were to be held two months later another twenty people could be there, but they would be all new acquaintances.

You see, Pat was a hard man to be in relationship with. He has this thing about money. People are always robbing or cheating him. Often Pat accuses staff or roommates of theft. And so on.

He perseveres. It is possible for him to call you thirty times a day or night (38 times is the record) with the latest story of embezzlement. He is so convincing, but he wears you out. Even his mother, now in her eighties, still finds his accounts persuasive.

Patrick's preoccupation was and is phenomenal. Today, however, while his fixation on money remains, so do eight of the original members. They are rock-solid members of Pat's Personal Network.

The reason is simple. They got to know each other. They were honest enough to admit their frustration and annoyance at Pat's repeated interruptions. Before they became totally exhausted and bailed out, they came up with a strategy.

Each member took on a different task. Joe agreed to be the money man, to help Pat with his finances and to respond to any concerns he might have. All inquiries or entreaties about money were to be referred to Joe. If Pat called another network member with a particularly engaging account of the latest misappropriation, they could plead ignorance and remind Pat to call Joe.

Meanwhile Joe and Pat made an agreement to limit the money calls to three a week.

The network members learned a deep truth. They surrendered to the mystery of Pat's fixation. They didn't try to change it. Years of behavior management had already been invested in that approach. Instead they danced around it. Like all good leprechauns would.

Mark

Dance me outside

Mark had lived the life of a hermit for 17 years. After high school graduation, the failing health of his parents, his lack of friends and his own allergies gave him little motivation to venture outside. His parents had died a few years back and his older brother had moved back to the family home to keep an eye on him.

Fortunately Mark's allergies were serious enough to require monthly visits to a specialist. If it weren't for the allergist appointments he may never have gotten out of the house. Strangely, he would only sit in the back seat – a hold over, we were told, from the days when his dad used to take him on a weekly drive.

On one of the visits to Mark's specialist, his brother noticed a PLAN brochure in the doctor's office. He was about to be married and he and his fiancée were planning to get their own house. His brother, although extremely conscientious, did not have the time to devote to creating a life for Mark.

That's how we got involved.

During our first dozen or so meetings Mark wouldn't make eye contact. He sat in front of the TV and watched the weather channel. He seldom responded to any inquiries. We felt certain this was also his main activity when we were not around. A full-blown recluse was in the making.

In desperation our facilitator suggested a ride in her car as a way of getting to know Mark. Anything to get him away from the weather channel. As they approached the car, Mark headed for the back door. "Come and sit beside me," urged the facilitator. He did. That was the first step.

A few months later as Mark and his brother left for a doctor's appointment, Mark's brother held the back door open for him as he had hundreds of times. Mark opened the front door. Mark's brother could not believe it.

The religious icons throughout the house suggested to our facilitator a possible church connection. That was the second step. Three different members of a welcoming church congregation began to take turns bringing Mark to Sunday service. And yes, he sits in the front seat.

They began visiting computer stores during their drives. That was the third step. It led in turn to more steps that eventually led to a course in computers at the local community college.

By now Mark is using public transit to attend his courses. And he sits wherever he likes.

•

The nucleus of Mark's Personal Network is firmly in place. Now they are meeting to

continued on page 90

continued from page 89

discuss plans for Mark's 35th birthday party – his first ever. Vickie has been invited to attend the meeting. She asks Mark about the party.

"Will there be lots of people?"

"Yes," says Mark, "lots of people."

"Will there be a cake?"

"Yes," says Mark, "there will be a special cake baked just for me because I have allergies."

"I know," says Vickie. "Will there be music?"

"Yes," says Mark, "there will be lots of music."

"Will there be dancing?"

There is a long pause. Mark is lost in contemplation.

"Yes," says Mark. "Dancing, yes, I'd like that."

Norman

A brother's letter to PLAN

For over a year now my friend and brother Norman has been associated with PLAN through his Personal Network. I've watched Norman grow dramatically in confidence, in interpersonal relations, and in verbal skills. Norman's world has expanded due to the Personal Network that now surrounds him.

Lydia, Norman's Personal Network facilitator, has been effective in bringing his Personal Network together. Now Norman is friends with Lydia's husband, Mike. Norman and Mike have enjoyed, among other things, skating, bus riding, and simply "hanging out." This friendship with Mike has been very important to Norman. Although he has five loving brothers, including myself, I feel we have not always helped Norman become an adult. Norman is no longer "Normie."

Norman's relationship with Mike has given him a new, adult standard by which to measure his other relations. He now desires – practically demands – that relationships with him be on an adult level. I say, "Way to go, Norman!"

Another member of Norman's Personal Network who has been very important is Patsy. She has helped him learn valuable skills in a one-on-one relation with a young woman, which is something that has been noticeably lacking in Norman's life in the past.

Being in the network I have learned as much about myself as I have about Norman. His growth has challenged me to grow as well and together we are now involved in regular activities such as bowling and soccer. We share a new and dynamic friendship which encourages us both to meet each other's needs and to meet the needs of the important others in our lives.

Michael

Letters to PLAN

When Michael's mother died, his Personal Network became his sole source of support. Michael is a keen letter writer to PLAN. Here are excerpts from two of his letters.

Dear PLAN:

Since I started with my Personal Network, it has been an interesting and very positive experience for me because it is helping me prepare for my future. I am thankful to have wonderful friends come to my first meeting, although I was somewhat disappointed that some couldn't make it to the meeting as they had other things to do.

I have admiration and respect for my Personal Network facilitator, Ken. He knows what he is doing and is a great friend; he understands people who have disabilities. By working together with my facilitator and people in my Personal Network, I will be guaranteed a positive and hopeful future.

Two years later:

Dear Ken and members of PLAN:

The birthday party at the Unitarian Church on July 13th was excellent. I'm pleased a good number showed up, but with regret plenty of people invited couldn't make it because summer is a time when people are away on vacation.

The food was wonderful and I liked the cake for the occasion. It's great to have a party like this one to show that there are people who are caring, loving and supportive. I was so happy to get plenty of cards.

This is my first birthday of being on my own. This year I won't have to worry about my mother and no more stressful situations of being concerned whether she'll get better or worse now that the Lord has taken my mother home to that wonderful and happy place where there's no more illness, no more pain, no more suffering. She won't have to go to hospital again.

On the day of my 50th birthday, July 17th, I had lunch at the Sirloiner, and some of the people from my Personal Network showed up. This helped make my day a very pleasant one.

Debbie

My friend Rick

I first met Rick four years ago when I was working for PLAN. At the time I needed someone to help me get the newsletters folded, stuffed and mailed. Rick volunteered. I liked Rick immediately and soon after, when I was asked if I would join his Personal Network, I didn't hesitate to say, "yes."

I'll never forget the first Personal Network meeting that we held. Rick's circle of friends really only consisted of his immediate family, and I thought to myself how limited his social and emotional support was. Rick was very shy. It was difficult for him to participate in our discussions and he often let us make decisions for him. The Rick I know today is quite different!

Over the years the Personal Network has grown and there is now a mix of family, neighbors, and friends like myself. We have helped Rick find job opportunities; we've facilitated social activities; and we've just "been there" when he's needed to talk. The most important thing, though, is that he's become part of our lives.

Rick has been part of my family since before my son was three and before my daughter was born. He often comes to stay for dinner or overnight. Sometimes he invites my husband, who works near his apartment, over for lunch.

Recently Rick moved to his own apartment. The Personal Network pitched in to make it happen for him and we are in regular contact with him to see how things are going. Rick is a changed man from when I first met him. Being self-sufficient has given him a new confidence and he is much more outgoing. In fact, he often turns down my invitations because he's too busy!

It's been a great four years and I'd like to thank Rick for being my friend. It's not often I get to make friends with a truly kind and sincere person like him.

Patience

The Gentle Art of Facilitation – 1

Patience is the art of hoping.
VAUVENARGUES

In any contest between power and patience, bet on patience.
W. B. PRESCOTT

The waiting room was empty when I arrived. I had made a special effort to be early. The appointment was at 1:30. I was facilitating my first network and I knew it would not be easy. I had met Rose once before in the company of her family. Today I was meeting her alone.

Rose had been resistant to the idea of a Personal Network. Her parents definitely thought it would be a good idea. Perhaps to deflect the pressure, Rose acquiesced and agreed to my visit. Was it my imagination or was her ambivalence mixed with hostility?

Rose was described as a challenge – a temporary return to the mental health institution was the result of yet another setback. A thorny personality.

Nearly an hour had passed and there was still no sign of Rose. Was she trying to tell me something?

I decided to look around, exploring the deserted halls and locked doorways characteristic of all institutions.

There she is. This must be the clubhouse Rose talked about. What a cloud of smoke. Everyone is smoking. My eyes are stinging. I'll have to wash my clothes when I get home. And so warm. And loud. Still I can see the attraction. It's an oasis of conviviality compared to the barrenness elsewhere in the institution.

"Hi Rose, remember me, we met at your parents' place last week."

Well, she's definitely not pleased at the interruption. She's carrying on with the card game. They're all smiling, exchanging glances, keeping me at bay. Turning the tables. Rejection is a two-way street. However I mustn't get discouraged. I was not promised a smooth ride. This heat is unbearable. Is it the temperature or my embarrassment? I'll faint if I stay here much longer.

"Do you mind if we sit outside for awhile?"

A long pause and finally she gets up and leads me into the garden. She doesn't look at me and she doesn't say anything. We sit on a bench. Two women side by side in complete silence.

It's getting late. I wonder what time it is. I have to be home by 5:00.

"Do you have the time, Rose?"

Rose is not answering. I know she hears me. Am I being tested? For what? Now what?

At last, acknowledgment, "It's 4:15."

"Thank you."

Perhaps in a hint of acceptance, Rose replies, "I think you'll make a good friend."

Listening

The Gentle Art of Facilitation – 2

Listening is a mysterious, nurturing force. When we are listened to, deep dormant seeds of creativity begin to sprout. Under the warmth of silence, new life springs. When we are listened to with the same intensity most people display only when they are talking, we can be re-created. When there is an original sound in the world, it awakens a thousand echoes.

"I broke the windows in the lobby to that building. I hated living there. It was stupid of me. That's why I went to jail."

Her staccato outburst surprised me almost as much as her confession. A raging torrent of revelation compared to previous chats. We hadn't done much talking since I began working as her facilitator. Our best times were silent times. They were slightly unnerving at first, but I was beginning to enjoy them. Sometimes we'd sit for hours braiding our relationship in the caress of silence. Familiar to each other's presence, yet strangers as to the content of our lives.

Now after two months we were out for a walk in her old neighborhood.

"I didn't know you were in jail, Rose."

"There's lots of things about me you don't know," she countered.

We sat on the park bench facing her old apartment.

Suddenly she began to sing. A tenor voice, at ease and completely in pitch, the voice of a musician bursting with talent. As a humble choir member I appreciated her talent.

"You have such a beautiful voice," I remarked, "Did you ever play a musical instrument?"

Flute, as it turns out. She saw Paul Horn communicate musically with the whales at the Vancouver Aquarium when she was young. She studied with the Royal Conservatory for years. She even got to meet Horn. Boxes of music books were in storage somewhere. Like much of her life, banished from her daily existence. Was there a new life to be mined from those discarded cartons?

Inspiration does not come like lightning to me. My response that afternoon surfaced gently on the hymn of silence we had composed. Minutes passed before I understood.

"When's your birthday?" I asked.

"November 19th."

"I'd like to buy you a music book as a present."

And finally the bud, like the first signs of spring we were enjoying.

"Maybe I can practice and play for you sometime," she replied.

Courage

The Gentle Art of Facilitation – 3

Courage is not about forcing change through the application of brute strength and sheer will power. It is to be attentive, observant, and calm, acting with intelligence, intuition, and confidence. Courage is first about inner strength, not to be confused with passivity or distancing oneself from the challenge. The French word coeur (heart) is embedded in our word courage and that is what we believe is at the core of our facilitators' work – summoning their inner strength and trusting their heart.

I knew she liked movies. Everyone knew that. Delight was evident whenever we strolled past the cinema on Main Street. I even knew her favorite actor – Tom Cruise.

So there wasn't much chance to avoid *Jerry McGuire*.

We took our seats midway down the aisle. Right in the middle of the theater. I should have known better. What a fuss she made. It was clear she didn't like something. Maybe it was our seats. Every eye in the place was on us, not Tom Cruise.

"Shut her up." "Get her out of here." Those were the kinder remarks. You can imagine the rest. So we did get up and instead of leaving we moved a little closer. Maybe she felt confined, maybe it was too noisy, maybe the other people were disturbing her with their rustling. I should have known better.

This might work. Not too many people around us now.

Oh no, she's still upset. I wonder what is bothering her. People are not going to like another commotion. I wish I knew what she's trying to say. Here comes the usher. "I'm afraid you'll have to leave," he insists.

Stay calm, I remind myself. Resist the temptation to flee.

"I'm real sorry about the noise. She loves movies and she particularly loves Tom Cruise. I know she wants to see this movie and I'm not sure what she's upset about. Would you mind if we moved a little closer to the front? Will you escort us?"

Magically he cooperates and so does Betty. So that's what she was trying to say. Front row center. I should have known.

Creativity

The Gentle Art of Facilitation – 4

Creativity is not just about exceptional achievement, reserved for the great and brilliant. It is also about responding to the ordinary with inspiration and meaning. It is about reflection, inspiration, and the commonplace. Trumpets rarely blast and cameras rarely roll when parents are inventive in their daily tasks of creating a home and raising children. The same is true for the daily work of facilitators.

Peggie is not the most communicative of persons. Since she does not express herself in a typical manner, the onus is on the visitor to take the lead. Unless you have shared experiences and interests, you can quickly run out of things to say. Then there is the gauntlet you confront whenever you visit her. Staff hover, usually parking themselves in the front room, making any form of communion awkward.

The discomfort of exploring a new relationship was eased somewhat by the book of photographs and pictures prepared by our facilitator. However, even that exchange was useful for only ten or fifteen minutes.

After months of trying, our facilitator began to brood. She had run out of ideas. Fortunately, this state of emptiness was really a time of incubation. She happened to be watching reruns of "Mr. Dressup" with her children one morning. "Mr. Dressup" is an acclaimed Canadian children's program now in syndicated reruns. Its star, Ernie Coombs, is a friend and colleague of Fred Rogers – the grandfather of the gentle approach to children's entertainment. Mr. Dressup has a battered box full of mystery and delight. He calls this old box his "tickle trunk."

Click. Tickle was the key word. It resonated immediately. Our facilitator phoned a friend who works at the local community center and booked a room – a room with padded gym mats on the floor. She arranged a meeting with a few of the people who had expressed an interest in getting to know Peggie. They gathered in the room with Peggie and began to play games on the mats. Peggie loved to be touched and tickled and her potential network members were being given a chance to see her at her best.

Facilitator ingenuity worked. The small group of four has remained together for nearly three years. In the nicer weather they join with the local walking club and hike the dikes of a local river.

Genius

The Gentle Art of Facilitation – 5

The mark of a genius is a willingness to explore all the alternatives, not just the most likely option. People with genius make novel combinations out of barren possibilities and prepare themselves for chance. The connections and relationships they make mystify the rest of us. Here are some examples of facilitators with genius.

Maria and Andrea

Five years is enough time, you would think, to get acquainted. Not, however, if you are Maria and you believe your role as facilitator is to get to know who a person really is. She reminded me of how complex we all are during a recent car ride with Andrea. The tears drifting down Andrea's cheeks were yet another prompt of how little Maria really knew about her friend, who is unable to communicate in traditional ways. That Maria would notice was significant. That she would appreciate the emotion behind the tears was genius.

Eunice's kitchen

Kimberly's get acquainted visit with Tom's mom, Eunice, began and ended in the kitchen. In between, Eunice produced a special request birthday cake for a grand-daughter's birthday (decorated with a Spice Girls theme), two lemon pies (with real meringue), four dozen peanut butter and chocolate chip cookies, "for the older kids and adult guests," and two pie crusts to be frozen for another time. In addition, she made supper for herself and her husband. Even though her own children were grown, she was still wedded to the kitchen by utter passion. Jokingly, she spoke of the family sprinkling flour over her grave and setting the temperature to 350 degrees.

"When Tom was younger he loved to be in the kitchen when I baked. I'd place a bit of dough on his wheelchair tray and he'd do his best to flatten it out," Eunice recalled. "I'd help him make his mark in the dough and we'd bake it. He was so proud."

So when Kimberly asked Tom, "Would you like an opportunity to cook?" his answer was obvious. So, too, was the challenge of Tom's limited physical dexterity.

Undaunted, Kimberly set out to fuel Tom's infatuation with baking. A diatribe against electric breadmakers overheard in the aisle of a drugstore sparked the idea. Tom could punch and pound, flatten and turn, couldn't he? Of course he could. He'd been doing that since he was a child. And he had his own flat surface.

In short order, Kimberly set up a baking circle with Tom and three other virtuosos. Their specialty: bread and pizza crusts, both of which require a lot of kneading. As "authentic" breadmakers, they, too, scorn electric breadmakers. Elbow-deep-in-flour is the only way to go.

Bert and Mel

Head bowed, weighed down by a camera, Mel managed to avoid eye contact with everyone except family. Unbearably shy, he would shrink into the wall at any social gathering. He accessed the world through the lens of a camera. If you got too close, he would take your picture.

Bert knew that getting to know Mel would be a challenge. Meetings were out of the question. However, he was just about as crazy about cars as Mel was about cameras.

So Bert and Mel gathered in Bert's driveway around the open hood of the car, chatting about engines and photography courses. In time they began to discuss Mel's plans to move into his own place.

Worksheet 5

THE WEB OF FRIENDSHIP

The sample web has already been filled out. To fill out your own web:

1 Write your loved one's name in the center circle.

2 The inner circle represents the area in your loved one's life that is filled with people s/he trusts, feels comfortable with, and confides in. They can be friends or family. Put anyone in a paid position at least one circle out. The people in this circle will have a freely given reciprocal relationship with your relative, based on friendship and respect.

3 The remainder of the web represents the rest of the people who are involved in your loved one's life. Write their names down, using the distance from the center to represent how close their relationship is.

4 If you wish, the dotted lines can be used to indicate the different areas in your loved one's life. For example, family in the top section, friends on the left, school and work in the other quadrants. This will help you to visually demonstrate the interrelationships in your loved one's life.

5 When you have completed this picture, think about how you can strengthen the web, by joining up the people in your loved one's life. In a different colored pen, draw in all the potential connections.

Sample Web

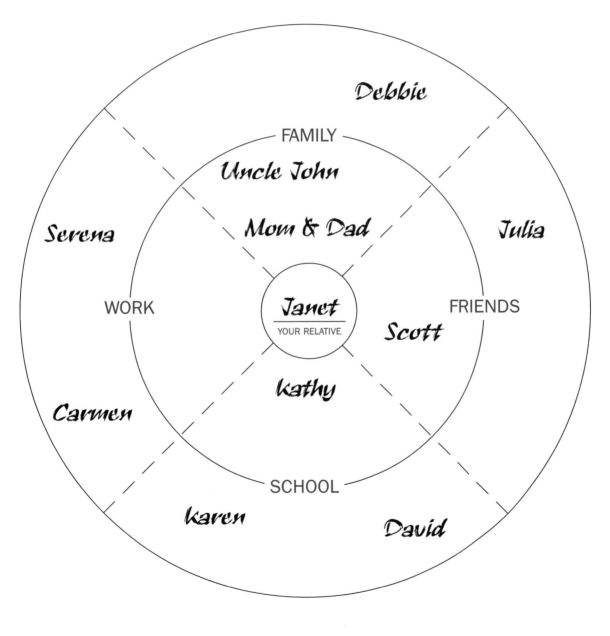

Your relative's web

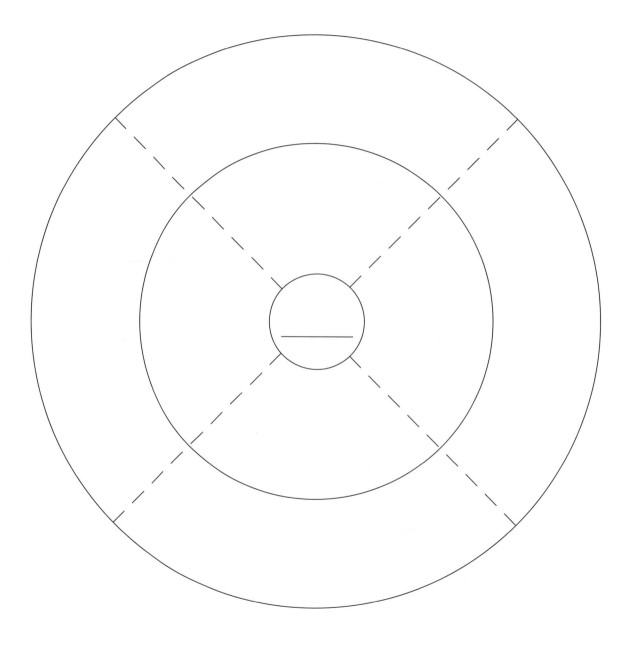

A GOOD LIFE

Worksheet 6

PERSONAL RESOURCE MAP

All of our network facilitators complete a personal resource map. To fill out your own personal resource map, list the people you know in each of the three categories. Can you think how to connect them with your relative?

You are a patron/customer at _____

_____

_____

_____

_____

You are a friend, acquaintance, co-worker, or neighbor of _____

_____

_____

_____

_____

You are a member of these groups or organizations _____

_____

_____

_____

_____

creating
a home

Mid pleasures and palaces though we may roam,

Be it ever so humble, there's no place like home.

John Howard Payne

Home alone, too

"My wife and I had always expected that Rick would stay in our home. We thought the local association might take it over after we died. They could turn it into a group home. Then Rick and others like him would live there. After my wife died I carried on with the same expectation.

"Then I attended a workshop on 'Letting Go,' sponsored by PLAN. I began to wonder whether I was holding onto ideas that weren't in Rick's best interest. I had no idea if he would enjoy living with other people. I didn't know how he'd react to having staff supervising him. Well, actually I did know. Rick had lived in a group home years before and it hadn't worked out.

"Maybe I'm being a little stubborn here, I thought. Maybe it would not be best for Rick after all.

"I decided to take it up with Rick. He didn't think too much of the idea at first. At least that's what I thought because he mumbled, 'I don't know.' Little did I know I had stumbled onto a secret.

As I later found out, Rick had begun to express an interest in moving out. He just hadn't mustered the courage to talk to me about it.

A neighbor from across the street who had known Rick since he was a baby had been coming to network meetings since they started. He never said anything, but he kept coming. Several people, including George, wondered why. However, when the topic of Rick's moving came up, the neighbor sprang into action. It turned out he was a property developer and he knew of a vacancy in an apartment building that was centrally located, on a bus route, etc.

George still wasn't convinced. "I thought it was too big a jump from living with the old man to being on his own. Then I heard this apartment building had the nosiest landlady in the city! That satisfied me. If she knew everybody's business, she would certainly know Rick's. I was confident she would keep her eye on Rick.

What clinched the move in George's mind was the fact the apartment was situated directly over the laundry room. Rick is a big hockey fan and makes a lot of noise when his team, the Montreal Canadians, is winning. "I thought Rick's feet stomping would irritate anyone living below him. Fortunately washing machines and dryers don't mind the noise."

So Rick moved out last February. "It's a

continued on page 108

Creating a home

home is something we long for. Think of the millions of people stirred by the scene in the movie *E.T.*, when the lonely, forlorn and abandoned E.T. whispers hoarsely to his boy companion and would-be rescuer, "Home, Elliott, home." It would be fair to say millions of people of all ages and from every culture wept in response to this universal longing.

The value of home is universal. People everywhere recognize home as a place of haven. It is no coincidence that the logo of the International Year of the Family, in 1994, was a heart-shaped roof. Home is synonymous with family and with relationship. In fact the word "home" comes from a Sanskrit root meaning a safe place to lie down; a separation of outside from inside, defined by a threshold. Be it ever so humble, home is a sanctuary and a place of intimacy.

Home is fundamental to a good life for ourselves. Home expresses something fundamental about all of us. Step Three reflects our expanded and maturing vision of home. Above all, this chapter reflects our belief that our relative's home must be defined by their personality, respond to their lifestyle, and embody what is most fundamental about them.

As we begin to think and plan our response to the question of home we are faced with three main challenges:

> There is nothing like staying at home for real comfort.
>
> JANE AUSTEN

continued from page 106

start," says George. "The apartment's his home now – he doesn't have his old man to bug him there.

"There have been no big problems. He took it in his stride. Actually he has matured quite a bit as a result of the move. He likes to boast that he knows all 15 people in the building and they all talk to him. What a difference from his old neighborhood where so many of the people he knew had moved away. And I must admit I like the idea he is surrounded by people who accept him and in their own way check up on him."

And there's more. Rick has just found a two-bedroom apartment in the same building. Bob, his friend since childhood, is moving in with him. George suspects that Rick has at least one more move ahead of him and that it will be into a place he owns himself. George will be able to help because he recently sold the family home. "No need to hold onto something that big," he said.

- rescuing our understanding of home from the limited perspective contained in the phrase "group home" and its equivalents.

- reflecting more deeply with our family member with a disability on the qualities that make a place a home.

- controlling the home environment – creating an opportunity through home ownership and other forms of tenure for our relative to have stability, choice, and control in their living environment.

Home – the idea we live in

He is happiest,
be he king or peasant,
who finds peace in his home.

GOETHE

Few languages offer as many alternatives to "home" as English does. Think of abode, dwelling, cottage, bungalow, shelter, domicile, sanctuary, residence, hearth, and threshold. Home is a metaphor of limitless possibilities. Home is a place we want to be. A place where we can simply be.

Home occupies a powerful place in our individual and collective psyche, carved into everyone's hearts and minds as surely as the St. Lawrence and the Mississippi Rivers cut through the heart of North America.

Getting from house to home isn't easy for any of us. For some it is an endless journey. Remember Robert Frost's magnificent elegy *The Death of the Hired Man*? Frost confronts us with the differing perspectives of the farmer and of his wife as they discuss rehiring an old farm hand previously dismissed. The wife, obviously moved by the man's distress, says, "Warren, he has come home to die." To which the husband cynically replies:

Home is the place where when you have to go there,
They have to take you in.

For years that definition satisfied me as representing the best home could offer. I completely missed the functionality and limitation of such an interpretation. After all, family is kin, and kin is obligation. They have to take you in, nothing more needs to be explained, end of story.

A recent look at Frost's poem uncovered a deeper meaning. It is reflected in the farm wife's quick reply to her husband's smug, superficial taunt. Through her, Frost repositions the concept of home beyond the husband's cool cynicism.

I should have called it
Something you somehow haven't to deserve

Home, as the farm wife understood, has nothing to do with rewards and punishments. It has nothing to do with wood and nails, bricks, and mortar. Rather, it is about sweat and laughter, bruises and tears, rug stains and cobwebs, flowers and slammed doors, failures and promises, kisses and fingerprints. Home is where we become, where we are authentic.

Getting from house to home is even more difficult and challenging for our friends and family members with a disability. From the words of an embroidered cushion that rested on the couch in my grandmother's kitchen, "It takes a heap of living to make a house a home." Many of our relatives live in that deranged juxtaposition of words known as a "group home." This adroit term, unintentionally perhaps, camouflages the limitation of what the human service system can offer or create for those who live in such a place.

Too often, group homes are not sanctuaries for the people who live there. They are simply places of work for the staff who come and go. And come and go they do, often reaching turnover rates of 200 per cent a year.

Group homes can excel at providing a place to sit, eat, dress, and sleep. Often they do not reflect the relatedness of people, places, and things. They do not nurture relationships among the people who live there, or help them understand their connection with nature, or with the everyday things they use.

Not all group homes are hostile to the heart and spirit. However, it takes exceptional people to make a group home a home. One of PLAN's founding parents has not sought to

The fireside is the tulip bed of a winter day.
PERSIAN PROVERB

change the living arrangements for her son for one simple reason. Every time she calls or visits the group home where he lives there is laughter, surely one of the languages of home. Similarly group living arrangements like those of the L'Arche communities create welcoming, nurturing environments that qualify as home to us, despite their large size. Jean Vanier, the founder and inspiration behind the L'Arche communities, believes that people with intellectual disabilities are people of relationships and heart. The homes created by L'Arche communities are intensely focused on relationships. No doubt this is why so many of the people in these communities flourish.

The continuum of status

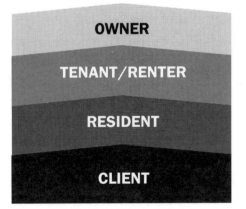

From house to home

Worksheets

Two worksheets are located at the end of this chapter, starting on page 138. Take a look at them now, and plan to fill them out when you've finished this chapter.

WORKSHEET 7 **Welcome Mat**

This worksheet will assist you and your relative to explore the hopes and dreams they have about a home of their own.

WORKSHEET 8 **When Is a House a Home**

This worksheet provides some simple guidelines and questions to help you evaluate the home-like quality of a community residence.

A home of one's own

A home of one's own. This is a significant dream for most of us. A home, particularly one we own, represents stability and security. It ensures privacy and gives us an opportunity to shape our living space according to our wishes and creativity. Home ownership is also a good investment and a hedge against inflationary times.

Most of us view home ownership as a given – a goal we will achieve sooner or later. This is not so for people with disabilities. For most it is not even a consideration; it is not even in their vocabulary. It is a dream neither they nor their parents dare consider for them. The closest many of us get to the dream is a secret desire to leave our home to an agency that will turn it into a group home our relative may inhabit life-long. Other than that, ownership is simply out of the picture. Or so we think. That secret desire is a critical thread, however. So don't lose it. As we pull it, it will lead to other possibilities: stability, permanence, predictability, control, choice and status.

Choice, control and status

Homeowners have status in our society. The pride of ownership is one of our more important cultural values. Home ownership is the fulfillment of a dream even if we have a hefty mortgage and are "renting" the money from a financial institution.

We see no reason why people who need staff support for their personal care should be denied the benefits of a home of their own. People's lives change dramatically when they control their own living arrangements.

Many of us cannot afford to assist our sons and daughters to purchase their own home. We're still paying down our own mortgage! However, there are alternatives to home ownership. Housing equity cooperatives, land trusts and co-housing provide many of the advantages of home ownership. If these options are not available or appropriate, we suggest you consider rental. Rental accommodation, particularly long-term leases, can allow people to establish a sense of their own place and maintain control of their living environment. Being a tenant provides a much different status than being a resident of a group home.

Even if you cannot afford to buy a dwelling at the present time, we suggest you reflect on the issues raised in this chapter. "Controlling" our relatives' home environment is one way we can increase the amount of influence and direction they will have over their lives.

Home ownership means. . .

- Control over where you live
- Stability of tenure
- The opportunity to build up equity
- A financial and emotional investment
- A hedge against inflation
- Privacy
- A sense of place

- Choice
- Contemplation
- Hospitality
- A haven
- Security
- Safety, comfort
- Sanctuary

Limitations of current housing options

In building the future for your son or daughter, you are the architect.

ARTHUR MUDRY

Despite the millions of dollars governments spend on the cost of accommodation and shelter for people with disabilities, little of it assists them to control or own their home. They have no security, tenure, equity, or choice. The money is directed to landlords, non-profit agencies and private vendors who usually own the houses and provide "residential support services." As a result, more and more families are looking for alternatives.

Regardless of whether your son or daughter is currently living with you or in a residential service provided by someone else, you have likely experienced some or all of these frustrations:

- Limited new housing spaces become available each year.
- Waiting lists are long.
- Housing is not available in neighborhoods your relative is familiar with.
- Group homes often become places of work for staff rather than homes for the people who actually live there.

Making homes out of houses

Here are some questions that will get you and your family thinking about establishing a home for your relative:

1 What kind of home can you imagine your relative living in?

2 Have you talked to your relative about a home for them?

3 What kind of housing are they interested in?

4 Where would be a good location?

5 Who would be interested in supporting your relative to establish a home?

6 Who among friends and acquaintances would make compatible roommates?

7 What kind of support would they need?

8 How would they like to decorate their home?

9 What would the entrance or threshold look like?

10 Which rooms would contain their favorite possessions?

- Staff turnover can be high.

- Someone else decides who your relative lives with.

- Individual needs may be secondary to those of other roommates.

- The number of unrelated people living together is higher than typical.

- Rules, procedures, and protocols abound.

- The people who work there, rather than the people who live there, often shape the personality of the home.

- There is anxiety about family involvement.

- Licensing restricts the character and look of the house.

- Agency priorities and politics influence what happens in the house as much as the needs and interests of the people who live there.

- Government funding varies from year to year.

- The people who live there form relationships with staff rather than with each other.

- There is limited involvement with neighbors.

Choice is the key

One alternative is to put control and direction in the hands of our relatives, or at least in the hands of their representatives, the people who love them and who have been selected to provide advice and guidance.

The goal of home ownership has become an increasingly attractive option to parents who want a secure housing option to complement the other elements of the Personal Future Plan they are developing. Whether the home is owned directly or owned on their behalf through a trust, they see their sons or daughters living in a place they choose, with people they choose, with staff they choose to hire (or fire), for as long as they like. Actually that sounds too clinical. They see their child or relative residing in a

> To me owning a home is like getting your freedom, freedom out of the dark ages. That was my dream. I wanted to see how it would feel to own my own place.
> DOUG BROOKS, HOMEOWNER

good friendly neighborhood, within walking distance of stores and other amenities, greeted by neighbors and shop-keepers, living with a good friend, hosting dinner parties, and relaxing in a home designed and decorated to their tastes. Does this sound too good to be true? Read the article "Lynn – A home of her own" on page 132, and consider the housing examples at the end of this chapter.

Critical components of home ownership

As you would expect, taking matters into your own hands requires more work. It means paying attention to a number of critical components, including:

Financing the purchase

Unless you are independently wealthy, this is the most formidable and intimidating challenge. Our goal is to see all governments provide more favorable tax treatment for families who assist their relative with a disability to purchase a home. The funds governments allocate to agencies for housing charges could be reallocated to individuals to purchase their own home.

Until this happens, families have opted to:

- Re-mortgage the family home.
- Seek support from grandparents.
- Form a partnership with other parents to purchase a home.
- Take out a reverse mortgage.
- Work with financial institutions to purchase homes previously foreclosed on and available at a cheaper price.
- Locate developers who will reduce the price on some of their units in return for zoning concessions from municipalities.
- Earmark part of their estate to establish a housing trust exclusively for the purpose of purchasing a home.

Home control means...

- Choosing where you want to live.
- Choosing whom you will live with.
- Choosing the staff who will support you.

- Purchase life insurance to finance a home or establish a housing trust upon their death.
- Rent out the other bedrooms to help finance mortgage payments.
- Leave their home in their will to their child with a disability.
- Find a non-profit service provider willing to own the home jointly with their relative.
- Finance the down payment and structure the mortgage so that government benefits cover the monthly mortgage costs.
- Find a foundation or association willing to: underwrite the risk for high ratio financing; provide interest-free or low interest first or second mortgages; provide a deferred second mortgage to the purchasers, or help with a down payment (loan or gift).
- Push for individualized funding so that government dollars can be used to purchase a home.

Ownership

Many individuals are vulnerable to exploitation by unscrupulous predators. Many of our family members are not capable of managing money. You may wish to structure the ownership of the home so that unprincipled people will not have access to this valuable asset.

Here are some home ownership options you may want to consider for your relative:

- Direct title.
- Joint ownership by you and your relative with a disability.
- Ownership with another person or agency.
- Ownership with another family.

- Co-op housing, particularly co-ops in which they can build up equity.

- Co-housing. All financing (for each unit and the common areas) comes from each owner.

- Ownership by a trust in your relative's name (or by joint trusts if two or more people with disabilities are involved). The trust(s) can be established:
  - while you are alive, or
  - through your estate after your death.

Types of co-ownership

If more than one individual or family owns the home, you must choose one of these legal co-ownership options:

- joint tenancy; or
- tenancy in common.

Housing Types

Just about anything is possible:

- single family

- condominium, strata or row housing

- housing cooperative unit

- co-housing

- apartment

- mobile home or trailer

- infill housing (e.g., converting a garage into a small housing unit)

- renovation of an existing house

- purpose-built housing designed for your relative's needs. Example: "pod-like" bedrooms with shared kitchen, dining, and lounge areas.

Maintaining government benefits

- Make sure a person with a disability is allowed to own a home and still receive government benefits in your jurisdiction. A home may be an "allowable asset" or an "exempt asset." Most jurisdictions permit people with disabilities to own their home and still receive government benefits.

- Some jurisdictions will deduct any contributions you make to the mortgage from your relative's government benefits. They consider such support unearned income and deduct it dollar for dollar from the amount of monthly government assistance. Check to determine the situation in your area.

- In some jurisdictions, the housing or shelter component of the monthly government assistance an individual receives is awarded on the basis of actual costs up to a maximum dollar figure. Many families structure their down payment so that the monthly mortgage payment is the equivalent of this maximum amount.

Taxes

Home ownership has its privileges. These include exemptions on capital gains tax, eligibility for homeowner grants, and local municipal tax breaks. It can be worthwhile consulting with a mortgage lender or non-profit housing developer to determine which benefits are available in your jurisdiction.

Ongoing maintenance

If you purchase a house, you will need to make arrangements to cover:

1 The ongoing mortgage payments provided you have not purchased it outright.

- Will government income assistance be enough to cover mortgage payments?

> Roommates will come and go, support services will change, that's a given. But whether I'm around or not, I know that the house, the home, will be there for my daughter.
> MOTHER – NEW HAMPSHIRE'S HOME OF YOUR OWN PROJECT

- Will your support for mortgage payments jeopardize your relative's government benefits?

- After your death, have you made provisions for the mortgage to be paid from a trust?

2 The major maintenance, repair, and insurance costs as well as property taxes.

- Will you pay for these yourself while you are alive? Or will you establish a living trust for this purpose?

- Will you establish a trust to cover these costs after your death?

- Who will initiate, handle, and oversee completion of major repairs?

NOTE It is critical that you consult with a knowledgeable lawyer to establish the trusts referred to above. For example, you may want to ensure that you do not jeopardize your relative's entitlement to government benefits.

3 The minor, ongoing maintenance.

While you can do this yourself in the short term, you may want to consider contracting with a property management company to provide this service. In addition, this may be a service you will need to request your trustee to provide. If your relative lives in a condominium or cooperative, property maintenance is already built into the monthly housing agreement.

4 Monthly expenses.

Don't forget such items as heat, light, phone, and cable charges. They all add up.

Negotiating funding for program support staff

Unless you have the private means to pay for staffing supports, you will have to negotiate funding from government. Generally government is becoming more interested in supporting people to live in their own homes. After all, it represents

Our belief is that everyone is ready to live in their own home. The issue is support. There is nothing magical about any building that we have seen anywhere in the country. What we know is that the magic is with the people who surround the person, and what we need to do is provide support to people so that they can live in and control their own homes.

JAY KLEIN, NATIONAL HOME OF YOUR OWN ALLIANCE

big savings to them if the capital costs of the home are not their responsibility. We suggest you use the leverage of your contribution when negotiating the necessary supports. You can argue that since government is not providing all of the financing – and is therefore saving housing costs – the least they can do is finance the staff supports.

Selecting compatible support staff

Not every staff person will be comfortable working in your relative's private home. Many will see it primarily as their workplace. We suggest you spend time clarifying in writing the values that are important to your child or relative. Whenever you hire from an agency or association, become familiar with their operating philosophy. Interview their executive director. Visit some of their programs. Get to meet the people who receive services from them; talk to their families. Remember, staff are working for your relative.

Consider making a room available at reduced or no cost in return for a student or other responsible adult living in and keeping an eye on things. Alternatively, you may be able to find a family willing to share a home with your family member in return for support.

Since old habits die hard, do not be afraid to let staff go if it appears they are not compatible or are uncomfortable with the home your relative is establishing.

Choosing a compatible roommate

There is no scientific approach to this challenge. Some people are easy to get along with. Others aren't. Often you won't know until you try. Many of the people who are now living in their own homes first tried living "on their own" in some form of rental accommodation. Then they invited someone to live with them. This is an excellent way to test the kinds of support they will need. It also enables people to have a better sense of what they want in a roommate.

> I want to remind myself and others that our homes can become sacred places, filled with life and meaning. We do not need cathedrals to remind ourselves to experience the sacred.
> GUNILLA NORRIS

Joint Tenancy

Property owned jointly by two or more persons in which the surviving joint tenant(s) becomes the owner of the entire property when one of the joint tenants dies.

Tenancy in Common

Property owned jointly by two or more people. Upon the death of one of the tenants-in-common, ownership of the deceased's shares is transferred to the person's estate, not to the other joint owner.

Technical advice for construction and renovation

We'll leave you to your own devices with this component. You will be able to access building contractors in your area far better than we will! Accessible building design advice would be available from local disability resource groups if you would like additional expertise. Other parents are a good connection for families who are considering construction or renovation.

Monitoring

Even though you have made all the arrangements in response to every eventuality, something is bound to go wrong. Count on it. You need to make arrangements in advance for an individual or a group of people to monitor the housing arrangements you have established. This can be a role for your executor or trustee(s). Another valuable group will naturally be your relative's Personal Network. These people will ensure the services required and the arrangements you have made are actually being delivered. They can also assist your relative to cope with any changes that occur. Another monitoring solution is to create a PLAN-like organization in your area to oversee the variety of arrangements you have made. See Step Seven for more information.

> A house is a garment, easily put off or on, casually bought and sold; a home is skin. Merely change houses and you will be disoriented; change homes and you bleed. When the shell you live in has taken on the savor of your love, when your dwelling has become a taproot, then your house is a home.
> SCOTT RUSSELL SANDERS

Homecoming

Times are changing. As the community living movement matures more of us are seeking alternatives to traditional residential arrangements. So are our relatives.

Many more people with disabilities are about to become homeowners. They are gaining a measure of choice and control over their lives they have never experienced before. When established with due respect and consideration for the issues identified here, long-term housing arrangements provide families with another concrete component of their Personal Future Plan.

As government financial support for social housing declines or is eliminated, families will have to examine other sources of financing. If families see themselves as part of the solution they may want to approach government to secure more favorable tax treatment for the housing investments they are prepared to make on behalf of their son/daughter.

Government saves money when the capital costs are borne elsewhere. In addition families will then have strong leverage with government to secure staff support. Surely government will be willing to provide operational support if the

Words of Advice

Rent first, purchase later

If you are considering purchasing a home, encourage your relative to try a rental arrangement first. You may avoid a costly mistake. Most people move at least three or four times before they develop a sense of the kind of place they would like to live in and who they would like to live with.

Create flexibility

No arrangement is forever. Many of us will live in or own more than one home. Give your trustee(s) the flexibility to sell or otherwise dispose of the property, and to change housing arrangements in response to changing circumstances of your relative. This applies even when it is the family home that is willed to the trust.

Seek advice before purchasing

There are a number of individuals and agencies with expertise in the key factors to consider when planning a home for people with a disability. Many of these are other parents. Seek their advice before you lay your money down.

capital costs have already been taken care of. With such tax and trust concessions, more and more families will be willing and able to invest in the housing future of their children and to support those whose families are unable to.

Governments could also redirect existing housing subsidy dollars. We think it makes more sense to use these to create long-term housing tenure. In the United States for example, a national "Home of Your Own" initiative assists people returning from institutions to become homeowners. See page 125 for details.

Creating a home cannot be done in isolation from the other steps. Without the existence of a network of personal support, our sons and daughters will be just as isolated in their own place as anywhere else. Often it is the Personal Network that will ensure a house becomes a home and remains so. Similarly, you will need to use your will and trust agreement to formalize the arrangements to own or rent as well as to take care of maintenance. Step Five, Ensuring Choices, will provide you with some options to protect your relative against exploitation and to assist them make housing-related decisions.

We conclude with the centuries-old blessing: Safe home!

Young families, take heart

Purchasing a home for a loved one with a disability may seem a long way off for those of us who have to deal with the little matter of our own mortgage on the family home.

Don't despair; you can still nurture a sense of place, a sense of the qualities that make a house a home. The details will take care of themselves eventually.

Here are some suggestions of what you can do:

- appreciate the sense of place you are developing in your child
- create stories about the places your family has lived in
- observe the places where your child feels comfortable and safe – factor these into their dream of home
- keep a souvenir box
- buy them furniture they can use forever
- include them in household chores
- take pictures of favorite places
- encourage them to take care of a plant
- teach them to dwell in loveliness and hospitality

The American National Home of Your Own Alliance

The American National Home of Your Own Alliance is the pre-eminent resource on home ownership for people with disabilities. Evolving from New Hampshire's Home of Your Own Project groundbreaking work (no pun intended), the Alliance has inspired and created new possibilities for individual controlled and owned housing and support. The project exemplifies how to blend and structure non-traditional income streams and government subsidies to support home ownership for people historically excluded from the housing market.

They have been able to support a highly motivated group of home purchasers by:

- Creating greater flexibility in underwriting, thereby enabling people without savings or established credit and dependent on government benefits to qualify for mortgages.
- Convincing government (state) financing authorities to revise their underwriting criteria to allow the use of public benefits as a source of income to qualify for loans and allowing the 5% needed for a down payment to come from monies other than borrowers' funds. This flexibility was necessary because people receiving Supplemental Security Income (SSI) and Medicaid Waiver funds cannot have savings or resources in excess of $1500–2000. They can however own their own home without jeopardizing benefits, provided they live in the home.
- Personalizing and restructuring agency budgets so that the line item for housing was committed to mortgage payments (principal, interest, taxes, and insurance). This served to stabilize housing costs not always possible in a speculative rental market.
- Collaborating with agencies willing to assist individuals select their home and guarantee long-term personalized support. In some situations agencies also contributed money for down payments, closing costs, monitoring of long-term housing maintenance as well as guidance and intervention before problems arise.
- Blending funds from a variety of sources (legal settlements, inheritances, family gifts, local grants, private foundations, service clubs, contributions from the seller, community block grants and U.S. federal HUD funds) for down payments, closing, renovation/repair and long-term maintenance costs.

The culmination of their efforts and their proudest moments are the mortgage signing ceremonies – the practical manifestation of their creativity and ingenuity and the extension of the American dream to people with disabilities.

Examples of housing solutions

Given the complexity of issues and the unique circumstances of each individual and family, the following examples should serve only as illustrations of what is possible.

EXAMPLE ONE
Norman – proud homeowner

Background

Norman lived on the family farm in rural New Hampshire with his parents until his mother's heart attack hastened a move to the State School. Most of the next 25 years were spent there. Eventually he moved into an apartment and now thanks to his brother, his support team and the project coordinator of New Hampshire's Home of Your Own Project, he lives in a three-bedroom home with a large yard, located in a friendly neighborhood. Norman, now in his fifties, hosts barbecues with his neighbors, has joined a local church, and visits his mother, who lives in a nearby nursing home.

Financing

Norman was pre-qualified for a mortgage based on an agency budget that served as his income verification. However, since the house he eventually chose required rehabilitation, he needed approximately $16,000 to close on his home. Fortunately, he was able to access funds provided by the New Hampshire Housing Finance Authority to build a ramp and a deck.

Features

- Community groups, in particular, church resources, were used to locate homes for Norman to check out.

- Since Norman doesn't speak, he communicated his

feelings about the homes he viewed by facial expressions and gestures.

- Normal often hosts visitors interested in the project, including Eunice Kennedy Shriver.

Norman's story is reprinted with permission of the Home of Your Own Project.

EXAMPLE TWO
Patricia – living in an apartment

Background

Patricia is a 38-year-old woman who lives on her own. She receives the maximum benefits available from the government for adults with disabilities. After sharing a rental apartment with a friend for three years, Patricia moved into a housing cooperative where she stayed for two years.

Patricia's grandmother had left her a large sum of money in a discretionary trust. John, Patricia's father, is trustee.

When Patricia decided to move out of the housing co-op, she and her dad decided to look for an apartment unit she could own. They found an affordable two-bedroom condominium unit, centrally located near a large shopping center, close to major bus routes and a short walk to the train.

Financing

The apartment unit cost $125,000.

- Patricia's dad contributed $12,500 of his own money.

- The discretionary trust contributed $97,500 in a no-interest second mortgage.

- Patricia took out a first mortgage for $15,000.

Features

- Patricia has title to the apartment.

- Since her dad owns only a tenth of the apartment,

Patricia is the principal owner. As homeowner she is eligible for the homeowner's grant. Also since this is her principal residence, the apartment is not subject to capital gains should it ever be sold. If her dad owned it he would pay capital gains because he already owns one home.

- The fact that Patricia's father owns approximately a tenth of the apartment prevents a dishonest person from persuading Patricia to sell or to order major repairs.

- Should the apartment ever be sold, Patricia's father would get his money back and the amount of the second mortgage would be returned to the discretionary trust.

- The mortgage payments plus hydro and maintenance costs are equal to the shelter component of the Income Assistance Patricia receives.

- Patricia does not have to worry about major maintenance costs. These are covered by her condominium fees.

EXAMPLE THREE
Thomas – staying in the family home

Background

Thomas is a 48-year-old man who currently lives with his parents. His parents want him to remain in the family home after they die. When that day arrives, the house will be placed in a trust for Thomas' continued use. To support Thomas, the family has arranged to establish two trusts (a residential trust and a family trust – described below) and a microboard (described on page 199). They have also arranged to recruit a "support family."

Financing

The parents' estate plan provides for the home, including furnishings, to be left in a discretionary trust for the primary use and benefit of Thomas. The family calls this the "residential trust." The trust would have a small amount of funds to cover minor repairs.

A separate discretionary financial trust will provide additional assets to cover maintenance of the home, property taxes, extraordinary expenses, and the quality of Thomas' life. The family calls this the "family trust."

Government will be asked to contribute funding towards the daily support needs of Thomas.

Features

- Thomas continues to live in a familiar environment.

- The financing provided by government for Thomas' support needs will be less than that required for a conventional group home.

- None of the money from government will be applied to the capital cost or maintenance of the home.

- There will be a small "microboard" of five people (two family members, an advocate, a co-trustee, and a Personal Network member). This microboard will have the authority to contract with the government for funding on Thomas' behalf. This funding will allow them to contract with service providers. They will also monitor the quality of the care he receives.

- Thomas' brother and his wife will live in the home with Thomas and provide a caring and harmonious living environment. In return, they will live rent-free and enjoy the home as is customary under traditional rental contracts.

- Should it become necessary to sell the home, the will contains a provision that the trustees can do so and use the funds from this transaction to acquire an equivalent home for Thomas' benefit. Any surplus funds will be placed in the "family trust."

EXAMPLE FOUR
May – living in a co-housing development

Background

Mr. and Mrs. Chang have purchased a three-bedroom town-house unit in the Windsong Co-Housing development in Langley, British Columbia for their daughter May.

Co-housing is a term applied to housing projects where the owners pay the costs for their own unit as well as their portion of the common area. Co-housing attracts people who want to recreate a "village atmosphere." It is a modern way of building a personal network or creating a supportive community, and this is what interested the Changs. People share meals together and are committed to building a safe, caring place for everyone.

The Changs have worked out an arrangement to obtain an affordable unit for their daughter and at the same time maintain a modest retirement income for themselves. Since they purchased their unit before the project was built, the Changs were able to ensure that the unit and common areas are barrier-free and wheelchair-accessible.

Financing

Mr. and Mrs. Chang purchased the unit outright and gave May a demand mortgage.

The monthly mortgage will be recovered from three sources:

- May's monthly government benefits.
- Rental of one of the bedrooms to a third party who will provide some support to May.
- Government, which is currently funding May's shelter costs at a group home she lives in.

Features

- The parents, who are retired, derive all their income from investments. They sunk their investments into the unit for May but they will derive a monthly income from the mortgage payments.

- May enjoys the benefits of living in a supportive community.

- Windsong incorporates a glass-covered pedestrian street. Each of the 34 units opens onto an unheated glassed-in atrium as well. These design features are perfect for May.

- May has title to her unit and therefore is eligible for the homeowner's grant.

EXAMPLE FIVE
Surrinder – living in a condominium near the family home

Background

Mr. and Mrs. Singh purchased a two-bedroom condominium for their 28-year-old son, Surrinder. The complex is located within three blocks of the family home.

Features

- Ownership of the home is between the parents and Surrinder. As financial protection, the parents have enduring power of attorney.

- Upon the parents' death, complete ownership of the home goes to Surrinder. Surrinder's sister and her husband will have power of attorney.

- One of the bedrooms will be rented to a roommate for Surrinder.

- A committee comprised of a representative of the family, the service delivery organization, and the family of Surrinder's roommate will oversee the maintenance and operation of the condominium.

Lynn

A home of her own

Like many senior couples who have worked hard all their lives, Arthur and Hazel own their own home. Like many couples, they felt they had accumulated sufficient assets to leave a trust fund for their daughter, Lynn, after they died. Unlike many couples, however, Arthur and Hazel have found a creative way to use their assets for Lynn's benefit today.

In response to a crisis in Lynn's life that left her without a secure place to live, Arthur and Hazel purchased a house for their daughter. "We had always intended to leave our assets to be divided among our three children after we die. We simply shifted that inevitable line forward 20 or 30 years to secure what Lynn needs right now."

Until the age of 28, Lynn had enjoyed a happy fulfilled life in the family home. Then Lynn moved into a group home. Lynn became increasingly depressed to the point of being unwilling to leave the house. "It was as if she descended deep into a cave," recalls her father. "The chaos to her psyche in that particular situation was devastating to Lynn. She had lost contact with the world."

She had moved into the group home with high expectations, excitement, and enthusiasm. Their daughter's change from a curious, gregarious and hospitable young woman was attributable in Arthur and Hazel's estimation to the routine and regimentation imposed by the operators of the home. Her friends and family couldn't come and visit her without scheduling in advance. She had little privacy; staff hovered around during visits. Outings were discouraged because Lynn's excitement when she returned upset her roommates, who did not have the same opportunities. She wasn't allowed to keep her cat. Staff took her African violets away from her as "punishment."

Lynn spent two subsequent years at Birch Clinic before her family was able to look for a place in the community again. However, the options all looked the same. "Group homes seemed little more than mini-institutions. Agency homes did not feel like the homes the rest of us live in," Arthur said. They vowed that Lynn would never again live in a home that wasn't her own.

That's when they decided to buy Lynn her own home. They had two criteria. First, her home should be within walking distance of the family home. Secondly, it should be near to the shops, recreation center, and library. It seemed like an impossible dream.

But dreams do shape reality, and with

persistence and good fortune they were able to find an old small house within two blocks of the family home. After months of exhaustive renovations, Lynn had her own place to her satisfaction. This special moment was enhanced because Lynn could share it with her new housemate, an old school mate and long-time family friend, Sarah.

Arthur and Hazel re-mortgaged the family home. As Arthur describes it, "We've been paying rent to the mortgage on our own house for most of our life. We're just continuing this practice in order that Lynn may have her own house. The mortgage collateral is on the family home so if anything happens to us, Lynn's house is secure."

Next, Arthur and Hazel had to find compatible caregivers. This proved to be a difficult task. Lynn and Sarah needed support in the evening between 3:30 and 10:00 p.m. Since this was Sarah and Lynn's home, not a place of work for staff, the interviews were exhaustive. Eventually they settled on an agency, largely because the executive director expressed his commitment to keeping the emphasis on Lynn and Sarah, and "their" home.

The arrangement is perfect for all concerned. Week-day support is provided by a live-in university student who appreciates a break on the rent and the opportunity to get away on weekends to study.

Additional weekend support comes from a young woman with a new baby. Next to cats, babies are Lynn's most precious joy. To Lynn's delight the dining room has become a child's play area.

As for Lynn, she is the perfect hostess. Among the many events she presides over is PLAN's Christmas party, which she has hosted for the past three years.

Watch out, Martha Stewart.

Nothin' as lovin' as something from the oven

My childhood summers are associated with my grandparents' kitchens. All our visiting was done in the kitchen. Just about all living was done there too. Certainly not in their parlor or living room. In my grandparents' homes, living rooms were closed to ordinary people. Priests and doctors were received there until we got to know them or they us. And dead people were waked there. There was no living done in those living rooms. We used to sneak into them during the summer, my cousins and I, because they were cool – no air conditioning in those days. Musty, waxy, cool, sheet-draped chairs and shiny, crackling linoleum but minus the boiled tea, baking powder biscuits and Spam sandwiches, readily available in the kitchen.

Home is where the kitchen is. My grandmother knew that. Her low, soft, happy whistling accompanied her well-worn linoleum path, even at ninety-one. Setting the bread to rise on the stovetop. Stopping for a sip of cool well water that we proudly fetched from the neighbor's because our well had gone dry.

Big old kitchens, with comfortable couches. Neither of my grandparents had a dining room. Big kitchens were enough. Big arborite tables crowded with books and unanswered mail to be shoved aside at meal time or for a quick game of cards.

Always euchre. Always a quick game. Right after supper, clear the table and begin.

Home is where the stove is. The staff in Kathryn's group home know that. They work hard to make mealtimes special. Trouble is, Kathryn's body gets nourished but not her soul. Last month a new supervisor took over. Now the food is served from the stove into serving dishes and placed on the table. Dining is meant to be elegant and she is determined. My daughter was just getting used to walking to the stove to fill her plate from the pots – the functional preference of the last supervisor.

Over in the corner where the wash stand might be, hangs a discreet bulletin board with shift assignments, learning objectives and med. charts.

What Kathryn misses out on, what we all miss out on, is the loving turbulence of my summer kitchens, the lazy meandering, noisy, conversation-rich, cleanups. The reverie, warmth and acceptance of grandmother's oven. Instead, eating seems almost a shameful, messy interlude in an antiseptic environment. Our kitchens are becoming more like the parlors of old. Our homes more like our kitchens.

Desperado

Wayne met me at the door.

"Will you be my father? Please be my father. Can I come and live with you?"

I muttered something irrelevant and slunk into my seat. Gone was my Super Advocate's swagger.

Aside from Wayne, his grandparents and his network facilitator, the meeting included a group home supervisor, the director of residential services, a vocational coordinator, a government social worker, a public health nurse, two residential workers, a specialist in behavior management, and me. I was there at the invitation of Wayne's grandparents and his network facilitator. I was supposed to deal with the "bad guys."

Their agenda was clear. Wayne was being bullied into leaving the group home he'd lived in for ten years.

Over the long holiday weekend Wayne had begun pushing his roommates around as they waited to be picked up by their parents. After they left he had thrown a glass at the lone staff person on duty and then locked himself in his room. In panic, the police had been called. Wayne's violence was "escalating" and he had to be moved – for his own good and for the safety of others. The specialist in behavior was reciting the options.

The nurse, having witnessed my personal disarmament, slipped in a question from the side. "Couldn't Wayne go visit with his parents on holiday weekends?"

The answer was a tragic echo from the early post-war era. Wayne's parents had died in a car crash when he was three. The same accident had injured his head. He went to live with his grandparents. Eventually he had been placed in care. His grandparents had tried their best. They lived in the Yukon and couldn't get down south as easily anymore. And Wayne had no way of visiting them.

The spell was broken and a new insight gained. The rogue question stimulated a different interpretation.

A pattern emerged. Wayne's outbursts were linked to holiday weekends and summer vacations. While his roommates went home, Wayne stayed. The skeletal staff had chores. Cleaning, not caring, was their primary task. Wayne was left on his own, abandoned once more.

Wayne's desperate search for a father shows us that memory, no matter how faded, is a close neighbor to our dreams.

POSTSCRIPT It took us eight months, but we did it. Wayne now lives with a family, a young couple with a baby. He has found a family he is devoted to, a mother with enough room in her heart, and a father who doesn't flinch when called "Dad."

Sam and Morgan

The séance of home ownership

Lawyers and accountants are the last people most of us would associate with the occult or paranormal. So you had to be there to believe it. I wasn't but John was. John headed up PLAN's HOME Advisory Service at the time.

There were seven of them: three lawyers, two accountants, and of course Sam and Morgan. They represented all the parties to the agreement – the mortgage lender, the Community Living Society, the government lending agency, and the two happy homeowners-to-be.

John had brought them together, a magic act in itself, six months of work culminating in the all-important mortgage signing. You'd expect gravity to be on its best behavior as befitting the solemnity of the occasion.

Sam and Morgan's townhouse had been put up for sale. It was obvious to everyone that they had made the place their home over the past six years. The realtor was the one to take action.

"It's a shame you can't buy the place," she lamented.

"Yeah," agreed Sam, "we should buy this place."

This place was a three-bedroom townhouse in a new suburb of Vancouver. A great location – a quick hop to rapid transit, a quick skip to Sam's job, and a quick jump to Morgan's volunteer position at his church. The community center was nearby, and the local Starbucks. All the regulars knew them.

Ken, the executive director of the Community Living Society, agreed with the realtor and with Sam. And he was in a position to do something about it.

He approached his board with a simple analysis. Over their lifetime Sam and Morgan would be paying landlords at least two or three times the worth of a mortgage. Why not investigate a home purchase for them? The board agreed.

Besides, as Sam's mom said, "None of us want to take that bed down the stairs again!"

That's when John went into action. He developed a co-ownership, "tenants-in-common" agreement, secured high ratio mortgage financing protected by the government lending agency, and attracted a lender comfortable with the arrangements. Most banks were concerned about lending money to a non-profit society without personal covenants from members of the board of directors. But Canada's largest credit union, VanCity Credit Union, wasn't.

It took a while, but eventually the alchemy produced a mortgage document everyone was comfortable with, including an agreement about transfer of ownership, should that ever become necessary.

Parents helped with down payments. The credit union fixed the mortgage rate a $1/4$ per cent lower than the competition. Sam and Morgan's monthly shelter allowance, plus their eligibility for the homeowners' grant met their portion of the mortgage, strata fees, and taxes. The high ratio financing allowed the agency to pay for its portion of ownership over time rather than as a lump sum. All the lawyers and loans officers were in agreement.

And now back to the meeting. The grand signing was about to take place. Everyone gathered around the oak table. Papers scattered about. If there was ever a time when every "t" would be crossed it was then. The cap of the thick, flashy, expensive pen was removed and passed to Sam. The moment had arrived.

Sam studied the document and declared, "I can't sign this."

"What's wrong?" came the solicitous response.

"Would you like us to explain it again?"

"Don't worry about your signature, just make a mark if you like."

"I can't sign this," Sam repeated.

"Why not?"

When you're in the starter's block, any unexpected stoppage becomes magnified. All this time, all the concessions and all the negotiations. One more delay was almost unbearable.

A sip of water, a cough, a cleared throat.

Everyone took a shallow breath, slightly off balance, waiting for Sam's reply.

"You've got the wrong address," said Sam.

A blast of exhalation, a chorus of distress, rapid movement of paper, incantations of the sober variety. Holy smokes!

Five people startled into action.

Suddenly the paper began to levitate, the water glasses shook, and then the table started to rise. Hands to paper, paper to table, table to gravity – the unbearable lightness of being in error.

That's how John described it and I have no reason to doubt him, have I?

Equally enchanting, despite the high-priced help, is that Sam – at least – had no doubt about where his home was.

Worksheet 7

WELCOME MAT

These are questions to discuss with your relative. These questions may be best answered by having your relative draw a picture or make a collage of cutouts from magazines.

What kind of home would you like to live in? _____
_____
_____

Would you like to live by yourself or with other people? _____
_____
_____

Who would you like to help you live in your own home? _____
_____
_____

What would they help you with? _____
_____
_____

Where do you want to live? _____
_____

Why do you want to live there? _____
_____

What do you want to live close to? (church, park, recreation center, bus route, stores, etc.) _____

_____

What is your favorite room? _____

_____

Do you have a favorite chair? Would you like to have one? Which room would you place it in? _____

_____

Where would you place your favorite things? _____

_____

What kind of furniture will you need for your own place? _____

_____

_____

Which furniture from your family home would you like to have? _____

_____

Would you keep a pet? What kind? _____

_____

Would you like a garden? _____

_____

Do you like to cook? Would you like to have a big kitchen? _____

_____

Would you like to have a quiet room? _____

_____

Which room would you like to have music in? _____

_____

Do you like doing dishes? _____

_____

Do you like to clean the house? _____

_____

Do you like to mow the lawn? _____

_____

How would you decorate:

Your living room? _____

_____

Your bedroom? _____

_____

Your entrance? _____

_____

What color would you paint the outside of your house? _____

_____

How would you welcome visitors to your home? _____

_____

When you came home at the end of the day, what would be the first thing you would

do? _____

_____

Worksheet 8

WHEN IS A HOUSE A HOME?

Here are some simple guidelines and questions to help you evaluate the home-like quality of residential services.

Whose house is it?

Does it appear as if the individuals who live in the house are the ones to determine its structure and tone? Or does it appear as if the house is geared to suit the staff hired to provide service?

Use your home and your own life as yardsticks for comparison. Do not accept, "Well, it's better than where they were." Instead, ask yourself, "Is it as good as I have now?" and "Is it as good as I would want for myself?"

Look around.

Are there locks where they are not needed (refrigerator, clothes closets, etc.)?

Are there no locks where they are needed (bathrooms, bedrooms, files, medicine cabinets, etc.)?

Do people have the same amount and variety of possessions and personal articles as other people their age? As much as you have?

What does it feel like?

Are the rooms comfortable? The couch? The chairs? Could you relax here? Does the place feel like a home?

Take a moment to listen.

Can you go somewhere for a little peace and quiet? Are there conversations among the people who live here?

Smell.

Do you get a scent of home-made dinner on the stove or dessert in the oven, or do you smell institutional cleaners and odors?

Taste.

Would you enjoy the food that is served or merely tolerate it?

Ask.

What are the rules? Are they excessive or overly restrictive? Do they make sense to you? Who makes the rules?

Infer.

Do the people who live here experience a home with some added support, programming, and needed supervision? Or do they experience an institutional program with a few home-like qualities?

Analyze.

What compromises have been made in the name of budget limitations, programming practices, staff needs, etc.? In what ways do these compromises detract from a home-like atmosphere?

Ask yourself,

"If an opening came up tomorrow, would I ask if I could move in?" If not, why not?

step four

making
a contribution

Good work that leaves the world softer and fuller
and better than ever before is the stuff of which
human satisfaction and spiritual value are made.

Joan Chittister

Tall in the saddle

"Rick always liked horses. No question about it," remembers George. "We had a small cabin in the Cariboo. Now that's real cowboy country. We spent as much time there as possible when he was young. Even after his mother died he liked going there. I didn't realize it at the time but it wasn't so much for the fish as for the horses. Unfortunately it was getting too much for me, too far to drive, and I had to sell it.

"Ah, but hockey – that was his passion. Especially floor hockey. Then all of a sudden he quit. Just like that."

George needn't have worried. There was not enough room in Rick's life for more than one passion and he had found a new love. To understand what happened we have to take a step back.

Rick's original facilitator had decided to travel and we recruited a replacement, Gwen. Given Rick's active network, she felt her contribution lay as a listener. Gwen wanted to get to know as much as possible about him, to dig deeper.

Rick, like many people sculpted outside the mold, had carried an invisible backpack for most of his life. The magnetic properties of mental handicap had attracted such destructive characterizations as "gruff," "uncommunicative," "detached," and "unemployable." His father admits that even those who cared about Rick could find those descriptions persuasive.

The value of a fresh perspective was soon evident. In her first summary, Gwen described Rick as easy to be with, "considerate" and "thoughtful" and "absolutely passionate about horses." Underneath the carpenter overalls, pockets full of pens and razor-sharp pencils, Rick was a cowboy.

A new view evolved.

The facilitator inspired everyone to look at the sculpture from a different angle. "Reserved" replaced "gruff." "Respectful" replaced "withdrawn." Good traditional cowboy qualities.

It all depends on your perspective.

"We knew he liked horses but we had no idea he had the 'fever,'" George recalls.

The trip from pedestrian to equestrian began with a two-week summer visit to a dude ranch. At George's treat the facilitator went with him. She left alone. Rick stayed on to work in the barns until fall. On his return he linked up with a wrangler he had met at the ranch, who joined his network.

continued on page 148

step four
Making a contribution

each of us, without exception, has a deep longing to give, to contribute, to offer, and to share what is meaningful to us. Unfortunately, this is often an experience our friends and relatives with disabilities are denied. We believe there are two distinct reasons for this tragic oversight.

One: there is no recognition that they have something to offer, to contribute, to give. Let's call that something their gifts.

Two: even if their contribution is recognized, they have little or no opportunity to make their contribution, to give their gifts.

And therein lies a paradox. A gift is not really a gift until it is given, is it?

Think about your own life.

Where would you be without your hobbies, your passions, your leisure pursuits, and your work? Aren't your talents expressions of who you are, of your essential self? We usually say, I am an accountant, a teacher, a mechanic, rather than, I do accounting, teaching, mechanics. In this context aren't we all artisans or artists? Pursuing something meaningful and sharing it with others – that's what we all do one way or the other, whether at work or our hobbies or volunteer activities. Certainly it's what most of us strive for.

Step Four is an extension of the discussion about the power of dreams and vision. It is about perceiving the gift,

> Work is love made visible.
> KAHLIL GIBRAN

continued from page 146

Soon that connection led to a paid part-time job at a local riding stable, a job he still holds. It involves a lot of shoveling but he gets to exercise the horses. And he gets paid. He soon got another part-time job – at a recycling depot. Another noble motive at work here, albeit mercenary. Rick is saving for a horse and he is in a hurry. He doesn't know the exact cost of feeding a horse but he knows "it's a lot."

These days the "unemployable" Rick gets up four mornings a week at 6:30, catches the bus to the stables, puts the coffee on, and begins his chores even before the manager arrives. The only corral he experiences now is the one for horses.

But that's not where the story ends. Just northwest of Kamloops lies the beautiful ski resort of Sun Peaks, which during the summer marks the beginning of British Columbia's largest cattle drive. For the past three years Rick has hired on as part of the crew. This year his facilitator drove him up, about a five-hour drive.

Picture this: Rick and the facilitator walking down to the bunk house and then over to the barn where his favorite mount has been reserved for him. He is in his element, a foot-long piece of grass hanging from his mouth.

There is a procession of greeters from the moment he steps out of the car.

"Hey Rick, welcome back."

"Hi big guy, where have you been?"

"We've put your favorite horse in the back stall."

With a smile as big as a barn door Rick turns to his facilitator and triumphantly declares, "That makes fourteen people I know."

acknowledging the dream, and translating it into action. This step adds the elements of passion and skill to the dream and vision you developed in Steps One and Two. We hope the equation provides you with a new way of thinking about work. Passion provides motivation, adds fuel, and transforms the dream into action. Passion gets you to act. Passion is about doing. Skill, on the other hand, cultivates and harnesses passion, enabling contributions of the head, heart, and hands to be made.

Step Four moves the discussion beyond both the contemporary perception of work and the traditional vocational services or employment training available to people with a disability. Instead we embrace the notion of work as vocation, which may or may not be associated with paid employment.

In short our four challenges are:

- recognizing the natural gifts of our friends and family members with a disability.

- validating their gifts – assisting them to appreciate and value what it is they already have.

- developing their gifts – providing them with the necessary skills to enable them to enhance their talents.

- ensuring their gifts and contributions are given.

> Service is the rent each of us pays for living – the very purpose of life.
> MARIAN WRIGHT EDELMAN

Understanding contribution means. . .

- Believing everyone has a gift.
- Validating previously unrecognized gifts.
- Developing the gifts.
- Ensuring all gifts are given.

Lakota gift finder

Two months before their annual Pow Wow, the Lakota Sioux set loose a gift finder. The gift finder's job is to make sure everyone brings a gift and to provide assistance to anyone who needs help to meet their commitment. The Pow Wow doesn't start until everyone's contribution is identified.

Seeking fulfillment and the common good

After food, clothing, and shelter, what's next?

The psychologist Abraham Maslow developed the idea of a "hierarchy of needs" which suggests that once your physical needs (food, water, sleep) are met, concerns about safety become dominant. Once these concerns have been tended to, love, affection and belonging emerge as central pursuits. But even these are not enough. There is still the drive to what he calls "self-actualize," to follow your calling, to act on what has heart and meaning, to seek fulfillment. If self-actualization is too psychological for you, substitute "to pursue your passion."

Maslow went on to say that fulfilling one's personal goals is compatible with the common good. He argued that the development of society depends on the ability of society's institutions and society's citizens to recognize and encourage the "potential for self-actualization." It doesn't take much imagination to connect work with individual purpose and link it with the real needs of the community. Realizing our gifts and achieving fulfillment makes us healthy, healthy people make healthy citizens, and healthy citizens create a healthy society.

There's a lovely scene in the award-winning documentary *And Then Came John* in which John announces to his startled family, "and now I will start my art!" For John, his art was his life, an expression of what was deeply meaningful to him. Having successfully completed a move from Los

> And there's a tremendous sorrow for a human being who doesn't find a way to give. One of the worst sufferings is not to find a way to love, or a place to work and give of your heart and your being.
>
> JACK KORNFIELD

Angeles to Mendocino, having developed friendships and obtained a job, John was now ready to "self-actualize"! After the basics, after belonging, there is more... much more.

In truth John likely had no choice but to start painting. Not pursuing his dream would have haunted him at some level as it does all of us who do not pursue our calling. As Shakespeare's Polonius put it: "This above all, to thine own self be true." Catholics list sloth as one of the seven deadly sins. The Latin for sloth is "accidie" – the sin of failing to do what you know you ought to be doing. The Hebrew root of the word sin comes from the verb "to miss," that is, to miss our calling, to miss our duty towards ourselves.

Subjects not objects

To believe that everyone has a gift, one must accept the essential humanity of our friends and relatives with disabilities. Humans are subjects, not objects. To be a subject is to interact with the world, to make a contribution, to have a gift. Unfortunately not everyone believes in the gifts of our friends and family members with a disability. To some, people with disabilities remain objects to be moved around at will. In our drive to "help" and "fix," the interests, talents and contributions of our friends and loved ones go unnoticed. They become people to whom things are done. They don't do. They are viewed not as subjects but as objects.

Many of the programs and services available for people with disabilities operate from this false value base. This is why the social, emotional and spiritual aspects of people are ignored. And why the possibilities for pursuing their passion are left unexplored.

Humans have a drive to become. We take pleasure in contributing, in doing our fair share, in being useful and in creating. That is the "being" part of human being. However, if the being part is ignored then the essence of being human is kept in the dark. The eighteenth-century philosopher George Berkeley declared, "To be is to be perceived." Perception of their "being," their essence, their gift, bestows a blessing on our friends and relatives with a disability. It recognizes their essential humanity. It ensures their contribution to the common good.

Citizenship – rights and obligations

When we think of citizenship, we usually think of the rights half of the equation but not the obligation half. The push for rights for people with disabilities has achieved significant changes. While much more needs to be done, we wonder whether it is time to renew our focus on obligations.

The French philosopher and mystic Simone Weil recognized the dangers inherent in focusing only upon rights. Before her death in 1943 she embarked on a challenging journey to create a Charter of Obligations.

We believe all discussions about the contribution of people with disabilities should take place within the context of this fuller and more balanced appreciation of citizenship. It provides a stronger base from which to achieve a safe, secure and prosperous future for our loved ones.

Society's pity, charity, and sympathy are not enough. Neither is government's largesse. Special government social programs are usually the last to be established but the first to be cut back. We predict the next advance in our grand movement toward full membership in society will be made

> If you deliberately plan to be less than you are capable of becoming, then I warn you that you'll be deeply unhappy for the rest of your life. You will be evading your own capacities, your own possibilities.
> ABRAHAM MASLOW

The gift of vulnerability

In rejecting the presence and contribution of people who live with disabilities, communities are missing something powerful. People everywhere are living in fear that they might some day have a need for support that is "unacceptable." This fear makes it impossible for people to share their caring in deep ways.

By exiling obviously vulnerable people from daily community life and interaction, we create a situation where "normal" people must hide their pain, or risk rejection. They deny the depths of both their wounds and their capacity to heal each other.

JUDITH SNOW

Charter of Human Obligations

As part of my contribution to the vitality of my community, I am obliged:

To show up and be present.

To marvel at the ordinary.

To see beauty everywhere.

To listen with silent intensity.

To serve with gentleness and respect.

To nurture with kindness and curiosity.

To play with enthusiasm and humor.

To make the truth visible.

To accept my vulnerability, and that of others.

To avoid idleness and to toil with love.

To embrace life with an open heart.

To sow seeds of tenderness.

To build a house of hospitality and affection.

To forgive gracefully.

To cherish a bold vision.

To care with compassion.

To perfect my life.

Everyone's will to work should be ensured. First, honorable and filling work. Second, a healthy and beautiful house. Third, full leisure for the rest of the mind and body.
WILLIAM MORRIS

from the base of citizenship. "Citizen" has greater value than "client" or "object of charity" or "special status."

The great Greek philosopher Aristotle suggested that it was the nature of humans to live in community and to take care of each other. The Greek word "philia" represents the love and sense of obligation people feel within community. Essentially Aristotle was talking about our moral responsibility towards each other.

Other philosophers, including Hobbes and Locke, took quite a different view of people and society. To these thinkers, people were by nature selfish and individualistic. They could live in community only if there were laws to govern and control their behavior. Much of the emphasis on rights has grown out of this tradition, and rights laws have been designed to protect vulnerable individuals from the harm others may do.

If our goal is contribution and community, an exclusive focus on rights may inadvertently limit the participation of our friends and relatives with disabilities.

One, it may tend to let people off the hook. They begin to

think, "Why should I get involved? Aren't their rights protected by law? It's not my responsibility."

Two, it may reinforce the tendency to segregate in much the same manner as the old services did by creating a category of distinct special needs.

Three, when rights are pushed to the exclusion of the responsibility to contribute, you may not be expected to contribute, and over time the impression develops that you have nothing to contribute. Then you are judged unworthy because of your lack of contribution.

Four, once rights are successfully achieved, the relationship between the advocate or rights champion and the person with a disability ends. Success erodes the connection; people move on to the next issue or cause. Citizenship, on the other hand, provides a foundation to continue the relationship. Simone Weil observed that rights are relative, only obligation is absolute.

Community depends on contribution

It should be obvious by now that we are on Aristotle's team. We believe that our responsibility towards each other is innate. This responsibility or obligation is therefore as critical an element of citizenship as are rights.

We think people with disabilities have obligations and should be supported and encouraged to make a contribution. Expectations of rights without expectations of obligations isolate us and weaken community. People with disabilities are an under-utilized resource in our society. If our communities are in as much trouble as we think they are, then we can't afford to waste a single resource.

Once the discussion is placed in the context of citizenship, we can then discuss the barriers to the effective participation in society of citizens with disabilities. Besides, it may be more timely and strategic to advance obligations together with rights. The great river of citizenship has begun to flow again in the public's mind. Not only should we "put in," we

Disability

It's ability to have fun
Ability to fall in love
Ability to have freedom
Ability to make friends
Ability to smile
Ability is a world
Ability to be responsible
Ability to be you
Disability

LIZ ETMANSKI

should also play a critical role in directing the flow.

Let's not be fooled. Obligation is part of a functioning community. Society does keep a record of our contributions. In the old days it was a lot more informal. Think of barn raisings and quilting bees. There existed a kind of community balance sheet. Implicit was the understanding, "I'll help you now because I might need your help later on."

All citizens are expected to build up credits in this reciprocity bank. If we are on the debit side exclusively, the record shows. It shows in how people with disabilities are judged to be worthy or unworthy to receive government support. We can think of many groups who receive government support without question, because the perception is that they are making a contribution. The balance sheet shows up in discussions about scarce medical resources, productivity, and access to medical treatment, education, and so on. The new unworthiness equation in the box on page 156 shows what can happen when the contributions of our relatives and friends are not factored into this unwritten balance sheet.

This is our major challenge: to prevent our relatives from being judged unworthy. The consequence of such a judgment is exclusion, segregation, and tokenism.

Perhaps a little reverse psychology is in order. If we can convince society that people with disabilities should fulfill their responsibility as citizens, then society will begin asking what it is they have to contribute. Then we can tell them about their gifts.

That will then lead to a discussion about structural barriers that limit or prevent their participation and contribution. Society will become motivated to ensure that their gifts are given. And that in turn will limit and perhaps eliminate judgments of unworthiness.

> The place to improve the world is first in one's own heart and head and hands, and then work outward from there.
>
> ROBERT PIRSIG

The new unworthiness equation

Make no mistake about it, society allocates its resources on the basis of perceived worthiness. In healthy economic times there is usually enough money to go around and government support is available to most. When the economy constricts, not only is there less to go around but some groups lose out.

Government decision makers, faced with more limited resources, draw a line between those who are perceived as worthy and those who are not. They discriminate.

In times past the line between worthy and unworthy was used to determine who would receive medical attention, who would live and who would die, who would be sterilized, who would be segregated and who could count on justice.

There was a perverse logic to their calculations that can be seen creeping back into public policy. We call this the New Unworthiness Equation.

Intellectual and physical limitations lead many people in society to assume that an individual is incapable. They have no experience to believe otherwise. Then they conclude the individual who is not capable should not be responsible for making a contribution. True, there is some acknowledgment of "specialness" which has led to "special needs" funding and inclusion in human rights legislation.

Unfortunately this benign conclusion is not the end of it. The "specialness" argument can often be a cover for sentimentality and prejudice. For a variety of reasons, including tough economic conditions, a moral judgment is made and the "not responsible" person can be seen as irresponsible for not contributing, for not being productive.

The individual is then judged to be unworthy for their lack of contribution or their "drain" on society's resources. This is how in some people's minds, intellectual and physical limitation becomes synonymous with unworthiness. They become linked to moral worth. Once

The new unworthiness equation

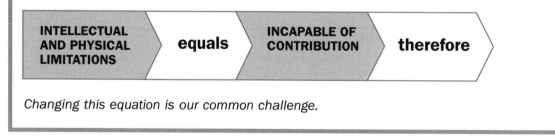

Changing this equation is our common challenge.

you are judged unworthy, it is easier to exclude, ignore or segregate. That is one of the critical lessons of the eugenics era. The elites who disdain those who are different use the unworthiness equation to justify their actions.

By not pushing for the full contribution of people with disabilities, for fulfilling their obligations as citizens, we may be conceding the grounds to those inclined to believe in the unworthiness equation.

Changing this equation is our common challenge and we may break the link at any stage. Step Five, for example, suggests new ways of viewing capability that deal with the first part of the equation. Asserting the obligation of people with disabilities to contribute assaults the equation at other stages.

The full participation of people with disabilities in society cannot be achieved simply by declaring their worthiness. It must be tackled at every stage of the unworthiness equation in order to ensure a different conclusion.

| NOT RESPONSIBLE | equals | NOT CONTRIBUTING IRRESPONSIBLE UNPRODUCTIVE | equals | UNWORTHY |

Gifts of the head, heart, and hands

Enabling contribution involves developing an appreciation of the skills, abilities, interests, possessions, passions, and character of our sons and daughters. Take a moment to reflect on these. You'll recognize it as the same process as you explored in Step Two, Building Relationships. Our participation in community, family, and relationships are based on these contributions.

Take another moment. How clearly does your emerging vision for the future (as discussed in Step One) articulate the contributions your relative with a disability could and should make?

One way to expand our appreciation for their contributions is to look for the ordinary as well as the extraordinary, for the active as well as the passive, for the obvious and the not so obvious, for the tangible and intangible, for the small scale and the large scale.

Read Judith Snow's definition in the margin on this page. Her definition includes the usual understanding of giftedness, that is, a special talent that only a few people possess. But it also includes the rest of us. All of us. Everyone has countless gifts, both ordinary and extraordinary. Not just the gifts that are recognized at the Academy Awards, or the Olympics, or with a whopping salary, but the other gifts, the gifts of loyalty, caring, hospitality, creation. To start with, Judith declares there are two simple gifts that everyone has and which form the basis of every other contribution.

The first pre-eminent gift is the gift of **presence**. You cannot create an opportunity for meaningful interaction if you are not there. Simply by being present, communion or fellowship is created. The exchange may be a helping hand, a spark of love, a moment of insight, a walk down an alley, a kiss in the dark, the comfort of silence, a pleasurable experience, an inspiring interchange, a great moment in history, a thrilling encounter, an enduring affair. It would not have happened without your presence.

A gift is pure when it is given from the heart to the right person at the right time and at the right place and when we expect nothing in return.
BHAGAVAD GITA

Judith's Definition of Gifts

A gift is anything that one is or has or does that creates an opportunity for a meaningful interaction with at least one other person. Gifts are the fundamental characteristics of our human life and community.
JUDITH SNOW

Mitzvah

The biggest handicap most of us face as parents, relatives, friends or supporters of people with disabilities is our ignorance of any direct experience of disability. Screening out our own bias of what is best for our children is a life-long job for many of us. We carry an invisible back-pack of stereotypes based on our non-disabled view of the world. Our insights can be feeble and patronizing. Eloquent expressions of life as a person with a dis-ability enlighten us. Most helpful are those accounts by people who become disabled later in life. Somehow an articu-late comparison of life before and after disability and a description of the transi-tion provides us with a basis for compari-son with our own experience.

One of the most stirring accounts we have encountered so far is contained in Bonnie Sherr Klein's beautiful portrait of her evolution: a brilliant filmmaker, the creator of *Not a Love Story* and *Speaking Our Peace* becomes a woman with a disability.

Her book, *Slow Dance – A Story of Love, Stroke and Disability*, is a deeply moving story of her recovery from two catastroph-ic strokes that nearly killed her. Incident-ally, the book is also an account of a lov-ing marriage: Bonnie and Michael's rela-tionship will fill you with joy, envy, and hope. Nowhere have we read as articu-late, detailed and gripping an account of the experience of disability. As Eileen O'Brien, Chair of DisAbled Women's Network (DAWN) Canada points out, "A new language is being spoken here: this is our experience."

Slow Dance is also the story of Bonnie Sherr Klein's awakening to a fuller appre-ciation of her many gifts, not just the gifts of a talented filmmaker. At the end of her book she invites us to ponder the wisdom of another gift – the gift of asking:

"What I have learned finally is that in asking for help I offer other people an opportunity for intimacy and collaboration. Whether I'm asking for me personally or for disabled people generally, I give them the opportunity to be their most human. In Judaism, we call this gift a mitzvah."

The second pre-eminent gift is the gift of **difference**. Difference creates meaning. If everyone were the same there would be no excitement, no mystery, no allure, no desire, no anticipation, no wonder or amazement, no motivation, fascination, inspiration, enchantment.

Variety is truly the spice of life. I'll borrow a charming example from Judith's recent book *What's Really Worth Doing*. Think of how many sonnets, songs, and poems have been written about a lover's eyes. Then think of all the optometrists and designers and retailers of eye glasses. Careers, lives, reputations, industries all based on eye difference. And of course you know what comes next. You are different from the next person in thousands of ways. Each person is a bundle of countless gifts because of difference.

Inspired by Judith and using Robert Pirsig's distinctions quoted at the beginning of this chapter, we suggest the following framework for liberating the contributions of our friends and family members with disabilities.

Contributions of the Head – things I understand. Things I know something about, enjoy discussing or listening to, learning or teaching about. Contributions of humor, wisdom, attentiveness, expertise, and taste. Gifts of presence and consciousness.

Contributions of the Hands – things I know how to do and like to do. Gifts of service, celebration, and communion.

Contributions of the Heart – things I care deeply about, love and appreciate. Contributions of grace, mercy, sensitivity, courage, compassion, acceptance, forgiveness, joy and intimacy. Gifts of difference and love.

Passion plus skills equals work

Another way to describe following one's dream and longing to contribute is to call it passion. Passion is very critical and fundamental. It is the fuel for our dreams, keeping them alive over the bumps and curves of life. However, passion has to be accompanied by doing and doing is enhanced by

> Why should we all use our creative power . . . ? Because there is nothing that makes people so generous, joyful, lively, bold and compassionate, so indifferent to fighting and the accumulation of objects and money.
> BRENDA UELAND

WORK means...

- following one's passion
- earning a living
- increasing self-esteem
- gaining job satisfaction
- being part of a team
- knowing your place in the world
- making choices
- meeting new people
- expressing yourself
- pursuing your dream
- being accountable
- making a contribution
- pursuing your potential
- being valued and relied upon
- acquiring and improving skills
- earning respect
- pursuing a vocation
- enjoying social opportunities

skill. Gregory Bateson advised that, "Without skill there is no art."

Remember we are talking about the pursuit of passion, not the pursuit of mind-numbing, meaningless activity. This is where a lot of our vocational, work oriented or supported employment programs fail. They are skill focused no doubt, but the skills have little to do with the passions of our relatives or friends.

This is a trap many of us fall into. How many of us are busy doing or earning but not being? We've become human doers and human earners as suggested by Joe Dominguez and Vicki Robin in their inspiring book *Your Money or Your Life*.

In the early 80's many of us were challenged by what was clearly an overlooked part of the integration agenda – the assertion that paid employment was a meaningful goal for people with disabilities. For some reason this was a harder conceptual pill to swallow than closing institutions and integrating other societal institutions such as schools or recreation departments. Many of us stumbled at the time and we're still stumbling. Today, nearly twenty years later, authentic examples of meaningful employment and supported employment are limited across North America.

Let's try another approach.

Imagine meaningful activity for your friends and relatives with a disability in a different way. Let's make the focus meaningful work, not paid work. Let's not confuse work with paid employment.

Essentially, work serves three different functions:

One, we receive a salary; we get paid.

Two, we receive personal satisfaction, deep pleasure, and fulfillment.

Three, we make a contribution to our community.

For many of our relatives the financial function of work will be critical and important. They will want to earn a living. For others this will be less so. What will be true in both

> Why should we be in such desperate haste to succeed, and in such desperate enterprises? If a man does not keep pace with his companions, perhaps it is because he hears a different drummer.
>
> HENRY DAVID THOREAU

situations is the value of pursuing work that brings meaning, fulfillment, purpose, and satisfaction to their lives. In fact, many of us are confronting the same dilemma. Witness the growth of the "simple living" movement.

Imagine careers based on your son/daughter's passion. Imagine employment training based on improving skills in one's area of passion. Imagine vocational assessment based on liberating passion. Imagine a job description as a passion promoter. Imagine marketing and job development based on contribution. Imagine rehabilitation defined as growth, stimulation, and fulfillment.

Conclusion

Work is a critical contribution to the exchange society expects of all its citizens. Recently this exchange has become unbalanced – linked almost exclusively with money and

---

Chartres

The historians among you will know that the cathedral at Chartres was built over many decades. The people who contributed the money must have been patient people. Their investment would not bear fruit until many years in the future, perhaps not even in their lifetime. One such benefactor, the King of France, grew impatient with the pace of development. He was planning a grand ceremony and delegated the archbishop to visit the site and report back to him.

The archbishop decided to ask three people working at the site about their work. He approached a stonecutter who was chipping away at a gigantic block of granite and asked him what he was doing.

The reply was blunt and gruff, "Can't you see, I'm cutting small blocks from this rock as

I've been doing all my life. I've shaped thousands of them."

He approached another person who was chiseling around a rectangular mold. The man replied with resignation, "I'm making gargoyles from a pattern. I've done lots of them over the years. I think they go somewhere up there; I'm not really sure. It's a job, and I've got a big family to feed."

Finally the archbishop paused before an elderly person who was busy sweeping the debris and dust from the construction site. This old man would certainly not live to see the completed structure. The archbishop asked the same question, "What are you doing?"

After a moment's pause, the old man looked up. His eyes sparkled. He replied: "I'm building a cathedral."

Creative minds have always
been known to survive any
kind of bad training.
ANNA FREUD

paid employment. Many of us who are searching for a balanced and healthy lifestyle are rejecting this perspective. Good work relies on the potent mixture of passion and skill. Good work connects individual calling with the real needs of the community. Good work is not about earning a living; it is more about being a good friend, neighbor, and partner; about being honest, courageous and caring; about the content of our character. Good work is the juncture where society's expectations meet our personal quest – to become who we are.

We invite you to work through the questions on Worksheet 9 with your friend or relative. Then you might want to take another look at Step One and the vision you are developing for the future. Are you satisfied you have created the opportunity, laid the groundwork, and built an expectation for the contribution your relative was born to make?

When our head, hands, and heart work together, literally and figuratively, good work emerges. Our sons and daughters, no matter the excellence or impairment of their brain, mind, or body will surmount these challenges by doing what moves them.

Desire – when respected – will win out, regardless of speed, dexterity, and ability.

Catherine

The gift of presence

In Nicola Schaefer's eagerly awaited update on her daughter Catherine's story, Yes! She Knows She's Here, *there is a moving example of the gift of presence.*

Catherine's roommate Sherrill tells the story in her own words:

After my father's sudden death down in Virginia, my move into Catherine's house was very stressful and sometimes I felt I would collapse in exhaustion. It was in this private holocaust that I first began to truly know who Catherine is.

One evening, as yet another thing went wrong, I fell on my knees beside her bed, crying. When I raised my head shamefully, Cath was looking at me with concern and as I moved near her, she reached out and shook my head. It was in that moment that I knew how truly present she is to others.

The opening between us widened in the ensuing days and I began to share with her what I was doing and feeling and to elicit her opinion on what she would prefer to do, eat or wear. I also began to read to her, something she seemed to genuinely enjoy.

I wasn't sure how much she was understanding, but I noticed that her reaction changed appropriately with the material content. At one point, while I was reading a poignant story that was particularly pertinent to our circumstances at the time, she began to laugh with a knowing look. I, too, began to laugh and realized that we were indeed truly present to one another. I knew then my own definitive answer to the question Nicola had posed with the title of her first book, *Does She Know She's There?* The gift of her presence is to allow those of us who are privileged to know her to experience just how simply living and loving is done.

Diana

The gift of communion

Diana is one of the busiest people we know, on the go from dawn to dusk. She has a seat on the local school board and belongs to numerous clubs and associations. Plus she watches out for her elderly parents who live in her basement suite. To top it off, she regularly minds her own grandchildren.

A phone call or visit with her is likely to be interrupted by a runny nose, sticky hands, or a referee assignment. Files are scattered among the freshly baked cookies; books are balanced on the toaster. We were skeptical about her participation in Joan's network. Where would she find the time?

Still Diana insisted, attending most of Joan's network meetings, albeit on the fly.

Then there was a shift in the schedule of Joan's caregiver. She had to attend staff meetings every Friday and would be unable to assist at lunch. Replacement staff would be available on a rotating basis. Joan balked at strangers feeding her. So did her network. Diana agreed to bring lunch and to assist on an interim basis.

Four years later Diana and Joan's lunch is the sublime interlude of their week. Diana's descriptions of the experience reminds one of the elaborate ritual associated with the Japanese tea ceremony.

The lunch is prepared in the morning by Diana. She packs it carefully in a wicker picnic basket along with her antique silverware, crystal glasses and her best Limoges china, covers it with a linen cloth and sets out for the fifteen-minute drive to Joan's house. Upon her arrival, she clears the table, spreads the cloth, and sets out the dishes. In the gloomy, gray days of winter they might light candles. When the sun is out they often head out onto the deck. The table is portable; it is the tray on Joan's wheelchair. The cloth has been sewn to fit.

They look at each other; they smile. Grace. And then, with composure and mindfulness, Diana begins to feed Joan. Spoonful after loving spoonful. Breaking bread. Taking time, slowing down, enjoying the intimacy, breathing. Being fully aware of the texture and taste. Savoring each slow and joyful bite.

"This benefits me," admits Diana. "Joan's gift allows me to close the window on my otherwise crazy week."

Nourishment, it is clear, is a sacrament.

The giving side of town

A friend of mine is a martial-arts type minister in a big city in Ohio. He enjoys twisting the Bible around, ratcheting a familiar quotation 180 degrees. Kind of mental karate. This is my favorite of his karate chops:

"Brothers and sisters, you are all no doubt familiar with what St. Paul says in the Acts of the Apostles: 'It is better to give than to receive.' Now I am sure that you govern your life by giving, not receiving, don't you? As I look out into the congregation I see you nodding in agreement.

I know you are doing your best to follow the Bible. Unfortunately your giving is hurting others and you must stop.

"You see, if it is indeed better to give than to receive – and we are all agreed that it is – then shouldn't you be allowing others to give?

"Many of you are involved in helping the elderly, people with disabilities, and the youth of the parish. But, you are so busy giving you haven't noticed you've left no room for them to give. You are depriving others of that most precious of gifts – the gift of giving. If it is truly better to give than to receive, then isn't your greater responsibility to see that everyone gets the opportunity to give?

"Don't you think they've been on the receiving side of town for too long? Isn't it time to get them on the giving side of town?"

Hey ho, hey ho!
It's off to work we go.

PERSONAL NETWORKS CREATE JOBS

Gordon

Gordon is big, strong, and strapping. Full of muscle power and energy. He also has a bushel basket of commitments. Sure he'd like to work, but only if it doesn't interfere with his passion for Special Olympics hockey. He wants part-time, seasonal work.

Most of us are thinking, "Get real, Gordon."

One well-connected Personal Network member has an idea. He has a construction business. How about a job stripping away forms after the cement has set? Perfect. Seasonal work, outdoors, good exercise, and decent pay.

Another member has a post office contact. The result: Gordon delivers flyers during Christmas rush season. Gordon is cited for being most reliable. Neither rain, nor sleet, nor snow...will prevent Gordon from staying in shape for hockey.

Erin

Erin is a recent graduate from high school. Loves measuring liquids. A perfectionist around the kitchen. The first dreaming/ planning session with friends and families yields a connection to a small entrepreneur who runs a coffee booth in the parking lot of a garden center.

Erin has beginner's luck. The Personal Network member who works at the garden center makes the introduction. Erin gets the job and her friend can keep an eye out.

Erin works out back of the booth, cleaning up. Lately she's been pouring regular coffees to ease the lineups at break. After work she practices the art of steaming milk with her buddy from the network.

Cappuccinos, anyone?

Frank

Frank can talk your ear off about war history. He also has a room stuffed with plastic model battle planes.

On his way home from a network meeting, Frank's brother-in-law notices a local hobby shop. On a whim he checks it out and makes two important discoveries.

One, there is a Plastic Model Society (PMS for short) and this store is the provincial headquarters. Two, they meet monthly at the local armory, which is full of war memorabilia. The Personal Network hits the ground running.

One year later, Frank is Vice-President of Special Projects for the Society and an assistant tour guide at the armory.

During a recent visit we asked if he was ever stumped for an answer.

"Heck no! You see that guy sitting over there?" – pointing to a uniformed commissionaire sitting inside – "If I ever get stuck, I just ask the old fart in the corner!"

continued on page 168

Pat

Pat has this thing about money. People are always taking it from him. Even though you have heard the story a dozen times already, you are almost ready to march down to the police station with him.

Pat's not the best of housekeepers. His room is cluttered with cans and bottles brought home for recycling. Not cashed in, however, due to the danger of theft!

Complaints from the group home. A Personal Network meeting is called.

Idea. Let's reframe this. Pat is an environmentalist.

Personal Network members help to organize the garage in the group home. Cans here, bottles there. An escort is provided once a week to the recycling depot and then on to the bank.

Is there money in recycling? You bet. Pat earns over a hundred dollars a week.

Michael

The biggest drain on Michael's trust funds is for postage stamps. He is Amnesty International's most prolific writer in British Columbia, using an old beat-up portable Underwood typewriter.

It was noisy and Michael likes to work late. Neighbors aren't as charitable at two in the morning, never mind the cause.

Let's look at an alternative, said his Personal Network. First a course on word processing, then a new printer and a computer.

One of the last of the ink-stained hacks to join the computer age is busy making up for lost time. Keep those stamps coming. Watch out, dictators.

Pam and Keith

There was something about telethons that appealed to Pam. She and her childhood friend Keith attended them all. The entertainment was a principal factor; so were the emotional presentations and donations. Most of all were the causes. Pam identified with them and she was determined to help. She wanted to be on stage one day. The first year she and Keith contributed their own funds. Next they collected cans and bottles. They worked hard at it but weren't satisfied with the results — even though they had collected more than $50.00. Not enough for a stage presentation.

Then they got ambitious. Or at least Pam did. There was no stopping her. Just ask Keith. They decided to hold a walkathon. They recruited participants by visiting churches — nine of them to be exact. It took weeks to make the contacts since the churches were scattered throughout the Greater Vancouver area. Every Sunday they would ride the buses for hours.

Their first walkathon was held in a

Vancouver suburb. Next year they moved to a larger venue, Stanley Park, where they raised $768.34. All of which was proudly presented on stage at Vancouver's Queen Elizabeth Theater to Bob McGrath of *Sesame Street*. He was not the only star attraction of the telethon. Just ask Pam's dad, Jack.

Pam

Pam sold her first painting when she was 37. By then watercolors were her chosen medium and she was in her semi-abstract period or as her father Jack claimed, her post-realism period. Not bad for a late bloomer who had come to her art only a few years earlier.

PLAN was having its first fund raiser, a prestigious event celebrating the fifth anniversary of Expo 86. A silent auction was part of the fund raising. The auction items included dinner on our wealthiest businessman's yacht, original memorabilia from Expo, ice wine, a trip to the next Expo and Pam's latest canvas.

We worried about Pam's contribution. Would anyone bid on it? Shame on us. It sold for the princely sum of $500.00. To a businessman who was a silent partner in a local art gallery.

Guess where you can purchase her art now.

Worksheet 9

PASSION PURSUITS MAKING A CONTRIBUTION

The following questions may help you expand your appreciation of the varied ways your family member makes or could make a contribution.

We suggest you use these questions as a guide to explore this challenge yourself. Then share them with others who know your relative well.

Most importantly, you can use them as a basis for discussion and interaction with your family member.

What contributions does your loved one make to your family? _____

_____

_____

_____

What are the three activities your friend or family member does best? _____

_____

_____

_____

What are the three skills they would most like to learn? _____

_____

_____

_____

_____

What are their passions? What gives them the greatest joy or pleasure? _____

_____

_____

_____

What kind of job (paid or voluntary) might be associated with their passions? _____

_____

_____

_____

Who are their heroes? In what ways do they inspire them? _____

_____

_____

_____

Which famous public personality, artist or athlete do they relate to the most? Why?

_____

_____

_____

What are their gifts of the head? What do they know about? (music, movies, singing,
playing music, computers, humor, languages, birds, sports, numbers, etc.)

_____

_____

_____

_____

_____

What are their gifts of the heart? (volunteering, listening, being with children, nursing, poetry, caring for others, etc.) _____

_____

_____

_____

What are their gifts of the hands? (recycling, gardening, cooking, walking, stamp collecting, quilting, fishing, arts and crafts, driving, plumbing, delivering, sewing, cutting hair, ushering, etc,) _____

_____

_____

_____

Which clubs or organizations do they belong to or have they belonged to?

_____

_____

_____

_____

Which clubs and groups are organized around your relative's passions and interests? (quilting, recycling, fitness, hobbies, causes, etc.) Which ones exist in your community?

_____

_____

_____

_____

_____

What could they teach others? What would they like to teach others? _____

_____

_____

_____

What support would they need to be able to teach others? _____

_____

_____

_____

What product or service would they enjoy selling? _____

_____

_____

If they could start a business, what would it be? _____

_____

_____

_____

_____

What are their favorite games? _____

_____

_____

_____

Are there other hobbies or special interests we have not covered? _____

_____

_____

What positive qualities do people say they have? _____

_____

_____

_____

What is their dream job? _____

_____

_____

_____

Have they ever made anything? Have they ever fixed anything? _____

_____

_____

_____

What is the greatest accomplishment of their life so far? _____

_____

_____

_____

What will be their greatest accomplishment? _____

_____

_____

_____

_____

If they could devote their life to only one occupation, what would it be? _____

_____

_____

_____

Can you imagine their most challenging characteristic turned into a gift or

contribution? _____

_____

_____

_____

Where in the community could they make their contributions? _____

_____

_____

step five

ensuring
choices

The best proof
of love is trust.
Joyce Brothers

More than we bargained for

"There was a period when Rick didn't live with us, you know. At the time we thought we were doing the right thing. He was getting pretty big and we thought he'd be better off with people his own age. My wife and I were both working, and we thought it would be best for all of us."

George's voice softens as he discusses what he calls Rick's "adventure."

Rick moved to a farm community where he lived in a group home with eight other young people his own age.

"At first it went OK. For Rick, that is. Not for us. We were in shock for weeks. Driving away from that home was the hardest thing I ever had to do next to burying my wife. Anyway, new people and new things to do everyday kept Rick happy for a while."

Rick is quite transparent. It is easy to tell if he's happy or not. He wouldn't tell George and his wife what was bothering him but after a while he looked so glum they knew something was wrong. It took them some time to get to the bottom of it.

One night George had popped over to the house to drop off some strawberries he had just picked at the U-Pick down the road. Staff were watching television and the residents were all in their rooms. It turned out that this was common practice. In fact, it was the nightly routine. The evening shift was sending everyone to his or her own room at 8:30 every evening. No one was allowed to watch TV, use a radio or tape deck, or make any noise.

"It was just like the bloody Air Force, back in World War Two," George explains. "No, it was worse. Lights out over there was at 10:00 p.m. for the crews who had to be up early for a flying mission. As long as we observed the blackout we could do what we pretty well wanted to."

Rick's life was completely regulated at the home, George explained.

"Their lives were controlled from top to bottom. Heck, in the six months he was there, he had four supervisors. It was a regular revolving door. Even the little things were controlled. No privacy, no respect, and no choice."

It was too much for Rick and his parents. George and his wife invited Rick to move back home.

"We thought we were giving Rick more choices when he moved into the group home. Instead, we got more than we bargained for."

continued on page 180

step five
Ensuring choices

how do we respect the choices and preferences of our relatives while at the same time keeping them safe? This balancing act is a tough challenge. Families find it difficult. So do professionals. So does government and its institutions.

On the one hand we want to protect our children from discrimination, exploitation, abuse, neglect and injury. We want them to be safe. On the other hand, we want to acknowledge their humanity, and to focus on similarities, not differences. We want to teach them to survive through adversity, as all of us must. We want to champion their autonomy and self-determination, to enhance their life's experiences, to nurture their abilities, hopes and dreams. We want to declare their worthiness.

We know a good life is a life with meaningful and authentic choice in it. We know our relatives have tastes, preferences and intentions, and we want these respected. However, it is a balancing act and we may resign ourselves to focusing on the safety side of the ledger. We may do this because we are not aware of the alternatives or because we have not met anyone willing to take the time to know our relative and to be respectful of the way they make choices. That may be why many parents are labeled over-protective or disrespectful of the rights of their sons and daughters. We don't agree with the criticism.

> Every blade of grass has its angel that bends over it and whispers, "Grow, grow."
>
> THE TALMUD

continued from page 178

One of the things that bothered Rick about his group home experience was the withdrawal of his spending privileges. Any of his own money, including the "comforts allowance" he received from government, had to be placed in a bank account that could be accessed by staff. And they often did, buying things he didn't ask for or want.

"Rick isn't a whiz with money but he is careful," George explained.

However, George was quite worried that some unscrupulous person would take advantage of Rick. He wanted Rick to have easy access to his money, but he wanted some checks on his spending. So he set up a trust. Not a discretionary trust but an income trust.

"I've got the local credit union acting as my trustee now. They're good at managing and investing the money. But just to make sure they keep Rick's interests in mind, I've appointed a co-trustee from the Personal Network. And to top it all off, my will instructs the trustees to also seek advice from PLAN. All this may sound complicated, but it acts like a system of checks and balances.

"When all is said and done, I'm finally getting what I bargained for. Rick's choices are respected and so are mine. You can't beat that."

Step Five is about resolving that contradiction. It is a gentle reminder that we can never be an authority on someone else's life. It is also a reminder that as our sons and daughters develop their own decision-making muscle and leave our orbit we can begin to relax, at least a little.

Count on this process being as challenging as it was or will be for your other children. Count on it being critical for everyone's growth and development.

For our sons and daughters to become authors of their own decisions they need to:

- be respected for their inherent decision-making ability
- develop an authentic decision-making voice
- receive support where necessary
- have genuine choices and options
- make decisions based on those choices
- have alternatives to legal guardianship
- be able to make mistakes

There are few legal options that recognize the decision-making capacities of our relatives with disabilities. That's why we have created a process and a form that encompasses and reflects the values and concerns of families. Step Five recommends that families create a Supported Decision-Making Agreement with their relative, and concludes with sample agreements you may wish to use.

Authors of their own lives

Who has the authority to speak for your son or daughter?

As parents, we may assume this authority when our children are young and we have temporary control and power over their lives. We know, or will find out through experience, that while we may have jurisdiction for a while over our offspring, we never have sovereignty. We have temporary stewardship, nurturing the seed of their character, but their essence, their defining image, their being-ness, came with their birth and belongs to them alone.

As the beauty and mystery of their lives unfold and as they find their place in the world, we are expected to provide nourishment. However, the kernel, their nucleus, is there from the start. We are observers waiting for the next twist of fate as their gifts and unique genius take root.

It does not really matter whether we see ourselves as an authority on our children. One way or the other, they are usually quick to let us know they have minds of their own. By the time they are teenagers, it is clear we are not an authority on their lives – or on anything else. We have to wait a little while before we regain status with them.

This process of our sons and daughters separating from our orbit, developing their own personality and making their own choices, is usually a bit messy. It can cause a lot of heat and friction. As parents, we are bound to be more than a little protective. As our children develop their own personality and begin to make their own choices, we have a ringside seat on the trials and errors of their decision making.

Unfortunately, it is not as easy for our children with disabilities to move out of our orbit and to become authors of their own lives. This critical stage may remain suspended permanently unless family and friends provide encouragement and support.

- Is it better to be safe than sorry?
- Is offering choice too chancy?
- How big a risk are we prepared to take?
- Can we balance safety with choice?
- Whom do you trust?

Supported decision making: a new response

Supported decision making can ensure that our sons and daughters become the authors of their own lives.

Imagine all the changes that have taken place in our world. Some are earth-shattering; some we barely notice. Change is a constant for everyone, including our relatives. Nobody really knows what they will have to adjust to in their lives. We can make some educated guesses, but there are no guarantees.

Rather than spending time trying to predict the future, we can focus on preparing for good decision making regardless of what arises. Good decision making ensures the best possible input is available to assist our sons and daughters adjust to change. Good decision making is supported decision-making.

Most of us make decisions with the support of others. We rely on people we trust, experts, celebrities, and opinion-shapers for their knowledge, experience and endorsement. They provide the context for good decision making. Despite

Supported decision making for our relative means:

- They actively participate.
- Their views are sought and taken into consideration.
- They are surrounded by caring, knowledgeable, trustworthy people who can assist with their decision making and communicate their decisions.
- Their needs are the primary consideration, not those of staff or the service system.
- The focus is on their abilities and wishes.
- All their choices and options are considered.

- Their tastes, preferences, motives, and ability to discriminate are taken seriously.
- Their risks, failures and mistakes are recognized as learning opportunities.
- Their intuition and feelings have as much weight as their intellectual ability.
- All their methods of communication, both verbal and non-verbal, are recognized as valid.

Worksheet

WORKSHEET 10 **Supported Decision Making**

This worksheet is based on the three major areas of decision making: health/medical decisions; financial decisions; and personal decisions. The worksheet is located at the end of this chapter, on page 222. Have a look at it now, and then fill it out when you have reviewed this material.

the need for our sons and daughters to make their own decisions, there is this sad reality: someone else usually makes their decisions, often without consultation.

In practical terms, our sons and daughters are offered few choices in their lives. As parents we can be guilty of this; so can service providers and professionals. Whatever the reasons – and most of us have the best of intentions – our relatives are given few choices and little control over their lives. Their decision-making ability is not exercised, is not accepted and is often ignored. This does not serve our children well in the present, and certainly will not serve them in the future.

From first to last resort, it's the relationship that counts

By now it should come as no surprise that we believe the only real protection for those you love is the quality of the committed relationships they have. To ensure good decision making for your relative with a disability, we suggest you make the concept of supported decision making the basis of your approach.

1 Do everything you can to enhance and validate the role of family, friends, and supporters as advocates and advisors to the decisions your son or daughter makes.

2 Identify and use the existing advocacy system for people with disabilities.

3 Consider a Supported Decision-Making Agreement. See page 203.

4 Identify people who would be willing to serve as temporary substitute decision makers.

5 If you must use the legal system, consider a guardian or conservator for specific reasons and on a time-limited basis.

See page 203.

There is no magic to the task of keeping people safe and respecting their choices. It is a matter of mastering the high wire. A tilt in the direction of over-protection creates a barren lifestyle. A tilt in the direction of complete autonomy without supports or safeguards is a license for exploitation. The risk in either direction can be minimized only when friends and family are there to provide support.

> Fear is the root of all exclusion. Trust is the root of all inclusion.
>
> JEAN VANIER

The institutional response

As parents, we know there are no absolute guarantees for keeping people with disabilities safe while at the same time respecting their choices. In the past, families have tended to rely on government and its institutions to resolve the dilemma. The three most common tools at government's disposal are funding for programs and services; regulations and policy; and legal guardianship. Let's examine how well these tools respond to the twin goals of keeping people safe while respecting choices.

Programs and services

A wide range of human services, professional supports, and social, health, and educational programs exist to support people with disabilities. However, there are some drawbacks:

- Funding for these programs and services is not guaranteed and must compete with ever-changing priorities.

- Staff turnover is high.

- Programs and services cannot respond to every area of

Diving

When I wrote this fictional meditation I had not yet read Jean-Dominique Bauby's extraordinary book The Diving-Bell and the Butterfly. *At the age of 45, French journalist Bauby suffered a massive stroke that left him without speech and movement. He was, as he says, "like a mind in a jar." Patiently, letter by letter, Bauby tells his story, using one eyelid to signal at what point in the chorus line of letters his friend is to stop transcribing. Bauby's reality is bright, vivid and compelling. I hope you have an opportunity to share his celebration of a profound journey by reading his book.*

What would you do?

You are heading to the grocery store on a beautiful sunny Saturday morning. You are a careful driver but your mind is elsewhere – on automatic pilot. Suddenly an approaching car jumps lanes and heads towards you. In a terrifying instant your life changes. After the impact you lose consciousness.

You wake up in the hospital. The pain is excruciating. You are unable to move your arms and legs. Then you discover you can't speak. A doctor and a nurse are hovering over you. They are asking a lot of questions. They want to know your blood type. You aren't able to respond. For one thing, you are in shock. For another, they

aren't watching your facial gestures and you have no other way of communicating.

Now they are explaining what needs to happen to you. No one seems to notice the fear in your eyes. You hear medical terms you don't understand. You're scared and all alone. Where is your wife? Have they tried to reach her?

Suddenly you are placed on a stretcher and rushed down the hallway into an elevator, then down another hallway and into an operating room. Your last thoughts before the anesthetic takes hold are of ...

Who would you think of? Your spouse, your children, your parents, your brothers and sisters, your friends? Or your lawyer, your mechanic, your dentist?

You do survive. The hospital is crowded but they manage to find a semi-private room for you. And they locate your spouse. She comes in several hours after you return from surgery. She immediately understands your terror. You are covered with blood. The needle from the IV tube is already causing noticeable swelling and bruising. Your wife calls a nurse.

They respond immediately. They are cooperative and friendly. They didn't expect you to wake up so soon. They were busy elsewhere. The IV tube is adjusted and they give you a warm sponge bath. Eventually you drift off to sleep, comforted by the presence of your wife. At least you are not alone.

When your wife and friends are around, you feel safer and your needs are met. They notice when you are uncomfortable. They do all the little things that make your stay tolerable.

On one occasion you had to contend with an inexperienced intern who insisted on giving you a needle in your arm even though he couldn't find a sizable vein. You were helpless to protest. Your arm became a personal challenge to him. When a colleague from work arrived, it was bruised and bloodied. Within minutes he had your wife on the phone. She spoke to the charge nurse and a notation was made on your chart. It won't happen again, they promised. It doesn't.

What keeps you safe during your hospital stay?

Who enhances the quality of your life while you are there?

Is it the hospital policy on care? Or is it hospital rules and regulations? Is it the professional training of medical staff? Or is it nurses and doctors who are paid to be there?

Most of us would say we were fortunate to have friends and families to mediate the impersonal nature of the care we would receive in the hospital. They guarantee your identity. They remove the cloak of anonymity. With them you become a person again. It's not that professional paid care isn't important; it's just that you are more than the sum of your health needs. Make no mistake about it, this move from being an object of service to a real person depends on your relationships.

Why would it be any different for people with disabilities?

It isn't. However, we often make the error of assuming professional paid care is all that is necessary to keep people with disabilities safe and guarantee choice. Programs, professional supports, rules and regulations have their limitations. Paid service is not a consolation for good old-fashioned human contact, warmth, and love.

It's as simple as that. Just ask anyone who has ever been in a hospital for any length of time.

human need, particularly the need for friendship and companionship.

- Control is invariably in the hands of the service provider, not the individual or friends and families.
- People can be isolated in services, preventing community connections and relationships from developing.
- Accountability is to the funding source, not to the individual receiving the service.
- Funding is based on what people cannot do. This places undue emphasis on their "needs" and "deficiencies" and ignores their abilities.
- People start to believe they are incapable and as a result they become even more dependent on professional support.

Regulations and policy

As our service delivery system has evolved and become more sophisticated, so have the rules and regulations governing practice and provision of care. Nevertheless, mistreatment, abuse, and neglect still occur. We know this from our own experiences as well as from the media's tragic portrayal of those who slip through the system.

In our rush to protect and prevent, we encourage government to create regulations. However, the expansion of government regulations eventually develops into a virtual straitjacket:

- Rules and regulations become more important than human flexibility and common sense.
- Following the rules is encouraged; creativity and initiative are stifled.
- Insurance requirements push considerations of risk and liability into the foreground.

- The sheer weight of regulations affects real caring.

- Everything important to people can be lost in highly regulated environments.

- A culture of mistrust is created in which there must always be someone to blame.

- Union agreements can create additional constraints.

- Bureaucracy is created to monitor the rules, adding another significant expense to the cost of caring.

- Staff morale declines as people are required to enforce regulations rather than provide support.

Legal guardianship

Our society has created legal mechanisms to allow another person to take over all the affairs and decision making of someone who has been judged incapable by court order. This guardian or conservator then has complete power to make financial, medical and legal decisions for the person.

Again, this system is not perfect. In Canada and in the United States, there has been a movement to reform outmoded guardianship legislation. Few jurisdictions have succeeded.

Here are some of the concerns about legal guardianship:

- Most guardianship orders are "all or nothing." Although individuals may need help only in certain areas of decision making, all of their financial and personal decision-making power is removed.

- A full guardianship order strips individuals of all citizenship rights. In the eyes of the law, they are no longer persons.

- Guardianship does not recognize that most of us make decisions in collaboration with others, be they friends or family.

- Ability to communicate verbally is traditionally associated with capacity.
- Obtaining a guardianship order is costly and time-consuming.

Five false assumptions

Do unto others as you would have them do unto you.

THE GOLDEN RULE

Society's quest to develop tools that keep people safe and guarantee the quality of their life is based on five false assumptions, as identified by David Schwartz in *Crossing the River*:

1 It is possible to create a perfect system.
2 All bad things that happen to people can be prevented with a sufficient body of law and regulation.
3 A paid professional's response is the only response to the situation of a person in need.
4 Safety and protection are ends in themselves, rather than a means to enhancing the quality of a person's life.
5 Systems have performed well in the past.

Should I consider legal guardianship?

Some families believe the only way they can have power to protect their adult son or daughter is to arrange for someone to become their legal guardian. This is a very intrusive and costly solution. From a practical point of view, we believe it is unnecessary.

Note: Parents are already legal guardians of their minor children. However, you do need to identify guardians for your children in case you die. See Step Six, page 243, "What happens if I die without a will?"

We believe that you can achieve what you want without resorting to legal guardianship. Before you accept our assurances, let's look at the major areas of decision making in your son or daughter's life. We think we can convince you that you can have your cake and eat it too. That is, you can keep your children safe and maximize their choices without resorting to legal guardianship.

Types of decision making

There are three broad areas of decision making that affect your relative's life:

- Health/medical decisions
- Financial decisions
- Personal care decisions

Health/medical decisions

You can divide this category into emergency and non-emergency decision making.

Most families are concerned whether their son or daughter will receive medical treatment in case of an emergency, especially if they are not able to give consent. In most jurisdictions, doctors are able to provide treatment in cases of emergency without having to wait for the consent of an authorized person.

For non-emergency health care, the experience is varied. Many adults with disabilities enjoy a long-standing relationship with their family doctor. They know each other's abilities and communication styles. In these situations, the capacity of the person with the disability to give consent is simply not an issue. The physician is willing to take the time to give individuals the opportunity to express their

Choices

Let's approach our relative's role in decision making by asking the following questions:

- What choices do they have now?
- What experience do they have with decision making?
- With support, could they be assisted to make decisions independently?
- What decisions can they make independently?
- What decisions will they need help with?

- What decisions will others challenge your relative on?
- What informal arrangements can be made to assist with decision making?
- What formal or legal arrangements other than guardianship can be made to assist with decision making?
- How do they communicate their decisions?
- Who understands their mode of communication?

What is freedom? Freedom is the right to choose: the right to create for yourself the alternatives of choice. Without the possibility of choice and the exercise of choice a man is not a man but a member, an instrument, a thing.

ARCHIBALD MACLEISH

wishes, or to let the decision be made with the support of family and friends.

In other families, it has become common practice for the doctor or health care provider to ask next-of-kin to authorize health care treatment for the adult with the disability. In many jurisdictions enduring powers of attorney for health care are available. In these situations supported decision making is already working.

Unfortunately, some health care professionals will provide major health care only if the adult with a disability has a court-appointed guardian. In these situations, the adult's ability to consent to treatment is challenged. Informal status for family members is tragically not recognized. Families and other groups have had to apply to the courts to become adult guardians in order to give consent to an operation or health care procedure.

A Supported Decision-Making Agreement (see page 203) anticipates your relative's health and medical decision making and creates a supportive process to accomodate them.

Financial decisions

In the past many families became their relative's guardian in order to protect, manage, and invest the financial assets of their adult relative with a disability.

This procedure had a number of disadvantages:

- obtaining guardianship involves the courts and is time-consuming and expensive
- reporting on the management and expenditure of money is tedious and costly
- further rights of the person with a disability are removed
- guidelines to protect the assets may be too conservative for productive money management

Less intrusive alternatives

Often the only disposable income available to people with disabilities is their monthly government assistance. As such, the risk of exploitation and mismanagement is lower. We have found the following useful for supported financial decision making.

1 Joint bank accounts.
2 Getting to know your local bank manager.
3 A pre-set ceiling on the amount to be withdrawn from a bank account.
4 Joint signatures.
5 Joint title on home ownership.
6 Automatic deposits and automatic withdrawals (e.g. for the rent).
7 Enduring or durable power of attorney.

   An enduring or durable power of attorney is a written document that allows a person to confer authority upon someone else to make financial decisions on her behalf.

When you confer this authority on someone else, you do not lose your own authority.

The person who conferred it can revoke the power of attorney at any time.

Conferring an enduring power of attorney is one way of establishing supported decision making about finances. However, you do need to make sure that this power of attorney is "tailor-made" to suit your relative's situation. This option may not work if your relative is not seen to be legally competent to confer a power of attorney.

Before you choose this option, it would be a good idea to seek advice from a lawyer familiar with disability issues.

8 Trusts.

Some families establish trusts, to take effect either when they are alive (inter vivos or living trusts), or after they have died (testamentary). Consult with your lawyer and accountant as to the advantages of each arrangement. For more details, see Step Six.

9 Personal Network sub-committees.

Some families are establishing a "sub-committee" of their relative's Personal Network to assist with banking and other financial decisions.

10 Supported Decision-Making Agreement.

A Supported Decision-Making Agreement would anticipate and provide support for all areas of financial decision making (see page 203).

Personal care decisions

This area of decision making can be the most worrisome for families. Many of our relatives will likely be dealing with paid caregivers or service providers for the rest of their lives.

As parents, we want to know that our sons and daughters

will have sufficient food and clothing, and that they will always have a place to live. We want to make sure that service providers and professionals do what is best. We want to make sure there is enough money to support the services and programs our sons and daughters need. Most of all, we want them to have choices, and to have those choices respected.

Fortunately, this is where parents are most knowledgeable. After all, as parents, we do most of the advocating and quality assurance right now. Parents know the necessity of being vigilant. "Checking in" is part of our job description. We know how important it is to be in regular contact with our sons and daughters and to maintain a relationship with service providers. We have a good idea of how much work this requires and how much time it takes.

Here are some alternatives to legal guardianship or conservatorship that promote good decisions in the area of personal care.

1 Relationships and personal supports

No one can ever take your place. So let us look at the best alternative: a Personal Network of family members and friends. The investment in a Personal Network will pay dividends, not only in reducing the isolation and loneliness of your relative but also as a support for decision making. Granted, networks can never replace you, but they are a natural source of assistance and the best guarantee of quality assurance. They can ensure your relative has choices in life. They can maintain contact with and monitor service providers. They can advocate with government should the need arise. They can be appointed as supported decision makers.

2 Advocacy

Given the limitations of the service delivery system, it is prudent to consider the role of advocates as a check and balance on the professionals involved with your son or daughter.

The best and most effective advocacy is self-advocacy by the individual involved. All other advocacy must be subservient to this principle. However, we do recognize that many people may need support and assistance to advocate on their own behalf.

There are two other types of advocates. First, there are those who know your relative and are in a relationship with them. They may or may not be knowledgeable about funding questions and service delivery issues. However, they do know your son or daughter, are in touch regularly, and will fight for their best interests.

Other advocates provide professional services. Some of these advocates are specific to the disability field. Some have a general focus and their expertise is available to people who are discriminated against.

3 Individualized funding and self-determination

Our friends and relatives with disabilities often need support to participate in and contribute to society. They require the services of staff people or the support of a program. Access to these programs and services are usually through a service delivery agency, which may be non-profit or private for profit.

This presents a number of problems. The individual may not need or want a service or a program. They may simply need a bit of support to follow their passion and participate in community. However, their only alternative for support is through the service delivery system.

Even if they want a program they will quickly discover that service providers receive their funding under contract from government. Often one agency or organization provides the full range of services needed by the individual. That is, they own or lease the homes, provide the staff, and offer vocational, recreational, and other support services. The result is that people who use these services often have very little say over what happens to them. Their life is controlled from dawn to dusk and accountability is weak.

Often the criteria for accessing the services are fixed and inflexible, and are not based on the uniqueness of each individual.

Many parents, advocates, and people with disabilities are now promoting a new approach – individualized funding. They believe that people who require support to participate in society can choose these supports freely only if they control the funding.

Individualized funding, also known as self-determination, provides money from government directly to people with a disability or their agent to assist them to purchase the particular goods and services they require to becoming a fully contributing citizen. The funding can be used to purchase formal and informal supports.

Individualized funding covers food, clothing, shelter, transportation, and technical aids as well as program and personal care supports. The individual, with the help of his or her supporters, can then determine where to live, who with, who to hire, and so on.

Individualized funding is based on the unique supports an

individual requires and is defined by that individual or in collaboration with trusted representatives. Individualized funding is paid directly to the individual often through a financial intermediary. Individualized funding is portable, cutting across government departments, jurisdictions, and programs. Individualized funding is not just about enhancing the individual's ability to choose the services he or she needs. It may be about deciding not to choose a service. It is about creating and maintaining a good life.

Individualized funding is not available in every community. However, more and more jurisdictions, including at least four Canadian provinces and 29 U.S. states, are examining and implementing individualized funding or self-determination. While not every location has embraced every aspect of individualized funding, the results to date are quite heartening.

A recent independent evaluation of one project concluded:

- costs to government were lower by twelve to fifteen per cent
- waiting lists declined
- individual choice and decision making increased
- individual and family satisfaction was markedly higher

Individualized funding in its full expression is a goal to strive for. As a general principle, we believe the greater the

Individualized funding

- Provides the means and the authority to make choices.
- Strengthens individual decision making.
- Facilitates control over your service requirements.
- Promotes citizenship.
- Saves government money.
- Requires strong social support (Personal Networks).

- Reallocates wealth to the individual.
- Allows for freedom of expression in the marketplace.
- Builds self-respect.
- Reduces victimization.
- Makes service systems accountable.

control individuals have over their funding, the wider their choices will be, and the stronger their decision-making muscle will become.

4 Microboards

One of the mechanisms used to receive individually assessed government dollars is a microboard.

A microboard is a non-profit society that exists only to serve the program and service needs of your son or daughter. A microboard is small (hence the name, micro) with usually no more than five committed family members and friends on the board of directors.

This board of directors receives funding from government on behalf of the person with a disability and either directly employs staff or negotiates with service providers to provide support services for the person. The board of directors, along with the person with a disability, directs and customizes these support services.

Microboards serve a variety of other purposes because they create opportunities for relationships of support to flourish. As a mechanism for direct funding, they allow people to achieve greater control over their personal support needs.

5 Supported Decision-Making Agreement

The development of a Supported Decision-Making Agreement by your relative would anticipate and support all personal care and lifestyle decisions they may make.

The enigma of competence

Intellectual ability is seen as the exclusive determinant of our competence to make decisions. We find evidence of this on a daily basis in the numerous decisions made on behalf of our relatives, because of their perceived intellectual limitation.

The focus on intellectual ability fails to acknowledge at least three other areas of competence:

- non-verbal, non-traditional communication skills
- ways of knowing and thinking beyond cognitive ability
- social competence

In the area of decision making our relatives suffer as much from stereotypical perceptions as they do from the limitations associated with their condition. Thus, they can become prime candidates for some form of guardianship or conservatorship.

Most legal jurisdictions rely on a version of the old I.Q. score to determine the ability of people to make their own decisions. Lawyers, guardians, and the courts apply what is called the U.N.E. test. Before individuals can be deemed capable of making a decision or signing a contract, they must *understand* the *nature* and *effect* of their decision.

We disagree with this emphasis on intellectual decision making for four reasons:

1 The link between intellect and decision making or common sense cannot be proven. (A few prime ministers and presidents come to mind.)

2 Most of us make decisions in a social context. We either ask people for their views, advice, and counsel, or indirectly incorporate the views and opinions of others. Whether we acknowledge their influence or not, the opinions of others, like gamma rays, bounce off us regularly. An important corollary of socially influenced decision making is that many of us are more likely to take the advice of those we trust – perhaps even without "thinking it through ourselves."

3 There is an emotional, visceral, or intuitive component to many, if not all, of our decisions. Take for example the decision to marry, to buy this house and not that one, to select a car, or to return to school.

4 There is more than one kind of intelligence. Howard

Gardner in his seminal book *Frames of Mind* describes seven intelligences, or ways of knowing. These are identified in the box below. Cognitive intelligence is the basis of the U.N.E. test. It is clear that it is only one form of intelligence.

We are not suggesting that thinking and reasoning skills are irrelevant when it comes to decision making. But we do think it is important to balance their value with the other elements all of us use to make decisions. When evaluating a person's competence, all intelligences should be taken into consideration.

Our own formula

Given the limitations of the U.N.E. formula, we decided it was time to develop a formula of our own.

First of all we redefined competence.

Competence is centered on the interaction between individuals and their environment so that they can grow and flourish.

Competence is related to:

- Support from others. We exist as part of a community or social collective and our survival depends on the

---

The seven intelligences

1 Linguistic
An interest in reading and telling stories.

2 Logical-Mathematical
An interest in arithmetic problems.

3 Bodily-kinesthetic
An ability to process knowledge through bodily sensations.

4 Spatial
An interest in images and pictures.

5 Musical
An awareness of sounds, including those others may miss.

6 Interpersonal
An ability to understand the feelings of others and to communicate with others in any way.

7 Intrapersonal
An ability to be aware of your own feelings.

---

contributions of each one of us. The larger group has a personal stake in supporting our decision making.

- An individual's natural drive to make a contribution. (See Step Four.)

- An individual's quest to achieve control over their world and their environment.

- An individual's situation and experience. The disabilities of the individual establish the context in which the capability of the individual must be achieved. A particular limitation associated with a disability gives meaning to and provides logic for the actions of our friends and family members with a disability.

- An individual's confidence in their abilities to perform or accomplish a task. Think of people you know who have natural abilities but who lack self-confidence and therefore appear incapable. Are they more competent than our friends and family members who have the courage and confidence to tackle situations despite the challenges of their disabilities and the handicaps imposed by society?

- Recognition of an individual's right to choose their areas of control and performance.

Then we identified the critical elements of decision-making competence:

1 **Trusting Relationships** – evidence of mutually supportive and nurturing relationships characterized by commitment, closeness, caring and affection, and by

---

PLAN's decision-making formula

Our formula can be characterized in this manner:

Decision-Making Competence = Trusting Relationships X (Understanding + Supports + Talents)

DMC = TR x (U+S+T)

expectations that one is valued, expected to contribute and respected for one's capabilities.

2 **Understanding** – awareness of one's limitations, realistic appraisal of one's capabilities, wisdom, confidence in one's worth and in one's relationships, in touch with one's feelings and surroundings, expressing emotion in familiar, relevant and meaningful ways. Having tastes and preferences, and the ability to discriminate, select and choose, intentionally.

3 **Supports** – assistance, options, opportunities and resources available to assist with decision making.

4 **Talents** – natural skills and abilities of the head, heart and hands. (See Step Four.)

Our definition suggests that intellectual ability is only one of many dimensions of competence.

In fact, the overarching element in all aspects of competence is our trusting relationships. These enhance the other elements and turn a potential liability into strength.

Supported Decision-Making Agreements

The law has not caught up with our evolving understanding of the various intelligences, the concept of social competence, and our personal experience with the decision-making capability of our friends and family members with disabilities. Many of our relatives need a process that ensures genuine choice but is also mindful of their vulnerability. To bridge this gap we recommend the creation of a Supported Decision-Making Agreement.

1 The process of creating a Supported Decision-Making Agreement (SDMA) is powerful and useful for assisting the individual with a disability to become accustomed to making decisions. Having the discussion is most important, whether you get it down on paper or not. Bringing concerns about medical or financial decision out in the open, communicating with each other, and

paying attention to these decisions are important aspects of the work of a Personal Network.

2 Supported Decision-Making Agreements are a tool to strengthen existing relationships and to involve others. The network becomes stronger. With a new mission the collective is galvanized, reconfirming its commitment to the individual.

3 The existence of a Supported Decision-Making Agreement creates at the very least moral authority for assisted or supported decision making. If enough people begin to use Supported Decision-Making Agreements, this moral authority will begin to nudge into legal authority. This is certainly what has happened with "living wills" and "health care consent forms." When the need arises, health care providers often utilize these even in jurisdictions that do not yet recognize their legality.

4 Supported Decision-Making Agreements can be used to enhance existing enduring powers of attorney.

SAMPLE

John Smith's Supported Decision-Making Agreement

1 Date

07 JUNE 1999

2 Identification

Name: JOHN SMITH

Address: 123 Main Street, Hometown

Telephone: 222-4567

Birthdate: 12.5.75

Health Care Card Number: 98765432-1

I am making this agreement because I need and want the support and guidance from my friends and family in making some decisions in my life.

3 Supporters

    1 Alan Affable – friend

    2 Brenda Busy – friend

    3 Corinne Cousin – family member

    4 David Dreamer – friend

4 Responsibilities of supporters

    a Financial affairs and legal matters: I would like the following two supporters, Alan and David, to support, guide and/or represent me in financial and legal matters. If either Alan or David is unavailable, I would like Brenda to act as the second representative.

    b Personal care and health care: I would like two of the following three supporters: Corinne, Alan and Brenda, to support, guide and/or represent me in health and personal care issues. If only one of these supporters is available, then I would like David to act as the second representative.

    In a medical emergency if two supporters cannot be reached, any one of the three supporters may act alone.

    I would like my supporters to inform my mother Margaret (222-8876) regarding significant health-related issues.

continued on page 206

I want the supporters to agree on their decisions. If there is a disagreement between the two supporters, the monitor will ensure that at least three supporters meet and are involved in making a decision that is acceptable to everyone present.

The monitor will be kept updated by the supporters on all major financial, legal, personal or health care issues.

5   Responsibilities of health care professionals

Any time there is any question regarding my health or well being my supporters must be consulted.

6   Monitor

Patricia – as a representative of Planned Lifetime Advocacy Network (PLAN)
Address: 101 Canada Way
Telephone: 256-1111 (home) 222-4848 (work)

My family and I are lifetime members of Planned Lifetime Advocacy Network (PLAN). PLAN has agreed to provide ongoing support, advocacy, and monitoring on my behalf.

If Patricia is unable to fulfill the role of monitor, the executive director or designate from Planned Lifetime Advocacy Network will meet with me and my supporters to choose an alternate.

7   Responsibilities of monitor

The monitor will maintain regular contact with me and with my supporters. The monitor has no decision-making power, and their role is to ensure that the supported decision-making agreement is reflective of my preferences. If there is a disagreement between the two supporters, the monitor will ensure that at least three supporters meet and are involved in making a decision that is acceptable to everyone present.

8   Effective date of this agreement and reviews of this agreement

- This agreement will be effective immediately upon being signed and witnessed.
or
- This agreement will be reviewed two years after coming into effect and every two years thereafter, or upon the request of myself and/or my monitor and/or my supporters.

Appendix A Description of supporters' relationships with John

Alan Affable

1234 West 1st Street

Hometown

Telephone: 456-7890 (home) 222-1023 (work)

I have known John since 1983. I first met John as his staff at a group home and have formed a close personal friendship with him over those years. Since John has moved to Hometown Central I visit weekly and visit on most holidays. I also organize the network functions for him.

Brenda Busy

5678 West 2nd Street

Hometown

Telephone: 987-6543 (home) 333-4567 (work)

I have known John since 1990. I first met him as a volunteer at St. Pancras Community Church. I have formed a close friendship with John. Over the past 6 years I have been visiting John on a weekly/biweekly basis. I am an active member of his Personal Network.

Corinne Cousin

6070 42nd Street

Hometown

Telephone: 987-1234 (home)

I am John's cousin and have known him all my life. I am an active member of John's Personal Network. John's contribution to my own family is very important to Stephen, my partner, and to our two children, his nieces Alice and Chantal.

David Dreamer

8090 93rd Street

Hometown

Telephone: 987-4321 (home) 286-6962 (work)

I have known John since 1989. I first met John when I was assigned to be his social worker. When John moved, my relationship changed from being his social worker to

continued on page 208

becoming his friend. Although I don't see John as much as I would like to, I feel I have a good understanding of his history and want to be a part of his future. I am a member of his Personal Network.

Appendix B Other supporters and their roles

1 Able Nursing Care Services, Nurse Nancy Drew, contact
Role paid nursing support to John. Nancy Drew's role is to provide all pertinent information to the supporters in areas of John's health and personal care.
Address: 610 Library Lane, Hometown
Telephone: 338-4420 (office) 682-1945 (pager)

2 Frank Friend
Role former support worker and friend. Frank Friend worked with John for approximately 3 years, and has maintained a friendship with John since moving to another job. Frank understands John's medical and personal care needs, and has supported John in many areas of his life. He has encouraged and supported the writing of this Supported Decision-Making Agreement.
Address: 206 Harmony Mews, Hometown
Telephone: 591-8044 (home) 476-8765 (cell)

Appendix C Expression of preferences

If I am able to give the supporters a clear indication of my preferences, either through eye contact or through body language, then the supporters will act based on my indicated preferences. If I am unable to give the supporters a clear indication of my preferences, then the supporters will act based on their relationship with me, their knowledge, and their shared past experiences with me.
I express my preferences in the following ways:

- When I am enjoying myself I smile and am alert.
- When I am not enjoying myself my body is tense, sometimes I grimace, I tune out or I'm non-responsive.
- When others are gentle with me I usually relax.
- I respond more readily to people I know well. If I don't know someone, I might not respond to them.

My likes: pasta, especially lasagna; loud, action-packed movies; pop music; sports; my network friends; my audio tapes; going to coffee house; off-beat humor, e.g. Mr. Bean;

basketball; surprises; cheesecake; chocolate; going for walks; visiting friends; talking to people on the phone; range of motion exercises.

My dislikes: meetings; slow, boring movies; spending money; shopping malls; cold foods and drinks; getting my teeth brushed.

Note This should not be seen as the final word regarding my preferences and communication.

Appendix D Informing relevant parties

I HAVE GIVEN COPIES OF THIS AGREEMENT TO:

Mother

Supervisors of Group Home

Family Doctor

Society which runs group home

Social Worker, Ministry of Family Services

Nurse, Able Nursing

Local Hospital

PLAN

Respirologist: Medical specialist

Neurologist: Medical specialist

Bank

Trust Company

Your Name   <u>John Smith</u>

Signature/ Mark   _____

Date   _____

or

This agreement has been signed in my presence and on my behalf by

Name   _____

Signature   _____

Date   _____

Witnesses

Signature of Witnesses (they also fill out Certificate of Witnesses)

Signature   _____

Date   _____

continued on page 210

Signature _____
Date _____

Supporters
Signature _____
Date _____
Signature _____
Date _____
Signature _____
Date _____

SAMPLE
Certificate of witnesses
Please print full names and addresses.

I, _____ live at _____
I, _____ live at _____
We certify that:
We witnessed the signing of the Supported Decision-Making Agreement made
by _____ (print full name of grantor).
We have both reached the age of legal majority.
Neither of us is a supporter or an alternate supporter. Neither of us is the spouse,
child, or parent of the supporter(s) or alternate(s). Neither of us is an employee or
agent of the supporter(s) or alternate(s).
We were present during the signing of the Supported Decision-Making Agreement.
We understand that the grantor has had the Supported Decision-Making Agreement
read or communicated to him/her and has signed it freely.

The truth of this statement is certified at _____ on _____

_____
Signature of Witness

_____
Signature of Witness

Key components of a Supported Decision-Making Agreement (SDMA)

1 The person with the disability must initiate the Supported Decision-Making Agreement.

2 A Supported Decision-Making Agreement should respond to three areas of decision making:

- financial/business
- health
- daily living or personal care

3 A Supported Decision-Making Agreement should convey an understanding that decision-making assistance will be based on the individual's values, beliefs, experiences, and preferences. It should not be based on what is felt to be in the individual's best interest. This may be a tough challenge for many of us.

4 A Supported Decision-Making Agreement should identify by example the manner in which the individual

- expresses preferences
- makes choices and
- conveys understanding

5 A Supported Decision-Making Agreement should identify the communication style of the individual.

6 A Supported Decision-Making Agreement should contain a clause stating that the intention is to assist and support decision making while at the same time recognizing the Supported Decision-Making Agreement does not have legal power. However, you may live in a jurisdiction where durable powers of attorney and health care consent agreements may be legal. In this case, a Supported Decision-Making Agreement should have legal status.

7 A Supported Decision-Making Agreement can identify one or more individuals to assist with decision making.

These people are called supporters. If more than one person is named as a supporter, the Supported Decision-Making Agreement should identify:

- each person's area of responsibility
- which person can speak on behalf of others
- a process for resolving disagreements

8 A Supported Decision-Making Agreement should identify an alternate or replacement, particularly if only one supported decision maker was identified originally.

9 A Supported Decision-Making Agreement should appoint a monitor who knows the individual and is willing to stay in regular contact with him/her. This could be an individual or organization; for example, PLAN is often named as a monitor on these agreements. The duties of the monitor should be spelled out and should include:

- ensuring the Supported Decision-Making Agreement is working
- preventing abuse and exploitation
- giving support and assurance to the individual
- acting as a contact for the individual and the supported decision makers

A word about communication

Many of our friends and relatives have a unique communication style, a mother tongue all their own. They may provide a response minutes or even hours after a question is asked. Their response may be a slight gesture or a groan. They may not verbalize in a manner that is easily understood. They may not verbalize at all. They may literally shrink and recoil from an undesirable choice. The process of understanding their wishes may be quite slow. We may be successful in understanding their wishes only some of the time. Regardless, we know (a) that they communicate and (b) how they communicate.

Unfortunately individuals with a non-verbal or non-traditional communication style can be judged incapable of making a decision purely on these grounds. If appropriate, we recommend that you identify the method of communication preferred by your friend or family member and write that into the Supported Decision-Making Agreement. Similarly, if they have difficulty physically signing the Supported Decision-Making Agreement, it is important that:

- they direct someone to sign the agreement on their behalf; and

- they locate an independent witness who is prepared to confirm their intention to sign the agreement.

What we have learned from creating Supported Decision-Making Agreements

A Supported Decision-Making Agreement:

- provides a vehicle for choice to be respected and supported

- strengthens the voice of the individual and ensures their views, values and beliefs are front and center

- is a declaration of commitment

- cannot be done without a network of support

- solidifies the relationship with the person and among members of the network

- provides status to family and friends

- involves a broad group of people who reflect the multi-faceted nature of the individual

- creates a working partnership among caregivers, professionals, friends, family members, and the individual

- brings families together, and reaches out to absent family members

- establishes legitimacy to the relationship between the individual and members of the network – you cannot get involved unless you have a relationship with the individual

- reinforces a focus on capacity
- provides a clear focus for the Personal Network, identifying specific tasks and practical jobs
- provides a clearinghouse, an identifiable group to bring information to and obtain information from
- does not happen overnight
- has moral authority and increases the potential for the individual's voice to be heard
- works best if you don't wait for a crisis but begin an open dialogue, with medical professionals for example
- provides a forum for airing conflicting views and for conflict resolution

The secret of good decision making

Ever made a bad decision or a decision you regretted? Ever changed your mind? You are not alone. Some of the poor decisions we have made are minor, some alas, are major and we would like to take them back. The same is true and will be true for our sons and daughters, all of them, including those with disabilities.

Decision making means taking risks, understanding consequence, learning from your mistakes and trying again. An

---

Tips for choosing supported decision makers

- How long have you known them?
- Do they have the time and energy to assist you?
- Do you trust them to carry out your wishes, beliefs, and values?
- Have you been able to rely on them in the past?
- Are they in regular contact with you?
- Do they live nearby?
- Are some members of your family more supportive than others?
- Do they have a special skill? (For example, are they good at handling money?)
- If you choose more than one person, can they work as a team?
- Are they good listeners?

old Chinese proverb says the risk is not in falling off the horse, but in lying there. A Personal Network in combination with a Supported Decision-Making Agreement will pick any of us up before the hooves descend. The secret of good decision making for our relative with a disability may be supported decision making.

Ulysses Agreements

Ulysses, Homer's epic Greek hero, was confronted with a number of challenging adventures. One of the more alluring was the task of sailing past the coast of the Sirens.

The Sirens were sea-nymphs who lived on a rocky island and lured mariners to their destruction with their sweet songs.

Ulysses, fearing the seductive powers of the Sirens and keenly aware of his own vulnerability, commanded his crew to fill their ears with wax and to lash him to the mast. He ordered the crew not to release him regardless of what he said until his ship had sailed beyond the Sirens' spell.

When he heard the Sirens' seductive music, he begged to be released so that he might cast himself into the sea. Obedient to his original orders, his crew bound him even more tightly. Protected in this way, Ulysses sailed safely on to his next adventure.

A number of mental health advocates have created a variation of the SDMA called a Ulysses Agreement.

This type of agreement lets individuals plan for episodes of mental illness that may leave them temporarily unable to make decisions of their own.

Ulysses Agreements describe the circumstances that trigger their utilization. They remind the crew:
- to remain faithful to the original instructions
- that it's time to act on the person's behalf
- what they should do

Ulysses Agreements can prevent the terrible consequences and disruptions that occur when someone is experiencing symptoms related to their mental illness.

Ulysses Agreements have been used to freeze bank and credit card accounts, to obtain treatment and to manage personal affairs. Doctors, banks, landlords, police, and other professionals have honored the Ulysses Agreement. The Ulysses Agreement can be a process that brings family members together to work in harmony with their relative who experiences mental illness.

Chris

A story of philia
I sat there amazed

"He could easily drown. I can understand his fear. Let's face it, all the pool staff are women. They're not strong enough to hold him steady. He needs big strong men in order to be comfortable in the water, particularly because his tracheotomy is open. No wonder he stiffens up. He's afraid the water will leak in."

They met me after work at the PLAN offices to review the Supported Decision-Making Agreement they had prepared with Chris. It quickly became clear I had nothing to add, so I excused myself.

They stayed on to arrange for the official signing at Chris' group home. They needed two witnesses. They also needed someone who knew him well enough to sign on his behalf. From my office I could hear snatches of their conversation, sprinkled with good-natured teasing, jokes and laughter.

They were discussing a trip to the pool for Chris as if it were an everyday occurrence. They might have well been discussing the weather instead of planning an adventure for a man with extraordinary physical challenges.

But this wasn't anything new for this group. Their commitment had reconnected Chris to two of his sisters after a 15-year absence attracted his mother to two of their monthly pot lucks and, as the pièce de résistance, they arranged for his first holiday – a week of fishing on the inside coast of Vancouver Island.

Not bad for a man who had spent fifteen years in hospital; not good that it had taken so long. Not bad that it was now happening.

As I sat there I thought about the mystery of it all. Four disparate personalities united through the bonds of love. Love for Chris. Trust in each other. A team of scuba divers, about to descend deeper into the reservoir of kindness they had created. They were ready for the next stage of engagement.

Alisha, gentle of disposition, steadfast and committed. Her connection to Chris was spiritual. In their presence, one would never doubt their ability to communicate beyond the blocked dam of words.

Adam, flamboyant and resolute, nothing but the best for Chris. A pub night out with the boys, Why not? An evening of fine dining. We will take five hours if we have to; the best seat in the house and damn the stares.

Lavonne, steady and wise, the matriarch. An alert eye ready for any sacrifice. Her renovated home, proof of her family's commitment to Chris. A barrier-free spare room at her expense – just for Chris. She hosts the potlucks, of course, and Chris loves her lasagna. Her place of hospitality is comfortable enough for Chris' conflicted mother to make a tentative appearance.

Theresa, precise and practical, nothing left to chance, no detail too small. The choreographer for the small dance troupe, the equipment manager for the team. Itinerary for a week in a tent, photo album for a lost family, signing arrangements for a Supported Decision-Making Agreement. Done. She coordinated them all.

The Greeks had an expression for it, "philia." The love of citizens for each other, neighbors caring for each other.

Philia – a willingness to assist, to support. Philia, personified by Alisha, Adam, Lavonne and Theresa agreeing to assist Chris with his financial and legal affairs, his personal and health care. Philia – evidence to anyone who would have us believe only the state should make decisions for people judged intellectually incapable. Philia – the missing link, confirmation of our capacity to care for each other.

"We declare our commitment to Chris. We will be his voice during medical emergencies, a sounding board for tough decisions, a portrait of his choices, a touchstone for what's precious to him, a cradle of inspired resolution, a vault of shared memories, an affirmation of his life."

Authentic voices for a new type of decision making – supported decision making. We are safe because we love and are loved.

I sat there amazed, bearing silent witness to the power of faithful friends.

Mark

Ulysses Agreement

Mark is a young man who has episodes of mood disorder. Each episode created great disruption in his life. Not only did Mark have to struggle to get treatment, he also suffered consequences. Sometimes his bank account was overdrawn; sometimes he lost his job or his housing.

After much thought and with the encouragement of his doctor, Mark decided to make a Ulysses Agreement with members of his extended family.

Mark's team members have acted on the agreement several times. They've used it to freeze his bank and credit card accounts, to help Mark get treatment, and to manage Mark's financial affairs. Financial institutions and professionals have honored the agreement.

Mark says that his Ulysses Agreement has "saved his life." After an illness, he no longer has to pick up as many pieces or start from the beginning.

My daughter Liz

I am because we are

Elizabeth Amey Kelsey Etmanski, or Liz for short, can turn a dry history assignment on New France into a love story between an Indian princess and a *coureur de bois* faster than most Grade Nine students at Hugh Boyd High.

She dreams of being a rock guitarist, idolizes Madonna, and can lip synch to most of the songs in *Wayne's World*. She can be extravagant with her make-up, prefers anything lacy, particularly black fishnet vests, and applies something called "white mud" to her face every evening.

Boys and romance are passions she shares with her best friend Rachelle and her sisters Catherine and Theressa.

We disagree on a number of matters — her Madonna dance moves, the state of her room, the frequency of her dishwashing and the need for her own phone. The latter seems an extravagance, since she has expropriated the portable one we already have, re-establishing her claim every time she walks in the door. I may be off the hook, however, since she has just seen the perfect electric guitar. It's bright red and costs "only $450, Dad."

She earns the occasional detention, would rather catch a video than do homework, and has a wicked sense of humor, especially about my bald spot.

Notwithstanding, she is an adornment to her dad's life, equal in beauty and charm to both her younger and older sisters.

Yet, there is darkness already threatening a corner of her future. Not that Liz is aware, fortunately. She sees the world as Timothy Findley describes it, "whole and green and alive with promise." The specter sadly is all mine.

In four years, she begins a high-stakes game of chance. On her 19th birthday, the law will silently confer the assumption of decision-making capability on Liz. It is a Pandora's present.

The standards of decision-making capability in our society remain firmly rooted in a narrowly defined, highly overrated form of intellectual ability. In our province, the legal test is your ability to demonstrate you understand the nature and effect of your decision.

Using that standard, Liz, who has Down syndrome, would most likely fail.

The utensils the law has to measure our worth have not changed significantly throughout this century. Neither has their intent. Verbal ability, proficiency of expression and abstract intellectual thinking remain the criteria for determining a person's decision-making ability.

As long as our society continues to ignore other factors that contribute to

continued on page 220

decision making, there is no equality in the assumption of capability; there is intellectual imperialism. IQ scores may have faded from use but their successors haven't. The law has embraced them all.

We know, learn, and understand even when we cannot explain. We learn through self-awareness, through our relationships and through confronting the challenges of our environment. We can know emotionally, spiritually, and intuitively. We can express ourselves through the medium of music, art, mathematics, relationships, and love. Our tears, laughter, smiles, and frowns reveal our trust, confidence, security, and wishes as surely as intellectual expression.

Ask yourself how you have made some of the important decisions in your life. Marriage? Children? Change of career? New car? Can you honestly say you understood the consequences of your decisions all the time?

How often did you rationalize afterward? And how often did you make decisions alone, completely cut off from advice, consultation, or influence of any kind? Is there really such a thing as independent decision making?

Our insights into the varied, complex and different ways of knowing remain half-eaten, too strange and threatening to be digested by the law. Its teeth are clenched. Liz and her abilities are a forbidden delicacy.

As an adult, Liz can anticipate the law ignoring her decision-making ability and ultimately usurping it. The law does not value her intuition, her compassion, her manner of expression and her relationships.

As a father, I am beset by burning questions. Which benign agents of society's institutions will challenge Liz's decisions? What choices and risks will they eliminate from her life under the guise of protection? How will the mask of caring prevent her initiation into life's mysteries?

When the law demands the password of her, will it appreciate the determination that convinced Powell's bookstore in Portland to search for an hour for a book on sign language when she didn't know its title? She knew it when she saw it, however.

Will it value her diplomatic skills, mature enough to find common ground even in irreconcilable positions? Will it honor her ability to assess emotions with uncanny accuracy and to read a room with more facility than any politician? Will it credit her storytelling, her humor, and her razor-sharp imitations of friends and family? Will it understand her motivation to plow through babysitting and leadership training courses even though she is just learning to read?

continued on page 221

My daughter has a wisdom that eludes many of us. She understands her limitations and adjusts with patience and eagerness. She negotiates the complexities and inequities of her world with more ingenuity, courage, and equanimity than she should have to. She offers, for all those willing to listen, a course in perfecting a life.

Yet, unlike her sisters, Liz is a candidate for exclusion.

No admittance. Access forbidden. Restricted. Off limits. Too risky. Vulnerable. Incompetent. Choices ignored. For your own good. Go directly to ... a program, a service, a professional, an institution, a legal guardian. Become a client, not a citizen.

We need laws that recognize Liz's talents and attitudes, including her ability to participate in caring, committed and trusting relationships. That's really what keeps you and me safe and contributes to the quality of our decisions.

If that kind of brilliance were to shine on the darkened corner of Liz's future, I know an Indian princess and a *coureur de bois* who would be pleased.

Worksheet 10

SUPPORTED DECISION MAKING

Use this worksheet to organize key decision-making information, issues and resources that affect the choices and safety of your relative.

A. Checklist

MEDICAL DECISION MAKING

YES NO   I (we) have discussed issues of medical consent with my loved one's doctor.

YES NO   The doctor accepts consent from my son or daughter for medical treatment.

YES NO   The doctor accepts my consent for medical care on their behalf.

YES NO   My son/daughter has developed a Supported Decision-Making Agreement and has discussed this with their doctor.

FINANCIAL DECISION MAKING

YES NO   I have set up a living (inter vivos) trust.

YES NO   I have set up an income trust.

YES NO   I have set up a discretionary trust.

YES NO   My son/daughter has a bank account.

YES   NO   Withdrawals from that bank account are protected by:

- joint signature for withdrawals

- my son/daughter is well known to bank employees

- funds in the account are kept to a minimum

YES   NO   My son/daughter has set up an enduring power of attorney.

YES   NO   My son/daughter has developed a Supported Decision-Making Agreement.

PERSONAL CARE DECISION MAKING

YES   NO   My son / daughter has an advocate.

YES   NO   The services s/he receives are monitored by a separate and independent agency.

YES   NO   Housing supports are kept separate from other services.

YES   NO   Staff understand and support the importance of family involvement.

YES   NO   Staff understand and welcome the involvement of friends and members of their Personal Network.

YES   NO   Service and program staff recognize the importance of offering and respecting my relative's choices.

YES   NO   Families and friends provide support by reviewing services and programs on a regular basis. (Note: This is different from the personal service plans developed by service providers.)

YES   NO   My relative has developed a Supported Decision-Making Agreement.

B. Information

GENERAL

Who does my son or daughter trust? _____

_____

Who would I trust to assist my relative with decision making? _____

_____

_____

Who understands my relative's communication style? _____

_____

_____

MEDICAL DECISIONS

Who is my son or daughter's doctor? _____

What assistance would my relative need to make medical decisions? _____

_____

_____

Who would my relative and I want to assist with their medical decision making?

_____

What aspect of their medical care do I think my son/daughter might understand?

_____

_____

What formal arrangements do I need to make to ensure medical care is easily

available to my son/daughter? _____

_____

My son/daughter's medical plan number is _____

_____

_____

FINANCIAL DECISIONS

My son/daughter's trustees are _____

_____

His/her financial advisors are _____

_____

My son/daughter has a bank account at _____

        Account number _____

Signing authority includes _____

_____

I have asked _____ to monitor the trust services and investment

advice available to my relative.

PERSONAL CARE DECISIONS

My son / daughter's advocate is _____

The independent agency that monitors services is _____

Friends and families should review services and programs at these intervals _____

_____

developing *your* will and estate plan

When someone dies,
a library burns.
Donald Scanlon, hospice worker

What the heck, it can't hurt me

"A lot of people my age have been thinking for most of their adult life about what will happen after they've gone. They hope their plans are adequate. Maybe they made a will 30 years ago. Or maybe they hope that plans will come together magically at the last minute. I don't think that's good enough.

"When you have a child with a disability you get lots of advice. But usually nothing ever materializes. You have to remember that every once in a while something comes along and it does work.

"I knew if I was going to make progress I had to take chances. What the heck, I said, it can't hurt me."

George's involvement with other parents associated with PLAN encouraged him to think about where he was going and what he wanted to achieve. "I call it putting your house in order. They got me moving but you have to be willing to do it. It means getting organized – getting all your necessary papers together.

"My original will is long gone. We made a new one just before my wife died. I changed it a year later to include some clauses I heard about from other families. Then I decided to change my trustee and to include a role for PLAN after I died. So I got another lawyer and she drafted a new will. It's never really over, you know. If I find out about something better and I'm still around I'll make changes again. Actually, altering your will is easy and not that expensive. Things are evolving and you are bound to get new ideas.

"My first goal was to make sure there were sufficient funds to look after Rick. I got advice on prescribed insured annuities and how to use life insurance to increase the size of my estate. There were things about life insurance I never appreciated. I just about doubled the size of my estate by buying a life insurance policy outright. And the money would be available for Rick immediately after I died. It wouldn't be tied up in probate and it wouldn't be taxable.

"These were the sorts of things I knew nothing about. The fact that other parents were exploring the same things gave me confidence."

George also decided to change trust companies. He thought they all were the same – straight business operations. Then he heard through the "parent grapevine" about one company that was sensitive to the needs of families. In fact, after the death of one parent, the

continued on page 230

step six

Developing your will and estate plan

You can never do a kindness too soon, because you never know how soon it will be too late.
RALPH WALDO EMERSON

this step is about passing your wealth and wisdom to the next generation, particularly your family member with a disability. Along the way you will encounter a document that eludes at least half of us – a will. And you will find advice that might increase your current wealth, which will eventually affect how much you can leave your relative with a disability.

The solutions we present in this step represent some of the best advice families have discovered as they traveled the path you are on right now.

The information in this chapter will:

- explain some of the issues involved in preparing a will when one of the beneficiaries has a disability

- urge you to consult a lawyer who is familiar with these issues and who will help you draft a valid will

- explain how you need to review your will periodically, and update it when necessary

- identify some of the critical elements of an estate plan

- discuss how to maintain government benefits

- point out the benefits of discretionary and supplemental trusts (also called special needs trusts)

- save you time and money

continued from page 228

trust officer got involved in the memorial service, even bringing his kettles and food to the reception after. The trust officer helped the son with a disability to move and now stays in regular contact, and often attends Personal Network meetings. George wanted that kind of service for Rick, so he shifted companies.

"I didn't figure I could take my previous trust officer out to lunch. Or for that matter that he would ever be interested in taking Rick out to lunch. I wanted a more personal approach and I got it."

For George, the company of other families helped get him moving. Looking back on it, now he realizes how easy it really was. The time spent was negligible compared to the time he had spent worrying.

Developing a will and estate plan need not be complicated, particularly if you have thought through the issues raised in the preceding steps. Most lawyers will be grateful that you are so well prepared. They find that people often come to them looking for the answers when in fact they are only highly skilled technicians. The job of future planning specialists is to respond to your vision of the future, not to create a vision for you. The work you have already done will save them time and you money.

This Step will not replace the need to make tough decisions. That's what Steps One to Five are all about. They are the critical steps because they define your vision and determine your goals. Your will and estate plan does not replace those steps. Rather, it assists you to reach your goals.

One final caution. Do not be intimidated by legal language. All professions have their jargon. We have tried to isolate most of the critical language so you have a handy reference (see page 259).

A few caveats about estate and financial planning

We are old enough to remember with fondness the response of the great vaudeville comedian Jack Benny, when confronted by a robber:

The robber demands, "Your money or your life!"

Considerable delay. No answer from Benny.

This step may not be for you

Before you become immersed in the language of will and estate planning, you may want to take the following quick test. You may be one of the lucky readers to whom this step does not apply. If you answer yes to any two of the following statements, you need read no further.

I like to pay taxes.
I am not old enough.
My family always gets along.
I will live forever.
The government will look after my relative.

The robber nudges him with his revolver, "Well?"

"I'm thinking, I'm thinking," replies Benny.

It's still an important question and a great answer. We'd like to think Jack Benny was pondering the important question of control. Does money control our lives or do we control money? Either way, estate and financial planning will help.

We are not estate and financial planning professionals. What little we know has been picked up from the experience of families and the professionals they have encountered who are sensitive to their concerns.

This section about estate and financial planning is not about details. It is about increasing the colors in your palette. For those wanting more details, there are many good books published on financial planning. Next to cookbooks, books on finances represent an expanding section of most bookstores.

If you are interested in saving taxes, offshore investments, diversification, the "rule of 72," joint and last survivor life annuities, consult these books. Or consult an independent, professional financial advisor. In most jurisdictions these individuals will be licensed, professionally accredited, and regulated.

For our part, we offer a lay person's guide to financial and estate planning. It does not hurt to know a little about the often-mysterious language of financial and estate planning.

Financial planning is the development of skills and knowledge to maximize and manage the financial assets you create for yourself now and in the future, including for your retirement.

Estate planning is the process of ensuring that your financial wishes are carried out after your death and that your beneficiaries receive the maximum benefit from the wealth and assets you have accumulated.

The link between financial planning and estate planning is direct. The better the job of accumulating wealth, the "richer" the estate you will have to leave.

Financial planning assists in the accumulation of assets.

Estate planning is the process of ensuring that your financial wishes are carried out after your death and that your beneficiaries receive the maximum benefit.

Each of us has a host of financial goals: day-to-day survival, paying the mortgage, putting the kids through university, setting a bit aside for retirement and the financial well being of our children. In this discussion we assume our chief concern is the financial security of our relatives with a disability – we want to maximize the amount of family wealth we can pass on to them. To put the challenge of financial and estate planning in plain language, we are looking at the creation of enough wealth to last not only for our lifetime but also for the lifetime of our son or daughter.

Estate and financial planning is not just for the wealthy or elderly. We have learned from our work with families that even those of us with little disposable income can create assets to pass on, regardless of our age.

Beginning to create your will and estate plan

Before you create your will and estate plan, you need to be clear about the details. Every family situation is unique. If you are going to rely on your family after you are gone, it's a good idea to discuss things with them beforehand.

Other valuable resource people you might consider talking to include: extended family and friends, members of your relative's Personal Network, members of your church congregation, and of course other families in similar circumstances.

In our experience parents have often been able to clarify their objectives by talking to others. The more open your discussions are, the clearer your objectives will be.

Eight key objectives of a will and estate plan

Most people want their will and estate plan to:

1 Pay their debts, taxes, and other liabilities.

2 Provide a separate independent income for their surviving spouse.

Worksheets

Four worksheets are located at the end of this chapter, starting on page 261.

WORKSHEET 11 **Your Net Worth**

This worksheet helps you figure out what your financial resources are. It is a good place to begin your estate planning. The worksheet is on page 261.

WORKSHEET 12 **Your Will and Estate Plan**

This worksheet will help you clarify your objectives in making a will. Take a look at it now. Before you make decisions about your will, fill out this worksheet in detail. It will prepare you for a visit to a lawyer. The worksheet is on page 263.

WORKSHEET 13 **Personal Inventory**

This worksheet helps you keep track of your documents, and lets others know where important information is located. The worksheet is on page 270.

WORKSHEET 14 **Your Will and Estate Plan: Summary Checklist**

Use this checklist to make sure you have remembered everything. This worksheet is on page 278.

ESTATE = Assets – Liabilities – Taxes – Fees + Life Insurance

3 Distribute their assets according to their wishes.

4 Maximize the size of their estate for their children.

5 Protect the estate of their son or daughter with a disability.

6 Ensure that there is a guardian for their children who are legal minors.

7 Avoid delays, family strife, needless taxation, costly legal challenges, probate fees and government involvement.

8 Allocate a portion of their estate to the charities and causes they are passionate about.

You will want to add your personalized objectives to these general objectives. Only when you are comfortable – well, reasonably comfortable – with your answers, are you ready for the technical solutions.

A Buddhist will

As you prepare your will, you will see clearly there is a dream floating in the sheet of paper. You will also see that a dream depends on fears and hopes. Without heartache and longing there will be no dream. Without love and belonging there will be no dream. You will see that without a dream there will be no vision either. Without a vision there will be no plan. Without a plan there will be nothing to share. There will be no conversation. Without a plan there will be no instructions. Without instructions there will be no will. So the dream is in the will. The existence of the will is dependent on the existence of the dream. Dream and will are very close.

As humans, we cannot exist without dreams. Dreams are vital to our sleeping existence. Sleep deprived of dreams means you wake up fatigued. You cannot rest without dreams. Dreams maintain your health. So too our waking lives are shaped by our dreams. Dreams shape our reality. We must dream. Dreams are vital to our existence. We are because we dream. Therefore, you can see your essence, your history, your life, your sleep, and your health in the will.

Our dreams also shape the reality of others. Let us think of some. The lawyer needs a dream to draft your will. So does the secretarial assistant. So does the computer programmer who writes the software the lawyer uses for drafting a will. So do the computer manufacturer, the computer salesperson, and the purchasing agent for the lawyer.

And if you look more deeply, with the eyes of a Zen master, with the eyes of one who is truly awake, you will see that will, dream, and paper are closely connected. You will see the cloud in the paper on which your will is written. Without the cloud there is no rain; without rain the trees cannot grow and without trees you cannot make paper. You will see that everything is there in the will: the sunshine that helps your family grow, that helps trees grow. The sunshine that grows food, that feeds the lawyer and the lawyer's family and your family and yourself. The food that keeps you healthy and enables you to dream.

The will does not exist independently. It is empty without its connections. It is also full of life, beauty, and truth, of eternity, of the universe. Out of emptiness, the will becomes full of everything.

In praise of the imperfect will

You've heard the facts before. Too many people either die without a will or with a will that's out-of-date. You want to avoid joining their ranks. But you don't have all the answers. You still need to work out a few more details. You're just about there. Maybe after reading this chapter!

We're sorry to disappoint you. This chapter will not help you create the perfect will. Neither will any other book. Or person, for that matter.

The challenges of executing a will are tough for all of us and have nothing really to do with having a relative with a disability. Maybe it has something to do with the word "execute." "Execute a will" is a curious phrase. It took us a long time to see the irony in the term. Too close to capital punishment for our liking. Yet that's how it feels sometimes, doesn't it? Completing a will is like being led to our execution.

Consider these amazing facts:

- Over 90% of the heads of North American family-run enterprises die without a viable estate succession plan.
- Over 80% of Americans will retire without a financial plan – they will be relying on social security.
- Over 50% of Canadians die without a will.
- Over 44% of parents have not appointed a guardian in their will to take care of their children, should they die before their children reach the age of legal majority.
- Only 3 in 10 family businesses survive to the next generation. 9 out of 10 fail to make it to the third generation.

Think of it. The heads of some of the most creative, determined and successful businesses cannot, will not, or do not plan for the future.

Don't make this mistake. Don't wait for something that will never happen: the perfect time to create the perfect will. Now is the time to develop and execute the "imperfect" will.

> People who never alter their opinions are like standing water and breed reptiles of the mind.
>
> WILLIAM BLAKE

We feel so strongly about this we might call our next book *In Praise of Imperfection*.

What's so great about perfection anyway? Where did we get the grandiose illusion that we humans can either be perfect or get things perfect? Surely that's the job of divine personalities. Our culture seems to value extraordinary athletic achievement, great beauty, and intellectual prowess — if you are to believe the advertisers. Few, if any of us, ever attain these standards. Yet we manage to get on with our lives.

That's what we want you to do with your will. Get on with it! Preparing and executing the "imperfect" will is not the least you can do; it's the best you can do.

Tips for wills and estate planning

The most indispensable person at PLAN is Jack Collins — our founding president. One of the reasons is that he knows more about will and estate planning than all of us combined. In fact we have an unwritten rule — refer every

It's never too late

Halfway through Marcel Proust's epic novel *In Search of Lost Time* one of the main characters, the writer Bergotte, dies. On the day of his own death, November 18, 1922, Proust summoned the maid at three in the morning to dictate revisions to the novel he had taken 17 secluded years to write.

He wanted to make corrections to Bergotte's deathbed scene based on his own experience.

Proust's novel was a work of lifetime dedication and a massive autobiographical monument. He was constantly revising, gathering more information, exploring new details, and adding new passages, like stamps to an album. *Rechercher*, "to search for" or "to seek" was a key word for Proust. He accepted that his novel, while entire and complete, would never be quite finished, would never be perfect and so he kept writing to the day of his death.

I know a lawyer who is equally passionate about wills. She sees our wills as the product of our lifetime task of reflection, research, recovery, and recognition — as creative works in progress. Not surprisingly, our lawyer friend draws inspiration from Proust. She recognizes the need to keep revising. She encourages us to think of our wills as our autobiographical classic, our own ongoing masterpiece.

question about wills and estates to Jack. We suspect he has met with more families and seen more wills than any lawyer. In fact lawyers and accountants and financial planners will often call him for advice and tips. His technical expertise is immense and his credibility among families is legendary. What follows are some tips from the jack of the trade.

- Your will is the foundation of your estate plan. Review it every two years and update it when circumstances in your life change.
- Codicils (additions and amendments to your will) are not costly.
- Start as early as possible to create an asset for your son/daughter with a disability.
- Consider life insurance. For a small monthly fee you can finance a policy whose proceeds can be placed tax free into a discretionary trust.
- Estate planning has nothing to do with wealth and age. If you want to leave something behind then estate planning is for you.
- Appoint executors and trustees who will outlive you.
- Ensure that your estate is not subjected to unnecessary probate fees.
- Talk matters over with other family members, particularly beneficiaries.
- Take advice with a grain of salt. Ask questions and get what you want, not what someone else thinks you should have.
- Keep all your personal papers in one place – a fire safe, safety deposit box, freezer (it's fire proof!), or lawyer's vault. Tell someone where you keep them.
- Review your financial plan in detail at least once a year.
- Review the beneficiaries of your pension and life insurance – which pass outside your will – each time you review your will.

- Giving to charity lessens the tax bite annually and is effective at reducing estate taxes.

- The year of your death will likely be your highest income year because most investments and registered retirement savings plans are deemed sold on the day of your death. Tax and estate planning is critical.

- Be sure to instruct your trustees to be generous in spending the income and capital from the trust you establish for your relative. Some trustees think their job is to preserve the capital for the next beneficiary. We, on the other hand, would be happy if there was no money left in the trust by the time our relative died.

- If your trust is not sufficiently large it may be too expensive to use a trust company because of the fees they charge.

- If you as parents own your own company, you may want to establish a trust, with your child as one of the shareholders. Find out the amount of company dividends that can be paid tax-free to your child each year.

- Personal Networks are an excellent source of trustees and executors and guardians.

- Avoid paying high service fees. Shop around for this service.

- The less money you have the more you need to plan.

- Maintain a sense of humor!

The color of money – now

It is impossible to experience one's own death objectively and still carry a tune.
WOODY ALLEN

Leaving assets for your relative with a disability in a discretionary trust is a major tool of providing for their future financial security. So much for the future, but what about the present? Many families lament they cannot share some of their wealth with their son/daughter right now.

In some jurisdictions this is not an issue. Families can assist their relative without jeopardizing their government

The weight

That infernal thing was heavier than I thought. I'm feeling lighter already. I sink into the plush, cloudy blue carpet as I am escorted past the receptionist onto brilliant hardwood that surrounds the elevator. A beautiful arrangement of flowers on her desk. Yellow lilies, brown stamens, Bird of Paradise, baby's breath and green, green ferns. Were they there when I came in?

I see trees of green
and red roses too,
I see them bloom,
for me and you.

I think we exchange pleasantries. I believe we shake hands. They'll file it with the wills registry.

And I think to myself,
What a wonderful world.

Hardwood shining floors, bright and polished in the foyer. I almost slip. I remember sliding/polishing the pasty waxed hallway at home in my dad's thick socks when I was a kid. The elevator floats to the ground.

I see skies of blue
And clouds of white
The brightness of day
The dark sacred night

I am whistling by the time I reach the sidewalk. What a relief to get the darn thing signed.

And I think to myself,
What a wonderful world.

The city smells so sweet. It is springtime.

The colors of the rainbow,
So pretty in the sky
Also on the faces
Of people passing by

Bursting with fragrance. Purple tulips, white flowering plum, and pink blossoming cherry. I begin to sing.

I see friends shaking hands
Saying how do you do
They're really saying,
I love you

I've never seen so many pregnant moms.

I hear babies crying
I watch them grow
They'll learn much more
Than I'll ever know

I start to skip. My will has been done.

benefits. In most jurisdictions, however, there are penalties. For example, a family paying for their relative's holiday trip would not be penalized in one place but would be in another. There usually are regulations for "unearned income" and "earned income." Both types of income are deducted, to varying degrees, from the benefits your relative with a disability receives from government. Earned income is often treated less harshly than unearned income. In British Columbia, for example, earned income from employment is deducted at a lesser rate than unearned income in the form of a family gift.

If you are independently wealthy you may decide to avoid the bother and simply provide your relative with his or her own income. However if like most of us you want to be able to supplement the government benefits your relative receives, consider the following options:

- Check the rules and regulations in your province or state to see whether family contributions are permissible for people receiving government benefits, and how they are treated.

- Create a living discretionary trust. This is also called an *inter vivos* trust. It is a trust that is established while you are still alive. It may have several benefits. One, there may be tax benefits. Two, you can watch how well your trustee(s) are doing and determine, while you are still alive, whether the arrangement will work. Three, in some jurisdictions disbursements from a discretionary trust are exempt income and therefore your relative may not be penalized.

- Check with a legal advocacy or disability organization in your community to clarify which assets your relative can have and still get monthly government benefits. Every jurisdiction is a little different in the amount and type of assets you can hold and still be eligible. Each province or state would have a different amount for the maximum liquid assets (cash, stocks, bonds, debentures) your relative is allowed to have without jeopardizing their government benefits. Most places allow your relative to own or have an interest in a house as long as it is used as their principal residence. Household furnishings and effects are usually considered as allowable assets as well. Some jurisdictions allow your relative to own a vehicle and some don't.

- Check the implications of adding financial and other "gifts" to the financial assistance your relative receives from government.

Essential questions about willing your wealth

What is a will?

A will is the legal document that tells people what to do with your estate. It helps make life easier for those left behind by providing a plan for them to follow. A will is the foundation of your estate plan, and its most important aspect.

Of mice and mothers (or, why it pays to know a little legalese)

In the prairie wheat fields a young family of mice was out for a stroll and an introduction to the finer foods of life. The cloudless autumn day was sunny and warm. Mother Mouse and family had not a care in the world.

Suddenly, a shadow blocked their path. A menacing barn cat, back arched, was poised to pounce.

As calmly as can be Mother Mouse gathered her children behind her. Summoning her energy, she inhaled deeply, exaggerated her size, and leapt forward barking, "Woof, woof, woof."

The cat twitched, executed a triple axle that would make a world champion figure skater rejoice, and fled.

Turning to her children, Mother Mouse advised, "Never underestimate the power of a second language."

What are the basic things I need to think about when I am making a will?

1 If your children are under the age of legal majority, you name the person who will be legally responsible in case you and your spouse die before they reach adulthood. A common term for this person is "guardian" but the terminology varies. (In Quebec, for example, this person is called a "tutor.")

2 You name the person who will be responsible for ensuring that the instructions in your will are carried out. This person is commonly called an executor. (In some jurisdictions this person is known as a personal representative.) In many cases your executor will need to submit your will to court so that the court can validate it – the process is called probate.

3 You indicate how you wish your estate to be distributed after you die. The property is divided among family (usually spouse and children), charities and others. A person who inherits or receives part of your estate is called a beneficiary.

4 You may create a special needs trust for your child or relative with a disability. Often this is called a discretionary trust or supplemental trust. They are important because they allow your relative to inherit funds without interfering with their public benefits. You identify a trustee and co-trustee to manage the trust.

What happens if I die without a will?

If you die without a will:

- Government will determine how to distribute your estate. It will decide how much goes to your surviving spouse and your children.

- The share of your estate designated by government for your minor children will be held in trust for them by a government trustee.

- The court may appoint an administrator for your estate. This may lead to family strife and extra legal costs if decisions are challenged.

- The court will appoint a guardian for your minor children.

- Distribution of your estate to your heirs could be delayed for a significant period of time.

- Your estate may be subject to needless taxation and fees if it has not properly been arranged.

What is a living will?

A "living will" is not a will in the conventional legal sense. The term is used to describe a signed document that sets out the person's wishes about the medical treatment to be provided or withheld in case of a serious accident, injury, or illness.

Living wills are also called "Consent to Health Care Agreements," "Health Care Proxy," "Advanced Directives," or

---

Do you have a child below the age of majority?

If you have a child who is a legal minor and you die without a will, here's what can happen:

You have no control over how your estate is distributed. Your spouse may not receive the amount of the estate you would have wished. Your child may not receive the amount of the estate you would have wished. You will not be able to protect the inheritance you want to leave your child with a disability.

You will not be able to appoint a guardian for a child. If there is no surviving parent who is the legal guardian, a public trustee or government agent may become the child's guardian.

Your child may not be able to access the funds you left for them. A government trustee could hold them in trust until the child has reached the age of majority. Your surviving spouse may have to apply to the trustee's office to access the money held in trust for the use, maintenance, and benefit of the children. This could be true for day-to-day expenses as well as any special expenditure.

When the child does receive the funds, they could come as a lump sum, and the child would not be able to take advantage of having the money placed in a trust.

To avoid a costly, complicated and potentially messy and heart-breaking outcome, you must make a will.

"Power of Attorney for Personal Care." Please see our discussion in Step Five on how a Supported Decision-Making Agreement can be used as a "living will" for your relative with a disability.

Living wills or their equivalent are legally recognized in some jurisdictions and not in others.

NOTE: For a complete list of definitions, see "Definitions of terms that could definitely derail you" on page 259.

What is a holograph will?

A holograph will is a homemade will, written in your handwriting and is signed by you. No witness is necessary. Some jurisdictions do not recognize a holograph will. Others do recognize holograph wills.

Which of my assets do not form part of my estate and pass outside the will?

Any assets held in joint tenancy with another person pass directly to that person on your death and are not governed by your will. For example, a home and bank accounts held in joint tenancy with your spouse go directly to your spouse on your death. Assets that are held outside your will are not subject to probate fees.

Life insurance policies with a designated adult beneficiary pass outside the will directly to that beneficiary. A discretionary trust can receive proceeds from a life insurance company without going through probate.

Usually retirement pension plans with a designated beneficiary pass directly to that beneficiary.

Quite often when a spouse dies, most of the family assets are held in one of these ways and pass directly to the surviving spouse.

Be sure to consult your lawyer about putting assets in joint tenancy with your children. There are dangers as well as benefits in so doing.

All flesh is grass and all its beauty is like the flowers of the field. The grass withers, the flower fades, when the breath of the Lord blows upon it.
ISAIAH 40: 6–7

Can I appoint a guardian for my child in my will?

If you have children who are legal minors, you should appoint a person to be legally responsible for them in your will – many provinces and states call this person a guardian. You should also appoint alternates in case the first person is not able to accept the responsibility.

Who should be the executor of my will?

The executor is the person who makes sure that the instructions in your will are carried out after you die. Normally you appoint your spouse as your executor, but you may need to appoint someone else. You should appoint alternates.

If you have set up a trust in your will, usually the executor and alternate executor will be the same as your trustees and alternate trustees. However, in some cases, for example where there is business to be managed, you may wish to have different executors and trustees. Talk to your lawyer about this.

What are the duties of an executor?

Some of the duties of an executor include:

- Arranging for probate of your will
- Locating and safeguarding all assets
- Itemizing and valuing all assets
- Paying outstanding bills, debts and taxes
- Distributing your assets to your beneficiaries
- Preparing and filing your tax returns
- Establishing a trust
- Keeping receipts and records of all costs of administering and distributing the estate
- Providing immediate management of all assets
- Redirecting mail, canceling leases, subscriptions and memberships

Choosing a guardian for your underage child

In our experience this is the toughest and most elusive question facing parents who have minor children. While there are no surefire solutions, here are some words of advice gleaned from our experiences with the families of younger children.

- Do not be afraid to talk about this with your spouse, partner, or close friends.
- Talk to other parents who have younger children with disabilities to get ideas and to share solutions.
- Choose individuals who share your views on parenting and on raising a child with a disability.
- Choose individuals who are good at making tough decisions. In the event you are not around, tough decisions may be required.

- Invest conscious time – schedule thirty minutes every weekend for a month in addressing this issue.
- Broach the subject with family members wherever they live. No expectations, just discussion.
- If you have someone in mind, be sure to confirm their willingness.
- Let your child/children spend weekends or holiday time with the people you have in mind.
- Establish a Personal Network for you and your family.
- Do not be afraid to make a choice outside your family.
- Send out a call for assistance.
- Do not give up.

Can my executor be paid?

If you choose a professional firm, credit union, bank or lawyer, they will charge a fee in addition to reimbursement for their costs. If you choose a relative or friend, you may wish to stipulate an amount in your will to compensate them for their time and the extra effort on your behalf. If no amount is specified most jurisdictions will specify the maximum amount an executor may take for his/her services. Check your province or state for the exact figure.

What is probate?

Probate is the name of the legal process that confirms your will. Normally it is the job of your executor to file for probate with the court. This process can be quite lengthy. Financial institutions will not normally release assets of your estate until your executor receives the grant of probate.

Probate fees are payable to the government and are paid from the proceeds of your estate. The fees vary; how much you pay depends on the jurisdiction.

How can I make a will that is best for my relative with a disability?

You can set up a trust in your will for the person with a disability. The best course of action is to talk to a lawyer who has expertise in providing wills and estates advice to families of people with disabilities.

What is a trust?

A trust is simply an arrangement where a trustee holds a sum of money or property interest for another person's benefit. The source of the funds may include a gift from a family member or an inheritance. A trustee may be one or more persons or a trust company or both.

Trusts date back to the Crusades when individuals were away for long periods of time and they needed the means by which an individual's personal and financial decisions could be carried out by someone else.

All trusts have three parties:

• a settlor – that is likely to be you

- a trustee — someone to manage the property or funds
- a beneficiary — that is likely to be your relative with a disability

There are two common trusts used by families of people with disabilities.

Income Trusts In an income trust your beneficiary gets a certain amount of money at regular times. For example, your child might get $600 each month. It is up to you to decide how much money will be paid to the beneficiary and when.

An income trust is usually set up when the parent knows that the child will not need government social security benefits in the future. Payments made from a trust fund to a person on government benefits may be deducted from that person's benefits. It depends on the jurisdiction.

Of divorces, separations, and second marriages

"Love is better the second time around." We agree with the songwriter on that. However, preparing a will and estate plan in such circumstances is a wee bit more complicated. Take our word on that.

We don't have ready-made answers. We do however have a growing body of experience. Here are some comments from PLAN members:

- A Personal Network can be a great help in communication and intercession among former spouses and a great source of support for your disabled relative.
- A singular focus on the future care of your disabled child concentrates the mind.
- A corporate or non-family member as trustee can mediate actual or potential conflicts between children from the first marriage and the children and/or spouse of the second marriage, staying clear of emotional conflicts and saving potential frustration and resentment. Naming your spouse as trustee over stepchildren may prove administratively awkward. They may have difficulty maintaining a neutral position.
- If you have amalgamated your assets (i.e. new spouse as beneficiary of life insurance, savings or joint ownership of house) they will likely pass outside your will to your spouse, leaving no assets to be distributed to the trust you wanted to establish for your child. You may have to dedicate the source of funding for the trust you want to create. For example, you could create a separate life insurance policy.
- Re-marriage invalidates your will. Write another one.

Discretionary Trusts Most families of people with disabilities choose to set up a discretionary trust in their will. You appoint a trustee (and possibly co-trustee) in your will as the person who will be in charge of the trust. You give the trustee the discretion, or power, to decide when and how much of the trust fund will be used for the beneficiary, your child or relative with a disability. Your trustee has the responsibility of guaging your relative's changing needs and deciding how the trust should respond to those needs.

What is the difference between an executor and a trustee?

Often they can be the same individuals, institutions, or firms. An executor is responsible for the disposition of your estate, which may include the establishment of your trust. A trustee is appointed to oversee the assets you have left in your trust. These assets could be a house, property and of course money. An executor's function usually ends when all the elements of your estate have been settled. A trustee's function continues for as long as the beneficiary is alive and until the trust is wound up. In effect, when the executor's job ends, the trustee's job begins.

What does a trustee do?

Choosing a trustee is one of the most crucial future planning decisions you will make. The person you choose may have responsibilities as a trustee for 40 years or more, so choose people you expect to live a long life.

The trustee:

- manages, or looks after, the trust assets; and
- makes sure your child or relative receives trust benefits according to your wishes.

The duties of a trustee include:

- exercising discretion to release funds when necessary
- providing investment and management of assets

- coordinating any maintenance/repairs of real estate
- preparing trust tax returns
- maintaining records of the trust

If you decide to set up a trust for your child or relative you will need to name the trustee in your will. It is a good idea to have more than one trustee. For example, you may want to have two trustees and two alternates, in case the original trustees die or cannot act or cannot agree.

Who should be a trustee?

In a living trust, you can be the trustee, or you and your spouse can both be trustees. You can share this responsibility with a trust company, if you want. When you are planning for a trust to take effect after you die, you may want to appoint a financial trustee and a personal trustee. Their skills may be different and should complement each other. One may be a good investment money manager and may keep accounts, manage tax returns, etc. The other may be in close personal contact with the beneficiary, your relative, and know what to spend money on.

You may consider using a respected trust company as one of the trustees. Some parents use a trust company as one trustee and a relative or family friend as the other trustee.

Living trust A trust established during your lifetime. Also called *inter vivos* trust. It contains provisions as to how trust property is to be dealt with during your lifetime and on your death. A living trust would seldom form part of your estate.

Testamentary trust Takes effect upon your death. It is part of your "last will and testament."

Income trust (or non-discretionary trust) Depending on the terms of the trust, an income trust pays out income on a regular basis from the interest and capital to the recipient.

Discretionary trust Trustee can decide when and how much of the trust to use. Also called a "special needs" trust.

Note Living trusts and testamentary trusts can be either income or discretionary.

The trust company can make sure there is experienced financial help to manage the trust. The relative or family friend should have a personal interest in your relative but must not be in a conflict of interest.

If you name a person as a trustee you should also name a successor in case that first person dies or moves or is not willing to continue. It is best if the trustees are people your child or relative knows and likes. The trustees and your relative will likely be involved with one another for a long time. A good relationship between them will benefit everyone.

At least one of the trustees should live close to your relative. If a trustee has close contact with your child or relative, they will understand their needs better.

The best source for trustees and executor is your relative's Personal Network.

Why should I make a discretionary trust for my relative with a disability?

There are four important reasons for establishing a discretionary, or special needs, trust.

1 It provides your relative with a source of financial support, worry free.

2 Your relative will still be eligible for government social security benefits because the trust is the legal owner of the assets, not your relative. (Different jurisdictions have different limitations on the size of the trust and different rules about what a trust can be used for without affecting government benefits.)

3 The assets in the trust are in safe hands and you do not have to worry about exploitation or the vulnerability of your relative.

4 You can direct who will receive any assets left in the trust after your relative dies. This person is called the residual beneficiary. (Please note: the residual beneficiary may appear to be in a conflict of interest if he or she is also the sole trustee of the trust. That is why we recommend co-trustees if the residual beneficiary is one of the trustees.)

Can a trust be reversed?

A testamentary trust takes effect upon your death and is funded out of the proceeds of your estate. You can make changes or cancel the trust by changing your will. Strictly speaking you are not reversing the trust because a testamentary trust isn't a trust until you die.

Once a testamentary trust takes effect (upon your death) it cannot be reversed. In remote circumstances it is possible the terms of the trust and the trust itself could be challenged, for example, if it was felt that force was used or the will was signed by someone deemed incapable of understanding what was signed.

A living trust or *inter vivos* trust can be designed as "revocable" or "irrevocable." A revocable living trust allows you, the settlor, to change your mind and reclaim some or all the assets you placed in the trust. Check the income tax disadvantages or penalties of using a revocable living trust. It may not be worth the effort of establishing one in the first place.

Does a trust pay taxes?

A trust pays taxes on its earnings and must file an annual tax return just like every taxpayer. The trust you establish for your relative with a disability may be able to use your relative's personal exemptions as deductions. Consult a tax accountant for more details.

Do trustees get paid?

Trustees are paid a fee for the services they provide. This fee is taken from your estate. Your beneficiaries or the court must approve the fee.

Fees are normally charged in three different ways:

Capital fee A one-time fee based on a percentage of the total amount of the capital in your estate.

Care and management fee An annual trust management fee on a percentage of the remaining capital in the trust.

Income fee An annual income fee not exceeding a certain percentage of the income (interest) earned each year.

Professional trust companies will definitely charge a fee to the maximum allowable although we have found that like many other things, trust fees are negotiable.

Check with a trust company or lawyer for the maximum fees in your state or province.

What investment powers should I give my trustee?

Trustees are limited by law to very conservative and safe investments. In your will, you may give them broader investment powers. For example, you may wish them to have the power to buy an apartment for your child to live in. Be sure to discuss this with your lawyer.

What happens to the money left in the trust when the beneficiary dies?

When you set up a trust in a will for a beneficiary, you must also state in the will who will get what is left in the trust when the beneficiary dies. This could be children, siblings, other family members, charities etc.

In choosing whom the money will go to, be careful to avoid a conflict of interest. The person receiving the money when the beneficiary dies should not be the only trustee responsible for spending the money on behalf of the person with a disability. To avoid the appearance of conflict of interest, appoint co-trustees.

If a clear conflict of interest occurs in a will, the government may try to alter the will. The government official responsible for this is often known as the public trustee. The terminology varies depending on where you live. (In Quebec, for example, the public trustee is known as the curator public.)

Eight tips to making your will if you have a child with a disability

1 Complete Your Net Worth worksheet (on page 261) to give you an idea of your assets and liabilities. Then complete Your Will and Estate Plan worksheet accurately (on page 263).

2 Decide how you want your estate distributed (e.g. all to wife and when she dies, split among children in equal shares).

3 Decide who will be the executor and their alternate.

4 Decide if you want to set up a discretionary trust for your child with a disability. If you do, decide who will be:
- the trustees of the discretionary trust and their alternates
- the beneficiary of the trust when your child dies

Ensure there is no conflict of interest.

5 Be aware that the following pass outside the will:
- life insurance with a designated beneficiary
- retirement pension plans with a designated beneficiary
- assets held in joint tenancy

6 If you have children who are legal minors, decide who you will appoint as their guardian.

7 Take all this information to a lawyer who has experience in wills and estates for people who have children with disabilities. Ask the lawyer to explain the tax and legal implications of your decisions. Also ask the lawyer about registering the will, once it has been drawn up.

8 Discuss your draft will with your trustees.

What is power of attorney?

A power of attorney is a legal document that authorizes one or more people to manage your financial and legal matters, for example, to sign documents, to deposit and withdraw money from your bank account, to invest your money, or to sell your house. In some jurisdictions, these powers extend to health and daily living decisions. Despite the name, the person you appoint as power of attorney does not have to be a lawyer.

People appoint someone to be their power of attorney if they expect to be out of town for extended periods of time, because they are ill, or because they need assistance. Powers of attorney take effect the moment they are signed. You can revoke a power of attorney at any time. Most jurisdictions require this to be done in writing. A normal power of attorney is valid only as long as you are legally mentally competent.

What is an enduring or durable power of attorney?

An enduring or durable power of attorney remains effective even if you become mentally incapable. A power of attorney can only be used in your lifetime and terminates on your death. That's when your will takes over. A power of attorney that does not have an "enduring" clause is not valid if you become incapable.

Seeking advice from professionals

There is no substitute for good professional help. There are lawyers, financial and estate planners, accountants and trust officers who have special expertise in helping plan for the needs of children and relatives with disabilities. They can help you maximize the size of your estate, save you money, and ensure that your instructions are written in proper legal language. They are guided by principles of confidentiality, prudent administration, and sound judgment.

As with all professional services, be a cautious consumer. Ask for referrals from other parents or check with a local organization that is working on behalf of people with disabilities or their families.

Life changes

No matter how exhaustive your preparation and thorough your study, your will and estate planning may never be complete. While preparing for this chapter we were consulting with one of the most prestigious estate planners in the country. He interrupted our interview to visit his lawyer. After over thirty-five years in the business he was still revising his will: his estate plan is still a work-in-progress.

Expect to revise your estate plan as life changes and you discover something new. The act of revision is relatively painless and inexpensive. And the peace of mind is incalculable.

Presente

There's an elegant Latin American funeral custom we'd like to import. Shortly after a relative dies, the grieving survivors travel through the town or village shouting the person's name and crying out, *presente*. Meaning, he or she is still present. In their hearts, in the air, a palpable presence is still available to inspire, teach and guide, still making a difference, still a factor, still loving.

North American funeral traditions aren't as celebratory. Low-key lamentation and quiet acknowledgment, usually in private, is more our style.

Our wills are a subdued form of *presente*. The great passions of our life are reduced to legal papers. Perhaps we'd embrace the elusive act of will making if we realized how precious this expression of our wishes was. Imagine our relatives brandishing our will and yelling *presente*.

Presente – our last best wishes.

Presente – our legacy to our family, friends, and community.

Let's liberate this vehicle from its legal chassis and form it into the artistic embodiment of a life well loved.

Shout it from the rooftops. I lived. I made a difference. Look out world, I'm still here.

Presente.

Bill

Will of steel

Bill Weeden had a stroke last fall. This came as no surprise to those who knew him. What he had been concealing did surprise us, though.

Within the parent movement he was legendary. Opinionated, indefatigable, bullheaded. Mind like a steel trap. If anyone knew what he wanted, it was Bill.

He was a familiar sight at parent meetings: right leg and foot vibrating, tight-collared and red-faced, he would openly question every presenter. We appreciated his challenges; they helped clarify our own views.

He attended just about every workshop with the same list of questions. We came to expect his early arrival. It was always a toss-up as to who would arrive first, Bill, or the presenters. Front-row center, he'd bring his bag supper and wait for his unsuspecting quarry.

He could be counted on to launch his favorite shibboleth at least once. Bill had a plan to develop a group home for his son – a home of his own design for 15 people with disabilities! He would make a significant financial contribution of course but government would need to make a long-term commitment to staffing. He was making government an offer they couldn't refuse, but they were! Wasn't this the best idea for securing the future? Why weren't the rest of us pushing for the same things?

The stroke was punishing. Bill had been living alone since his wife's death, and he delayed seeking medical attention. It was almost too late. Bill is paralyzed on his left side and is unable to communicate. Although he is in rehabilitation, he has lost most of his vocabulary. According to the lawyers he is currently unable to give consent. This is critical because Bill's stroke caught him unprepared.

The man with a will of steel, the unsinkable Bill Weeden, had no will! That was the chilling surprise. The man who knew the legal terminology and could converse with the best lawyers, estate planners and accountants had neglected the obvious.

Now Bill is a desperate man. You can tell when you look into his eyes. There's something else there as well: the old stubbornness. Desperation mixed with determination is a potent combination. We're convinced he will have another chance. This is one survivor we want to return to front-row center.

Definitions of terms that could definitely derail you

Age of Majority Once your child reaches this age, parents no longer are legally responsible or have legal control over their child. Age of majority varies from place to place but is usually between 18 and 21.

Assets Real estate, other physical property (jewelry, silverware, vehicles), shares in a company, a promissory note, cash, stocks, bonds, debentures, pension fund, insurance policies.

Beneficiary A person you leave things to (money, gifts, insurance policy, registered retirement savings plan, trust).

Bequest A gift of a specific item of personal property or a specific amount of cash identified in your will.

Codicil A legal document used to amend portions of your original will. You have to sign and witness it just as you do for a will.

Committee The legal term used in some jurisdictions to describe a person who is legal guardian for someone else.

Conservator Another legal term for adult guardianship.

Curator The term used in Quebec for a guardian for an adult.

Discretionary Trust A trust in which the choice as to how to spend the interest and principal is completely in the hands of the trustee.

Durable or Enduring Power of Attorney The power to conduct and manage your financial affairs even if you become incapable. See Power of Attorney.

Executor The person or professional named in the will who is responsible for ensuring the wishes in your will are carried out.

Grant of Probate This is the executor's proof they can act as your executor.

Guardian This term has two meanings. One, a person who has legal responsibility for children under the age of majority. In Quebec this person is called a tutor. Two, a person or organization named by the court to exercise any and all powers and rights over an adult and/or their finances.

Joint Tenancy Property owned jointly by two or more persons in which the surviving joint tenant(s) becomes the owner of the entire property when one of the joint tenants dies. (See Tenancy in Common)

Income Trust Depending on the terms of the trust, pays out income on a regular basis from the interest and capital to the recipient.

continued on page 260

continued from page 259

Intestate A person who dies intestate dies without a valid will.

Life Interest Benefit given to someone in a will which allows that person to have the use of the property or a certain sum of money only for the lifetime of that person.

Living Trust A trust that comes into effect during the lifetime of the person who established the trust. Also known as an *inter vivos* trust.

Non-Probatable Assets Assets that pass outside of the will. For example joint tenant ownership of real estate and bank accounts, designated retirement savings plans, life insurance and annuity beneficiaries.

Power of Attorney A written document giving someone else the authority to make financial and legal decisions on your behalf. Often used if you are going to be out of the country or want help in dealing with your financial affairs. See Durable or Enduring Power of Attorney.

Probate The procedure by which the will of the deceased person is legally approved by the court and documented. It also confirms the appointment of your Executor.

Revocation Canceling parts of or all of an existing will.

Settlor The individual who establishes a trust.

Testamentary Trust A trust set up in a will that only takes effect after your death.

Tenancy in Common Property owned jointly by two or more people. Upon the death of one of the tenants-in-common, ownership of the deceased's share of the property is transferred to that person's estate, not to the other joint owner. (See Joint Tenancy)

Testator That's you, the person who makes the will.

Trust A legal arrangement in which one person (the settlor) transfers legal title to a Trustee to manage the property for the benefit of a person or institution (the beneficiaries).

Trustee The person or company that manages the trust according to the instructions in the trust agreement or will.

Worksheet 11

YOUR NET WORTH

A great way to get your financial plan started is to figure out what you're worth today. To do this, fill in the blanks below.

	YOU	SPOUSE	TOTAL
Assets			
Cash			
Deposits			
Investments			
Pension			
Life Insurance			
Residential Real Estate			
Vacation Property			
Furniture			
Art/Antiques			
Other			
TOTAL ASSETS			
Liabilities			
Mortgage			
Bank Loan			
Credit Cards			

	YOU	SPOUSE	TOTAL
Other Loans			
Funeral Expenses			
Accrued Income Tax			
Other Obligations			
TOTAL LIABILITIES			
TOTAL ASSETS: $			
Less TOTAL LIABILITIES $			
Equals YOUR NET WORTH $			

Worksheet 12

YOUR WILL AND ESTATE PLAN

This worksheet is intended to:

- Assist you in compiling information to take to your lawyer when you wish to make your will.

- Make you aware of decisions you will need to make.

After completing the worksheet you will be ready to contact a lawyer of your choice to draft your will.

A   Personal and Family Particulars

Date _____

1 Full Name

Address _____

Occupation _____
(if retired, include former occupation)

Home Phone _____   Office Phone _____

Date of Birth _____   Place of Birth _____

Citizenship _____

Marital Status (including plans to marry) _____

Date of Marriage _____   Place of Marriage _____

Do you have a marriage contract? _____

Have you or your spouse been married before? _____

2 Spouse's Full Name (or Common Law Partner)

Address _____

Occupation _____

(if retired, include former occupation)

Home Phone _____ Office Phone _____

Date of Birth _____ Place of Birth _____

Citizenship _____

3 Children

(Please note each of your children and the children of your spouse or partner.)

Full Name   Date of Birth

_____   _____

_____   _____

_____   _____

_____   _____

4 Other Dependents

Is there someone who is dependent upon you for financial support?

Yes _____   No _____

If yes,

Name   Address   Relationship

_____

_____

B Will Particulars

1

a) Do you wish to leave the residue of your estate to your spouse if he/she

survives you? _____

b) If your spouse fails to survive you, do you wish to leave your estate to

your children? _____

c) What share do you wish each child to get? Equal shares? _____

If unequal, please specify who gets what. _____

_____

d) If your children are minors, at what age do you wish them to receive their

share of your estate? _____

e) If any child dies before you, what do you want to happen to his/her share of

your estate? _____

2

Who do you wish to be your executor(s)?

Name _____

Address _____ Relationship to you _____

Primary _____

Alternate _____

Joint with others named

_____

_____

3

a) Do you wish to set up a trust for anyone? _____

b) If so, who? _____

c) Do you wish the trust to be a discretionary trust? _____

d) Who do you wish to be trustees of the trust?

Names (in full) _____

Address _____

Relationship to you _____

Occupation _____

e) Who will be alternate trustees?

Names (in full) _____

Address _____

Relationship to you _____

f) Who do you wish to receive the money left in the trust when the person for whom

the trust was set up dies?

(i) the person's spouse _____

(ii) the person's children _____

(iii) others?

Name   Address

_____

_____

g) Is there a possible conflict of interest?

_____

4

a) Who do you wish as guardian(s) to your children who are under 19 years of age?

Name (in full) _____

Address _____

Relationship to you _____

Occupation _____

b) Who will be alternate guardians?

Name (in full) _____

Address _____

Relationship to you _____

Occupation _____

5

Do you have any specific articles and personal effects you wish to give to any particular person(s)? (Includes clothing, jewelry, household goods, furniture, automobiles, boats, art, etc.)

Name (in full) _____

Item _____

Name (in full) _____

Item _____

Name (in full) _____

Item _____

Name (in full) _____

Item _____

6

Do you have any cash gifts you wish to make to anyone? Yes   No

If yes:

Name	Address	Relationship to you	Amount

7

a) Do you wish to give your trustee power to buy, sell, rent, lease, or hold mortgages on property in which your child lives?   Yes   No

Whether it produces income or not?   Yes   No

b) What investment powers do you wish to give your trustee? You may wish to discuss this with your lawyer or financial advisor. Note that the investments trustees can make are limited by law and tend to be conservative.

_____

_____

8 (if appropriate)

Do you wish Planned Lifetime Advocacy Network (substitute name of local organization) to provide support to your child when you are no longer able to do so?

If so, contact PLAN to discuss incorporating appropriate clauses into your will that will enable PLAN to assist your relative.

C OTHER

1 Do you own property outside the state or province you live in?

_____

2 Other comments or instructions?

_____

_____

_____

_____

THIS WORKSHEET IS ADAPTED FROM
MATERIAL DEVELOPED BY DAVIS & CO.,
VANCOUVER, BRITISH COLUMBIA

Worksheet 13

PERSONAL INVENTORY

In the event of an emergency, it is vitally important that members of your family have access to your personal papers and records. This personal inventory will help family members know what your personal assets are, where they are, and whom to contact.

We suggest you fill this out and update it once a year. Keep it in a safe place away from your home and inform family members or your executor where it is.

Tax Returns and Income Information

These can be important in completing documents required for estate purposes. Where do you keep copies of your income tax returns?

_____

_____

Are your current earnings statements with them or kept elsewhere?

_____

_____

Money owed to you:

_____

_____

Where do you keep copies of notes, loan agreements, receipts, etc.?

_____

_____

Cemetery plot

If you own a plot, where is it located?

_____

Have you given funeral instructions by

Will?   Letter?   Pre-Paid Plan?   Other?

Other Property, Assets and Relevant Information

Social Insurance Number _____

Is there anyone such as relatives, a business partner, accountant, lawyer, or other

professional person who is familiar with your affairs?

Name _____

Address _____

Where were you married? _____

Houses and Real Estate

Records of purchase and sale or property can be helpful in preparation of various

tax returns.

I own the following properties.

_____ Sole owner or

_____ Joint owner with

Name _____

Address _____

Mortgage Value $

Tenants   Rental

Address _____

If you do not live on your own property, who is your landlord?

Name _____

Address _____

List other properties and investments in which you have ownership, and specify
what kind of ownership.

_____

_____

Where do you keep copies of deeds and mortgages, tax receipts, tax returns, etc.?

_____

_____

_____

Who prepares your taxes?

Name _____

Address _____

_____

Who is your general insurance broker?

Name _____

Address _____

_____

_____

Other Property

It is a good idea to maintain a list of your other tangible property.

Household furnishings located at

Jewelry	Appraised (A)	Estimated (E) value
Item	Replacement	Value ( ) $ _____
Item	Replacement	Value ( ) $ _____
Item	Replacement	Value ( ) $ _____

Automobile

Other

Savings and Deposit Accounts

I have the following accounts:

Account   Account Number

_____   _____

_____   _____

Do you have money on deposit or loans with banks, credit unions, or trust companies? If yes, give names, addresses, and account numbers.

_____

_____

Where are your passbooks/statements located?

_____

Securities

Bonds, share certificates, and similar documents should be kept safe from loss.

Where are your various receipts and certificates for investments located?

Are your records of purchase kept with them?   Yes   No

If not, where are they? _____

Who is your stockbroker?

Name _____

Address _____

If some of your securities have been pledged against loans, who holds them?

Name _____

Address _____

Life Insurance

Policies should be kept in a safe place. They are often an important means of raising immediate cash in case of need.

I carry the following policies on my life and they are located at:

1. Company _____ $ _____

Policy No. _____

2. Company _____ $ _____

Policy No. _____

Are you covered by group life insurance at your place of employment? If yes, where is the information about this policy located?

_____

Place of Employment

Who is the person to contact at the place you work?

Name _____

Name of Firm _____

Address _____

Disability Insurance

Quick access to such policies can help speed claims if you become disabled.

Do you have group coverage with your company of employment?

Yes   No

Are you covered by workers' compensation?

Yes   No

Do you have personal policies covering accidents and sickness?

Yes   No

If these contracts are not kept with your other policies, where are they?

_____

If there are identification cards of any of these policies, where can they be found?

_____

Trust Funds

I have established a trust for _____

_____

The trustees are _____

_____

I am beneficiary under a trust from _____

Papers are located at _____

Personal Certificates

These are often needed for insurance claims, pensions etc. where proof of age, marital status, or birthplace is required.

Do you have a safety deposit box?   Yes   No

Where is it located? _____

Where do you keep the key? _____

Where is your birth certificate? _____

Where were you born? _____

Date of birth _____

If you became a citizen, where are your citizenship papers? _____

Where is your marriage certificate? _____

Last Will and Testament

The date of my last will is _____

The lawyer who drew up my will is: _____

The original executed copy of my will can be found at: _____

I have named the following executors: _____

_____

Date Completed: _____

Name: _____

Address: _____

Worksheet 14

YOUR WILL AND ESTATE PLAN SUMMARY CHECKLIST

1 I have a valid, up-to-date will. _____

2 I have established a discretionary trust for my relative with a disability. _____

3 I keep all my records in a fire-proof and safe place. _____

4 I have made plans for the guardianship and care of my minor children. _____

5 I have made arrangements for my funeral/memorial service. _____

6 I have told at least one person where my records are kept. _____

7 I have taken advantage of the life and term insurance available to me. _____

8 I have done my best to minimize the taxes my estate will have to pay. _____

9 I have done my best to reduce the probate fees my estate will have to pay. _____

10 I have a charitable giving plan. _____

11 I have given my trustee(s) clear instructions about my wishes. _____

12 I have an enduring or durable Power of Attorney for my personal care and my affairs. _____

13 I have made arrangements for others to consent to my health care. (Living Will) _____

14 I have checked the laws where I live and know:

- estate taxes _____
- probate fees _____
- age of majority _____
- executor and trustee fees _____

A GOOD LIFE

- government regulations for discretionary trusts _____

- maximum monthly social security or disability benefits allowance _____

- how much additional income my relative can receive without reduction to their government benefits _____

- what assets my relative can own and still receive government assistance _____

- how the government will distribute my estate if I die without a will _____

securing *your* plan

Hope is the thing
with feathers that
perches in the soul.
Emily Dickinson

Back-seat driver

George took a hard look into the future and liked what he saw. He had become a lifetime member of the organization he had helped create. "I might as well throw my lot in with a bunch of old fogies just like me."

PLAN's commitment wasn't for George's lifetime but for Rick's. George liked that. PLAN agreed to keep a regular eye on Rick; to keep Rick's network strong and healthy; to help Rick with his money; and to provide regular advice to Rick's trustee. PLAN was prepared to keep a watchful eye on Rick as George's representative and carry out all arrangements as if George was still around.

In this regard PLAN really spells "continuity" and "relief" for George.

"You know, it's funny. The day Rick moved out was the culmination of an incredibly busy period, what with the move and all. By the time moving day came I was glad to see him go. After the move I sat down on the couch in the living room exhausted. I guess I thought I'd rest for the rest of my life. Well, that lasted for the rest of the evening.

That night was the longest and loneliest of his life. "You'd think at my age I'd be over those emotions," he confessed.

Now that Rick was taken care of, what was George going to do for the rest of his life?

Fortunately George is a half-full-glass kind of guy and he was able to turn his attention to other possibilities. One of them was Marge.

It seems she had some dreams that matched George's. The coincidence was inspiring. They had been dating on and off for a little over two years. She proposed; he accepted. They decided to sell their houses, buy a boat and move to the Sunshine Coast of British Columbia. They would be a short ferry ride from Vancouver and could fish and golf pretty well year round.

George had already started to take a back seat in his son's life. "I'm 74 next month," he observed. "I'm slowing down a bit. I guess I've earned the privilege of becoming a back-seat driver."

Securing your plan

b y this point you are fully prepared to re-weave the social safety net for your family member with a disability into a multi-colored tapestry of a good life.

For many of you that will be enough and you will need to read no further. However, if in the chilly hours of uncertainty, you still wonder what else you can do, read on. This book was inspired by a group of families who realized they couldn't catch the winds of fate by themselves. They knew they needed an anchor, particularly for the time they wouldn't be around. To stitch down their dreams, they created a different type of organization. In Step Seven, "Securing Your Plan," we will look at the worst that can happen in order to prepare for the best. We will also anticipate the future by reflecting on recent disability and social service history. Finally we will share the powerful story of what a small but determined group of families can do to create a safe and secure future for their relatives with disabilities. We hope it will inspire you.

To weave but webs,
To catch the winds.
RUTH SCHEUING

Searching for guarantees in an uncertain future

By now you are probably convinced that planning a secure future requires careful attention to a number of elements:

- the continuing involvement of caring, committed friends and family
- control over the home environment
- the contributions of your family member with a disability
- a properly drawn and executed will
- a special needs discretionary trust
- sensitive and caring trustees
- alternatives to legal guardianship

You will have thought about:

- how you want to divide your property
- which company or relative or friend might be a trustee or co-trustee of your discretionary or supplemental trust
- what services you may want from a lawyer, trust officer and financial planner

You may have a clearer idea about what your child's life will be like after you are gone:

- who their friends will be
- where they might live
- what their vocation might be
- who might serve as an advocate and monitor
- who will help them make decisions
- what role your other children and family members might play

And you have shared all of this with others...right?

If you are like us, you may still have one overriding concern: What happens if things spin out of control when I'm not here? What happens if as the poet Yeats observed:

Things fall apart; the center cannot hold;
Mere anarchy is loosed upon the world.

Who will be your eyes, ears, arms and legs when you are no longer around? Who watches over the people, services, and

Worksheet

WORKSHEET 15 **Securing Your Plan:**
Summary Checklist

This worksheet is located at the end of this chapter, on page 313. Have a look at it now, and fill it out when you've finalized the details of your Personal Future Plan.

institutions you are depending on? What is your backup if something unexpected happens? Who keeps all of the components of the Personal Future Plan functioning and connected when you die?

Together we are better

Our answer is simple. We have discovered strength in the company of others who share the same concerns, experiences, and values. That is why we created PLAN. Our goal was nothing less than the transformation of the family-based disability movement into a new force, one that operates parallel to the service delivery system.

We place our faith in families and in each other to provide guidance and direction to powerful new social organizations, capable of responding to the changing forces of time and focused on the future well being of our family members with disabilities.

Too much to hope for? Too bold? Too romantic?

Definitely not. At the end of the day the only certainty we have is each other. Families who have relatives with a disability are like a "tribe." We have a rich tradition that defines us, we have strong group loyalties based on our common experiences, vision, and values, and we have proven success at creating earth-shattering change. We can do it again and this time we are not alone. There are friends, caregivers, and other allies who care as much as we do about our sons and daughters with disabilities. The solution, as Jane Jacobs observed, is to put all our eggs in one basket and to treat them very gently.

> Hope is not the conviction that something will turn out well but the certainty that something makes sense, regardless of how it turns out.
>
> VACLAV HAVEL

PLAN provides two fundamental services to families:

1 We assist families to create a Personal Future Plan for the safety, security, and well being of their relative with a disability.

2 We make a lifetime commitment to maintain the Personal Future Plan when the parents become infirm or die.

Flowers and compost

When you think of it, a parent's job description is much like a gardener's. To nurture, to protect, to be alert to changing conditions, to provide shelter from the storm, to fertilize where appropriate, to enjoy all stages of growth, to savor the beauty of the moment and to appreciate the sweat of preparation. You learn a lot about life as a gardener. You learn, for instance, about the interrelationship between flowers and compost.

A beautiful rose that we have just cut and placed in our vase is very pure. It smells so fresh and fragrant. Its beauty is exquisite. Rotting compost is the opposite. It reeks and is full of decomposing garbage, waste and worms.

But that is only if we look on the surface. If we look more closely, we will see that in five or six days the rose will become part of the compost. The truth is, we do not need to wait that long. We can see it now. Take a deep look at the rose. Can you see the compost in the rose? Take another look at the compost. Can you see the rose in the compost?

The Chinese have a word for it

Networking is at the heart of Chinese society, a gift that remains alive through the exchange of favors and the growth of connections in an ever-expanding web. The Chinese have a special word for this dynamic: *Guanxi*. Roughly translated it means "lubricating relationships through connections."

Can you see its contents transformed in a few months into lovely vegetables, maybe into another beautiful rose?

If you are a gardener, you recognize the interrelationship between the beautiful flower and the rotting compost. You cannot have one without the other. They need each other. The rose and the compost are equal. The compost is just as precious as the rose.

If you are a parent you understand that much of the beauty you create arises out of life's darker moments or in response to threats on the horizon. This is true for our children. It is also true for us as a group of families. The parent-based disability movement arose at the end of the Second World War in the wake of the eugenics movement and the horrible atrocities committed against people with disabilities, and in reaction to professional advice to send our children away to institutions. Those early seeds of change, planted in dank soil, have blossomed into the most wondrous of plants. The parent-based disability movement was the first internationally based consumer movement. Before Ralph Nader, before consumer power and the other rights movements, we existed!

Across North America, in response to unsettling times and a realization something is missing, families are recognizing they may have to do it again. We don't pretend to have a crystal ball. Nevertheless we see some disturbing trends on the horizon. Think of them as the growing conditions any sensible gardener needs to be aware of in order to make appropriate plans. So let's descend underground into the compost and poke around for a while. Perhaps we'll see the beginning of another beautiful plant!

Disturbing trends

The great social commentator and thinker Ivan Illich makes a distinction between optimism, pessimism, hope and despair.

He uses the analogy of flying. Despite his knowledge of

science and physics, when he boards a plane he is pessimistic that such a heavy object can get off the ground. At the same time he is very hopeful about his chances. The point is simple. It is possible to remain hopeful while being pessimistic. We know that pain and tragedy will continue to exist. People with disabilities and their families are dealt their fair share. It would be foolish to deny this. However, there is also much to be hopeful about.

This is the spirit in which we approach the following disturbing trends.

Parents know how to turn adversity around; to create beauty out of ugliness; to see the rose in the compost. In preparing for a safe and secure future for our children, we need to understand the "composting" part. Facing what's out there with open eyes is a prudent response, wouldn't you say?

Funding cutbacks

Help us to be the always hopeful garden of the spirit who knows that without darkness, nothing comes to birth. As without light nothing flowers.
MAY SARTON

If your son or daughter is dependent on services delivered or funded by government, then the availability and quality of these programs are dependent on the future health of our local and national economies. Access to these services is also dependent on political priorities and political commitment. In many jurisdictions, governments have a statutory responsibility to fund disability assistance and supports for children, but not for adults. Regardless of age, there is no guarantee of the quality.

In the United States and Canada many analysts worry that national standards for the quality of human services programs are also declining. Cutbacks often masquerade as restructuring and centralization. Small, usually more responsive organizations are wiped out or amalgamated with larger service providers. Privately managed care and institutionalization are on the rise. The individual and their family have less of a say and a harder job to get heard.

Rationing of health care

Governments talk openly about the high costs of health care. They discuss introducing "user fees." Long waiting lists already exist for elective surgery, for cancer treatment, for heart operations. Hospitals and doctors are already making "triage" decisions about who will receive medical treatment and who will have to wait. A referendum in Oregon several years back voted the treatment of health conditions associated with disability as a lower priority for government funding than other more costly interventions. Can people with disabilities be assured of fair access to medical treatment in the future? Who will decide? On what basis? Who will monitor the decision makers?

Erosion of human rights

Since the 60's we have lived through an era of increasing respect for people of diversity. There have been hard-won gains. Many of these advances have been recognized in human rights codes and legislation. However, the increased focus on the costs to society of funding social and health services highlights how weak human rights guidelines are when the critical supports for people with disabilities are reduced or withdrawn. Human rights legislation does not prevent cutbacks. It does not prevent arbitrary decisions by institutions or caregivers or governments. People can have their "rights" and still be ignored. People do die with their "rights" on, as one commentator suggested.

New worthiness debate

The debates about "right to die" legislation, mercy killing, and our reverence for technology and medicine all reflect a belief that some lives are not worth living, or that quality of life is something that can be measured by others. We applaud the "Not Dead Yet" coalition for their steadfast opposition to this trend. We have witnessed the isolated but

> We must accept finite disappointment, but we must never lose infinite hope.
> REV. MARTIN LUTHER KING JR.

tragic deaths of people with disabilities at the hands of their parents, and the sometimes sympathetic response from media and the justice system. Some North American jurisdictions are already publicly debating the value of providing health care to people with disabilities even if the treatment is minor and inexpensive. Those may be the "lucky" jurisdictions because at least the biases are out in the open. Subtle funding shifts within the bureaucracy can happen without public consultation.

Changing tax laws and regulations

Governments are always looking for ways to raise more money or to save money. As discussed in Step Six, one of the few tool boxes available to families is legislation that permits them to set up discretionary trusts, without interfering with public benefits for their relatives with a disability. However, several Canadian jurisdictions have already attempted – without success so far – to require that the monies in the trust be used to pay for basic services and programs. Once the funds are spent, the person with a disability would live a poverty level existence.

All governments are looking at ways to tap into what has been called the largest inter-generational transfer of wealth in human history. Estimates vary, but trillions of dollars are expected to pass from one generation to the next over the next 20 years in North America. Will governments cut back, attempt to access trusts, and curtail the few exemptions available to families who are simply interested in preserving some of their wealth for the future support of their son or daughter with a disability? Who knows?

Limitations of human services

The history of the parent-based disability movement is full of unsung heroes and heroines. Mothers and fathers who, with persistence and singular initiative, created the wide array of programs and services we now take for granted.

Planning is bringing the future into the present so that you can do something about it now.

A. LARKIN

When we stop to think about it, we owe an immense debt to these pioneer parents.

In the ranks of parents living today are those who still remember the church basements, the bake sales, and the tremendous volunteer efforts required to gain acceptance and access for their sons and daughters in regular society. By the 60's most of these programs had become the responsibility of government. The 70's and 80's saw an escalation in their scope and number. Parent organizations grew from the tiny self-help groups that sprung up after the Second World War to the huge multi-service organizations with multi-million dollar budgets that exist today. There is now a wide range of employment, residential, social and recreational programs available in most jurisdictions to people with disabilities.

As they stood at the threshold of their own death, these pioneer parents began to realize the limitations of professional human services:

- Despite their years of dedication, none of the agencies they created were in a position to make a lifetime commitment to monitor and personally advocate for their children with disabilities.

- Despite the closure of institutions and the abundance of community services, their relatives were still isolated, lonely, and bored.

There were other cracks in the allure of professional services:

- Formal monitoring programs were non-existent.

- Staff turnover was high, creating instability and unpredictability.

- Control was in staff hands.

- Parents were sometimes viewed as liabilities, busybodies in conflict with the rights of their child.

- Services became less personal as organizations grew larger.

STEP SEVEN SECURING YOUR PLAN 291

- Specialized programs required knowledgeable advocates, which sometimes made it difficult for family and friends to keep up on their own.

New solutions for changing times

Given the general social and economic climate and the specific weaknesses surfacing within the service delivery system, parents began searching for other solutions to their dilemma: how to safeguard the quality of their children's lives on a long-term basis.

They discovered a new type of association. These organizations are generally called advocacy foundations although they are referred to by various titles: continuity foundations, self-sufficiency trusts, advocacy trusts, and private guardianship corporations. The oldest, based in Seattle, Washington, has been in existence for over thirty years. There are over thirty similar organizations in Canada, the United States, Australia, New Zealand, and England.

These non-profit societies were created for the sole purpose of providing lifelong security for people with disabilities. They make a long-term commitment to the people they serve and provide future planning services to families. We would like to introduce you to the one we have created. Perhaps there is a similar group in your area or there is the basis for creating one.

Planned Lifetime Advocacy Network (PLAN)

The Planned Lifetime Advocacy Network (PLAN) exists for one reason: to assist families create a safe and secure future for their relatives with a disability. The founding families wanted to create an organization that would not make false promises, but that would look at the fullness of people, not their emptiness. They knew there were no miracle cures. No magic solutions. No perfect vitamin combination. Just plain old-fashioned hard work.

Community is not built upon heroic actions but rather upon the love shown in the little things of daily life.

J. VAN

PLAN is an association of families who have a vision of an organization that will:

- be there to fight and advocate for their sons and daughters long after they themselves are gone, and
- offer families everything they need to know about planning for the future of their relative with a disability, including what they might be afraid to ask about.

They know from their previous experience that this means establishing an organization that is independent of government and financially self-sufficient.

PLAN is about:

- taking charge and directing the future welfare of our sons and daughters
- facing the future with our eyes wide open
- being as clear and honest as possible about limitations and possibilities
- creating power by working together
- focusing on abilities of our own, our children and our neighbors
- meeting government as an equal
- accepting that we are in the same leaky rowboat together
- putting all our eggs in one basket and treating them gently
- finding roses in the compost

PLAN – A model for creative problem-solving by families

The parents who created PLAN had a clear list of do's and don'ts. Do create an organization that can withstand the winds of change. Don't become dependent on government funding. Do develop a diversified funding base. Don't rely exclusively on service providers to keep our sons and daughters safe, supported and happy.

There was wisdom in their prescription. Many of these parents were founding members of what were then called Associations for Retarded Children. The organizations they created in the 50's evolved from small parent support groups to large service-providing agencies funded almost exclusively by government. They didn't want that to happen to PLAN.

These parents had found that when the time came to address their most pressing and intimate needs – their deaths, and the future security of their relative with a disability – the agencies' response was disappointing. There was plenty of good will, enthusiasm, and good intentions. However the best they could offer was service and program solutions in the here and now. In other words, because they relied on year-to-year government funding, they could not guarantee long-term security. As Mark Twain wryly observed, "when the only tool you have is a hammer then every problem is going to look like a nail!"

The parents knew the value of program support. They also recognized there was more to life than staff support. They needed a replacement for the job a parent or a family does. They needed an agent that was both tenacious and tender.

Perhaps it was their age. Perhaps it was a matter of time. Perhaps they needed a lifetime to sift through all the options before the truth emerged. Regardless, they had concluded that care could not be produced from a system. Caring is face to face. Caring is self-selected. Caring comes from a commitment to a relationship. Caring cannot be managed.

Since most of the parents were of retirement age, they could be forgiven for thinking it was too late to make a difference. Fortunately these "elders" took on what will probably be their last challenge and their greatest legacy. They decided to go back to basics and recreate the energy and passion of the early days of the parent-based disability movement. They did not want to be a negative force. They did not reject the individual rights and advocacy movement; they did not reject the service and program sector. They

I think these difficult times have helped me to understand better than before how infinitely rich and beautiful life is in every way and that so many things that one goes around worrying about are of no importance whatsoever.
ISAK DINESEN

Thinking in the future tense

Choice not coercion

Citizen not client

Companion not
caretaker

Consent not control

Contribution not
helplessness

Home not house

Hospitality not seclusion

Participant not recipient

Subject not object

Wealth not welfare

simply wanted to correct an imbalance and to restore
the family voice to a larger, more complex and mature
disability movement.

It has become more common in the past few decades to
expect solutions from government. It wasn't always this way.
The family-based disability movement has drifted in much
the same way much of North American society has drifted
in the past thirty years: onto the shoals of increased reliance
on government and onto professional, technical solutions
for all matters associated with disability. We have drifted
away from the grassroots problem solving, from the self-
sufficiency that was commonplace in the early days of our
movement.

These original PLAN families were determined to:

- return to a parent or family-based definition of their
  problems

- create parent or family-based solutions

- establish a parent or family-driven base to implement
  the solutions. Their vision was positive and hopeful,
  providing us with the opportunity to think, talk, and
  act in a new way. Here is what they have taught us.

Concepts and assumptions
that guide PLAN's work
Families must direct the future
of their relatives with a disability

There is no sense in looking for external solutions. There
are no miracle cures. The lead role is ours. Professionals
are there to assist but the direction comes from us. We are
the conductors of the symphony of caring, comfort, and
support for our relatives. No one else has the breadth of
vision and the passion. If we don't do it, who will? Other
families who have relatives with disabilities are the best
custodians of our vision for our sons and daughters' future.
They will provide the continuity of vision, commitment,
and energy.

PLAN's basic functions:

BEFORE YOU DIE
Future Planning Advisory Service

PLAN offers up-to-date information on all the elements of future planning. Through family visits, workshops, telephone referral, information kits, newsletters, publications, videos, mailings and personal contact, PLAN provides families with, for example:

- a seven-step process to complete a Personal Future Plan for their relative
- the latest information on preparing a will and planning an estate
- referrals to professionals sensitive to the unique issues a son or daughter with a disability presents
- advice on preserving government benefits
- sample will clauses

Creating and Maintaining a Personal Network

PLAN believes that now is the best time to consolidate friends and family into a Personal Network. PLAN's future involvement in the life of a person with a disability is conditional on the existence of a Personal Network and PLAN's active involvement with the individual, their Personal Network and their family. Without this personal and intimate contact with people and their families, PLAN would not be in a position to understand, let alone advocate for, the best interests of the person with a disability. PLAN will create and develop a Personal Network for people upon request.

Family Support and Advocacy

A common response from families associated with PLAN is the degree of support and comfort they themselves derive from developing a Personal Future Plan for their son/daughter. "This is just like the old days," is an often-heard comment. PLAN's program is based on family-to-family contacts. Parents co-present with professionals at every workshop. Parents make personal visits to other parents. Every family with a Personal Network is assigned a "mentor family" from the PLAN Board. Parents with Personal Networks meet regularly to share concerns and to seek advice from each other. Parents accompany each other to critical meetings as advocates. On a broader scale, PLAN serves as a watchdog on relevant tax, trust, and guardianship legislation.

Housing Control
Home Ownership Advisory Service (HOME)

PLAN offers a home ownership advisory service through a program called the HOME Advisory Service.

This service provides families with

hands-on advice and support to deal with the potentially complex issues of home ownership. For example, it helps families liaise with builders, developers, and financial institutions. It assists with negotiating a service contract or program supports with government. It provides referrals to knowledgeable professionals and helps with finding a friendly, compatible roommate for the family member with a disability.

AFTER YOU DIE

Lifetime Commitment

This is the fundamental function of PLAN. All families can take advantage of all the other services offered by PLAN. However, if they want an independent organization to watch over and protect the best interests of their loved ones after they die, then they must become a Lifetime Member of PLAN.

A PLAN Lifetime Membership means PLAN commits to overseeing and ensuring that the future plans families make are carried out. PLAN becomes the foundation on which families can rest all their other plans. PLAN can be the final check in the system of checks and balances they set up for their relative.

For example, Lifetime Members can expect PLAN to:

- assist and advise their executor and trustee(s) on decisions for the benefit of their relatives
- maintain the health of their relative's Personal Network
- visit their loved one on a regular basis
- monitor the services their loved one receives
- advocate for changes that will protect or improve their relative's quality of life
- carry out any specific wishes identified by the Lifetime Member
- oversee the housing arrangements they have made
- respond to emergencies and crises
- oversee any legal arrangements for supported decision making that they have made
- press for improvements to the tax and trust system

Relationships are key to well being and safety

Without caring relationships our relatives will get lost in the world of professionals and programs. All the money in the world combined with the most efficient service delivery system cannot substitute for the value of true friendship. As Billie Holiday sang, "Without friends I've got nothing." Programs and services should supplement, not supplant, relationships.

Our family members with a disability have both the capacity and the responsibility to become contributing citizens

If we don't believe this then why should others? One of the most important mindsets families can bring to any discussion is the mindset of fullness. A focus on the gifts and capacities of our relatives encourages participation and discourages victimization. One of the most important mindsets to discard is the mindset of emptiness. Our emphasis should be on acknowledging their gifts and on creating opportunities and expectations that their gifts will be given. Only then will the disability of isolation diminish.

Neighbors and community members are inherently hospitable

Contrary to popular belief and the headlines in the popular media, the average person cares and is willing to get involved. They simply need to be asked. They may need someone to reach out to them. But they will respond. They will accept our friends and family members with a disability into their clubs, organizations, and families; they will become their companions, associates, supporters and friends.

> To make a great garden one must have a great idea or a great opportunity.
> GEORGE SITWELL

An independent organization is best able to promote the best interests of individuals with a disability and their families

A family-directed independent organization is best able to stay focused on the essence of what constitutes a good life – relationships. An independent organization has a better chance of avoiding the seduction of professional and government directed solutions. Only an organization independent of government funding, with families in the directors' chairs, will stay disciplined and focused on our relative's best interest. Every penny from government has a string attached. Lots of pennies equal lots of strings. Lots of strings can be braided into a rope that allows government to pull us anywhere.

> I can't myself raise the winds that might blow us, or this ship, into a better world. But I can at least put up the sail so that when the wind comes, I can catch it.
>
> E. SCHUMACHER

There are limits to growth

Every social organism has its ideal size. Some of the most effective community groups, impacting thousands of people, have a small staff complement. PLAN was modeled after two of them, Alcoholics Anonymous, and La Leche League.

We trust future families to limit our growth. Staff should be kept to a minimum with maximum participation from families and citizen volunteers. Too many staff creates the potential to drift away from grassroots problem-solving. When the passion goes, so does the inventiveness. Beyond a certain size, we commit to helping new families create their own organization rather than grow larger ourselves.

PLAN's core values

PLAN has a high tolerance for ambiguity and a high regard for flexibility when it comes to supporting individuals with disabilities and their families. We are committed to using the insight and experience of Personal Networks to guide the development of any protocols or structures we may need. We will do whatever it takes to support an individual and his or her family. We are wary of prescriptions. We honor adaptation rather than rest on routine. We recognize the paradox of attempting to institutionalize flexibility. We are prepared nevertheless to live with the contradiction.

We do, however, have a low tolerance for any departure from our core values. A tight focus on mission is the glue that holds our porous organization together. We are absolute and unyielding on our three core values:

- relationships keep people safe
- organizational accountability must be to families and their relative with a disability
- financial self-sufficiency, no government funding

How is PLAN accountable?

To prevent the development of bureaucracy that becomes inflexible, PLAN has implemented the following accountability measures. These are in addition to the standard annual audit and annual general meeting.

1 Our constitution calls for a majority of board members to be family members.

2 Representatives from our board, called mentor families, check in with every family with a network once every two months. All concerns, complaints, and criticisms are reported back to a management committee, a Lifetime Membership committee, and our board.

3 Families who have networks for their relative meet regularly to share their experiences. Staff do not attend unless invited.

4 A bi-annual work plan is developed and approved in advance for each network and a monthly accounting for time spent is sent to each family.

5 People who do not like our service can leave. They are genuine consumers. They are paying for the supports they receive and are under no obligation to remain.

6 We have an annual Lifetime Members meeting, which is similar to an accountability session at a shareholders' meeting.

7 We have a three-year business plan, which is revised annually.

We are still not satisfied. We intend to create a social audit. We envision an independent audit of our organization (our personnel practices, satisfaction with our service, coherence between our values and our practice, and our faithfulness to our original values) conducted by an independent body that would ensure the organization responds constructively to the results. We expect this "social audit" will guarantee adherence to our core values well into the future.

PLAN – a creator of social capital

PLAN has been described as a "social enterprise," a new type of non-profit, deploying business skills in social settings to satisfy unmet needs, creating social capital instead of economic capital.

As a society we are at an impasse. We have a social welfare system that is ill equipped to deal with our modern social problems. A system that faces increased costs and increased demands yet decreased effectiveness.

Without detracting from government's continuing responsibilities, we are determined to look beyond the traditional social service system to develop lifelong security and well being for our relatives with a disability.

Instead we invest in:

- the capacity of families to solve their own problems
- the hospitality of neighbors and community
- the enlightened self-interest and social responsibility of the corporate sector
- the redirection of government resources to enhance individual, family, and community capacity

Features of social enterprises like PLAN

Here are a few features of social enterprises:

- Flat flexible organizations with a small core of staff, few resources, and a culture of creativity.
- Value is created by identifying underutilized resources (people, in kind services) and using them to satisfy unmet needs.
- Their currency is stories not statistics, theory or analysis.
- Their core assets are relationships, connections, networks, trust and cooperation. They use their connections to eliminate social exclusion.
- They work with all three sectors, at the juncture where the private sector, the government sector, and the voluntary civic sector intersect.

EC-powerment

"Advocacy Plus"

EC-powerment = Traditional advocacy + Collective economic wealth of families

We've often wondered about the word empowerment. There is something strange and disconcerting about having power conferred on you from the outside. So many people want to empower us or our sons and daughters. The term is well meaning but it becomes patronizing when others begin to "empower" us. We perpetuate our helplessness when we rely on others to give us power.

The parent-based disability movement has understood this for a long time. Realizing our personal strength as parents has been our major contribution to the international consumer movement. Combining our power has created a number of powerful advocacy organizations and the prototype for other disenfranchised groups.

PLAN has discovered a new type of power, economic power, which has added a critical dimension to our advocacy. We have discovered the economic force of our collective wealth can be useful for furthering a number of our objectives. Here's how.

1   There is a psychological shift when parents and families see themselves as an economic force. Try this the next time you are at a meeting with parents. Mentally calculate the combined assets in the room. What is the total of trust funds? Amount spent on life insurance? Wills? Mortgages? Investments? Then imagine yourself as an economic force negotiating with financial institutions or government officials. Imagine yourself as a potential investor, business partner, or funder attracted to a "market" of this size.

2   Financial institutions begin to view families and our relatives with a disability as a market worth catering to. The competition among financial institutions across North America is fierce. Each institution is trying to retain or increase its share of business. Remember those trillions of dollars being transferred from one generation to the next? Financial institutions are keenly interested in the flow of this money. We are representative of at least 10–15% of the overall market, a sizable share to develop or adapt financial products and services for. By pooling our assets with other families we are in a position to negotiate: for reduced fees for trust and legal services; for increased rates of return on trust fund investment; for having a bundle of financial products and services developed that meet our needs. Imagine, for example, a pooled or consolidated investment fund whereby individual personal trusts for each of our relatives were combined. Very quickly this fund would be in the hundreds of millions of dollars.

We predict that financial institutions will soon discover our economic power and develop products and services for families with disabled relatives as they have in the past for women and people who are retiring. At the very least, our collective economic power should increase the rate of return on invested trust funds and decrease the fees for trust management.

3 We can develop leverage when negotiating with government. Imagine a group of families offering to purchase homes or other supports for their disabled relatives in return for tax concessions or changes in regulations or policy or guarantees of long-term funding. Our willingness to contribute equals respect. Further, imagine the reception you would get if you were accompanied by your new-found corporate partners. Chances are you would be negotiating with treasury finance officials rather than social service bureaucrats.

4 We can develop a diversified funding base for our new organizations. Families will realize the value of independence and direct their charitable dollar your way. In PLAN's case they are also willing to pay fees for services. In addition corporations and foundations will be drawn to the positive self-sufficiency goals of families helping themselves. They will appreciate, and be willing to pay for, a partnership that assists them gain a better understanding of an important new market.

Using our collective wealth is a relatively new phenomenon for our movement but definitely worth exploring.

Creating an organization like PLAN in your community

We were visited recently by a sociology professor from another city. He was at a conference, had heard about us, and dropped by to check us out. He happened to be the father of a young woman with a disability and had been meeting on a more-or-less regular basis with other parents in his community.

These parents had come to the same conclusion as had the parents who formed PLAN. They recognized the inadequacy of service-based solutions and wanted to create something different to guarantee the safety and security of their sons

> Every time we say,
> Let there be! in any form,
> something happens.
> STELLA TERRILL MANN

and daughters. This wonderful visit reminded us of the spontaneous insight families around the world are having – independent yet common beliefs about what is best for their sons and daughters.

We believe this commonalty of perception, diagnosis and solution is no coincidence. It is a reminder yet again of the wisdom of families and of how much we have to share with each other.

Once a new way of thinking and acting picks up a certain critical mass it starts to erupt spontaneously, beyond the boundaries of known communication, and even faster than e-mail. It slips into the collective consciousness. PLAN has simply picked up on a frequency that families everywhere are creating.

We have had the good fortune to be able to organize an association of families to implement these insights. Many of you may want to do the same. If you have completed the previous six steps you will have developed a far more secure future for your relative than most people ever do. You do not have to create an organization. However if you are interested in doing so, here are a few tips to get you started.

- Understand and articulate your core values. Take as much time as you need to describe your beliefs.

- Cherish a bold vision. You are redefining how we care for each other. You are creating a better world for everyone. You are rebuilding community.

- Start with relationships. Build Personal Networks first. Build your organization around these experiences. Often people want to create a formal structure before they begin developing personal supports for their relatives. Resist the temptation. In our experience traditional structures inhibit relationship building. Let the relationships you develop inform the type of organization you want to create. Adapt as you learn what it takes to support individuals and their families.

- Accept that it takes time. Relationships take time and forming the organization will as well. It took us six years to develop the seven-step future planning process you have just read about.

- Respect stories. Statistics, theories and data are for researchers and scientists. The easiest way to keep your integrity and signal your differences is to stay in story-gathering and story-telling mode. That is what community is all about.

- Stay away from government funding. It has undermined too many great people with great ideas and good intentions.

- Keep your organization separate from service providers. A good life is broader than service provision.

- Honor your expertise. Your knowledge of what constitutes a safe and secure future for a person with a disability is worth money to law firms, trust companies, banks and credit unions, financial and estate planners.

- Negotiate bulk rates. Your collective buying power for such products as wills, life insurance, and trust services can lead to discounts, fee reductions and better financial and legal products and services for families.

- Think about forming strategic alliances with other non-profits, with businesses and corporations and perhaps with government. They can distribute your information, make referrals to you, and offer gifts such as free advertising, postage, technical expertise, and money. They can also provide you with a source of income.

- Take risks. The corollary is, you will make mistakes. Sometimes the risk lies in acting in ways non-profits don't traditionally do. For example, we charge a fee for our services. This was startling and shocking to many of us when we started. It took us years to publish our fee structure because we were so embarrassed. Even then the fees were so low we were losing money.

Sometimes the risk lies in doing nothing. The expectations of others can force you to make a decision before you are ready.

- Associate with those who act on their beliefs. Stay away from detractors. When you achieve success you will be surprised at how many people waiting in the wings are willing to join you.

- Stay single-minded. Keep the focus exclusively on developing safe, secure and enriched futures for your relatives.

- Trust your passion. Always. It has worked for us.

Let the beauty of what we love be what we do. There are hundreds of ways to kneel and kiss the ground.
RUMI

Chris

A new life for Chris

Chris lost his speech, use of his arms and legs, and his family all on the same day. He had just turned ten years old and was riding his mountain bike over the rise of a steep embankment. Losing control, he slid onto the freeway and under the wheels of a transport truck.

For the next ten years Chris lived in a children's hospital virtually alone and without visitors. Unbearable sadness mixed with faint hope eroded his family connections.

Fortunately, Chris had an ally in Alisha, a person who recognized Chris's special gifts. She met him while on a student placement at the hospital and formed a deep connection with him. She visited him regularly, long after her placement ended.

Chris is a good-looking young man. Jet-black hair and a winning smile. His eyes compensate for his immobility. They are a window into his thoughts, feelings, soul, and spirit. Expressive and penetrating, his eyes are his sole means of communication.

While Chris appeared unable to communicate and seemed locked inside a fragile and unresponsive body, Alisha and the hospital social worker recognized that Chris was frustrated and bored with his hospital routine.

They worked out a communication method using a simple yes/no signal with his eyes. Gradually a vision of what Chris wanted emerged. He wanted to move out of the hospital and to live with other men his own age. Alisha and the social worker recognized Chris would need a strong advocate to push for a chance at community living. There was a limit to what they could do inside the system. They also recognized Chris would need a group of caring, committed people who would monitor the quality of service he would receive in the community.

They approached PLAN. They knew of our work with families and wondered if we would provide the same support to someone without active family involvement. The hospital social worker had already secured funds from the government-run auto insurance system to finance the development of a Personal Network.

A new life for Chris began to take shape. A PLAN facilitator was hired for his network. A small group home was developed and Chris moved into the community with two roommates.

Chris's current life is unrecognizable from his previous hospital regimen. Members of the Personal Network visit regularly – reading with him, taking him on car rides, and watching football and hockey games on TSN. One of the highlights of Chris's life is the regular pub visit. While Chris doesn't drink he loves the atmosphere – the music, the games, the jokes, the camaraderie.

What makes these outings even more amazing is the level of commitment that has evolved among members of the network. They operate like the sophisticated inner mechanisms of a Swiss watch.

An outing for Chris is no simple matter. He has a tracheotomy and must be fed through a tube in his throat. Members of Chris's network have received training and are qualified to take Chris out on their own. They work as a team to ensure not only that he gets out but also that he is safe and comfortable. Last summer two of them went camping with Chris. Under normal circumstances these two people would not socialize, their personalities being so different. Yet through the miracle of Chris's presence the two arranged their summer vacation together and planned a week of roughing it in the bush.

Chris is no longer an anonymous statistic in a hospital environment. He is surrounded by people who care about him and have committed to a long-term relationship. Regardless of funding cutbacks and changing government priorities, Chris has a backup system – his friends.

Michael

What Michael's mother did

Michael was 50 when his mother died. The house they had lived in for 28 years was sold. Surely his mother could have protected Michael from the trauma of finding a new place to live?

In fact, Michael's mother had planned the future very carefully. Through her will she had directed her house to be sold. The proceeds were to be put into a discretionary trust for Michael. The house was her only asset and had to be sold to create the financial security she wanted for Michael. She had located a reputable trust company sensitive to her wishes for Michael. She was convinced the trust officer of the local credit union would spend the trust monies in Michael's best interests. Besides, she had a backup.

Michael's mother had become a Lifetime Member of PLAN. That meant she consulted with PLAN on every aspect of her future planning. Through PLAN she met other parents facing the same question: "What will happen to my son when I die?" Two years before her death she also asked PLAN to facilitate a Personal Network for Michael, so that he would have a circle of friends. Michael's mother knew she didn't have much time left. She wanted the comfort of seeing Michael surrounded by people who cared about him. She shared her hopes and dreams with them while she still could.

Being a full member of PLAN also meant that Michael's mother could direct PLAN through her will:

- to provide advice to the trustee;
- to maintain Michael's circle of friends;
- to monitor his services and health care; and
- to stay in regular touch with Michael lifelong.

Moving out of the family home wasn't traumatic for Michael. He, his mom, and his network had prepared for two years. The PLAN representative helped Michael find his new place. His circle of friends borrowed the truck, moved his possessions, built his bookcases, and hung his curtains. Even the trust officer got into the act, holding onto the family photographs and eventually placing them into albums with Michael after the move.

That's the backup Michael's mother had in mind when she signed a Lifetime Membership contract with PLAN.

Three steps back, one leap forward

One evening, George's weekly phone call was answered by an unfamiliar voice.

Rick, when he came to the phone, proudly announced he had a new roommate, one who could cook!

Ever since Rick's roommate Bob had moved out George had been concerned about his son's health. Rick wasn't a cook and subsisted on a diet of beans, lots of bread and chips, chips, chips. "When Bob left he took nutrition with him," was George's wry comment.

This new development raised the anxiety meter. Who was this guy? Where did he come from?

PLAN's facilitator received the next call – immediately. As it turned out she had just met Howard, the new roommate. Not wanting to alarm George, she had gone over to check him out first. Not only was there a new roommate but he had moved in a roomful of possessions.

It was time to call an emergency meeting of the network. George came down from the Sunshine Coast.

Rick thought the world of Howard and wanted him to stay. The woman who cleaned Rick's apartment had introduced them. In fact, she was Howard's ex-wife. While suspicious and concerned, the network members decided the best course of action was to keep an eye on the situation. They would let Howard know that Rick was surrounded by people who cared about him. They drafted a schedule and took turns "dropping in." The facilitator was given the task of speaking with Howard privately, to determine his plans, and to clarify when he would start contributing to food and rent.

Howard was charming. Of course he would pay. He was a little down on his luck right now but within a week or two he'd have some money. In the meantime Rick was eating regularly, had companionship, and the place was clean.

The weeks went by and Howard was still not making a financial contribution. The network members sent him a written request on Rick's behalf.

Howard responded by confronting George. Why wasn't he providing Rick with more money? What right did he have to keep Rick's money in a trust? Howard would be talking to the authorities about this! Didn't he know Rick had rights?

It was clear Howard was exploiting Rick – clear to everyone except Rick.

Rick found it hard to accept that his new friend would take advantage of him. We

continued on page 312

continued from page 311

realized later that Howard was threatening Rick. It was a very confusing time for Rick. It became impossible to speak to him alone.

Eventually Rick admitted Howard's shouting was getting to him. "I don't do nothing but he always yells at me. He calls me stupid. He laughs at me."

The letter to vacate the premises was sent immediately. Howard refused to leave. Reluctantly the network asked the police to assist with Howard's eviction. Upon hearing this, Howard left. He then called PLAN complaining about our facilitator and threatening to call the police, accusing Rick of exploiting children. Howard's true colors were showing.

Troubles continued. Howard returned to Rick's apartment and Rick let him in. This cat-and-mouse game continued for a few more days.

Eventually network members changed the locks, arranged for Rick to obtain an unlisted telephone number, and took turns staying overnight with him. They moved Howard's belongings into storage.

In time Rick moved again: once into the basement of a network member and later into a one-bedroom apartment he found for himself.

George was beside himself with guilt. He reproached himself for having moved out of Vancouver. This went on until one day his partner, Marge, challenged him.

"Death is not an option for any of us. This could have happened at any time. In fact you should be grateful it happened now. You've had a ring-side seat to watch Rick's network in action during a crisis."

George could see that Marge was right. The network members were a dream team. They'd had Howard on their radar screen from the moment he landed on Rick's doorstep and in a delicate but firm manner had shadowed his every move. They had kept Rick safe but in a way that preserved his dignity.

Worksheet 15

SECURING YOUR PLAN: SUMMARY CHECKLIST

I have completed all the following documents:

_____ A "family portrait" of my relative.

_____ My letter to the future, clarifying my wishes.

_____ A list of my relative's documents: Supported Decision-Making Agreement, birth certificate, social insurance card, health care card, etc.

_____ An up-to-date will that reflects my current wishes.

_____ A description of the purpose of the discretionary trust.

_____ An up-to-date list of my major assets and where they are kept (insurance policies, bank accounts, stocks, mutual funds, etc.).

_____ I have stored all these documents in a safe place.

_____ My executor knows where these documents are kept.

achieving a *safe* and secure future

I am unable, even at the worst hours,
to abdicate from the belief that the
two validating wonders of mortal existence
are love and the invention of the future tense.

George Steiner

epilogue

Building a house of stone

as you have seen, each step in *A Good Life* builds on the last one. By itself, each step offers greater safety, security and well being than many people with disabilities currently enjoy. However, the steps are interrelated. Taken together, they offer a system of checks and balances that has focus and integrity. They may not be foolproof, but they are thorough. And that's what is needed to replace what parents do now and to provide continuity from one generation to the next.

We urge you to work through each step. Each step builds an architectural structure greater than the sum of its parts. Remember the three little pigs? One thought a house of straw would be sufficient. Focusing on only one of the steps might be the equivalent. We do not believe that will be good enough. Similarly, picking a few steps and combining them will build you a house of sticks. Good until the first time it is really tested. With luck the big bad wolf will never find you. But why let better stand in the way of best? For best results think stone.

The house of stone will take time. It will require discipline and attention. If the wolf hasn't shown up at your door, that's the good news. The bad news is you're running out of time.

But take heart. There is magic and power at work here. Our sons and daughters are the perfect excuse for a whole

> We shall not cease
> from exploration
> And the end of
> all our exploring
> Will be to arrive
> where we started
> And know the place
> for the first time.
>
> T.S. ELIOT

new way of thinking and acting. You will discover this too. What you need to do is begin. Once you do you will witness the transformation of your basic intention into the most beautiful of stone houses, a castle. It's pure alchemy at work.

No one, not even the greatest artists or athletes, let alone those who have been involved in the future planning business for decades, is ever satisfied with their final product or effort. There will always be tinkering and adjusting. That's natural. The difference is you will be amending a plan that is already in place. The hard work will already have been done and the basics will have been covered. Putting turrets on castles is a lot different from building the big thing in the first place.

> It is not the strongest of the species that survives, nor the most intelligent, but the most responsive to change.
>
> CHARLES DARWIN

Summary: The seven steps to a good life

This book has presented seven steps for preparing a Personal Future Plan for the person in your life who has a disability. The brief summary below is for your handy reference.

STEP ONE Sharing your vision

Goal

Describe a vision of a desired future, of a good life, for your family member with a disability, and share it with others.

Your Challenge

Clarifying and sharing your vision before embarking on technical solutions.

Where to Start

- Have a discussion, have several, with your family member who has a disability.
- Complete Worksheet 1, Sharing Your Vision
- Complete Worksheet 2, A Family Portrait

- Complete Worksheet 3, A Letter to the Future
- Complete Worksheet 4, Parent Contract
- Keep going.

STEP TWO Building relationships

Goal

Build a strong network of caring, committed friends and supporters for your relative with a disability.

Your Challenges

- Letting go.
- Asking for help.
- Being open to the involvement of others.
- Believing people will care about your relative.

Where to Start

- Complete Worksheet 5, the Web of Friendship.
- Complete Worksheet 6, the Personal Resource Map.
- Identify caring people who would be willing to become more involved with your relative.
- Think of one thing that you could let someone else do with your relative, and ask them to do it.
- Keep going.

STEP THREE Creating a home
Goal

To develop a home which reflects the personality and lifestyle of your relative with a disability.

Your Challenges

- Rescuing your understanding of home from the limited perspective contained in the human service system's "group home."

- Reflecting more deeply with your family member on the qualities that make a place a home for them.
- Controlling the home environment – creating an opportunity through home ownership or other forms of tenure for your relative to have stability, choice and control.

Where to Start

- Complete Worksheet 7, Welcome Mat.
- Complete Worksheet 8, When is a House a Home?
- Evaluate the current/potential living arrangements of your relative versus the concept of home presented in Step Three.
- Talk with other parents who have created a home environment for their relative.
- Rent first, purchase later.
- Keep going.

STEP FOUR   Making a contribution

Goal

To build an opportunity for your relative to contribute to society and to work in a meaningful way.

Your Challenges

We could never learn
to be brave and patient
if there were only joy
in the world.
HELEN KELLER

- Recognizing the natural gifts of your family member with a disability.
- Liberating their gifts – assisting them to appreciate and value their gifts.
- Developing their gifts – providing them with the necessary skills to enable them to enhance their talents.
- Ensuring their gifts and contributions are given.

Where to Start

- Uncover their passion. Understand the gifts of the head, heart and hands of your relative with a disability.
- Complete Worksheet 9, Passion Pursuits.
- Keep going.

STEP FIVE Ensuring choices

Goal

What's past is prologue.
SHAKESPEARE

To maximize the ability of your relative to make their own health, financial and lifestyle decisions.

Your Challenge

Keeping your relative safe while at the same time respecting their autonomy and not limiting their choices.

Where to Start

- Complete Worksheet 10, Supported Decision Making.
- Discuss the concept of supported decision making with friends and family members.
- Complete a Supported Decision-Making Agreement.
- Keep going.

STEP SIX Developing your will and estate plan

Goal

To develop a will and estate plan which maximizes the wealth available for your relative after you die.

Your Challenges

- Getting started.
- Completing your will. Realizing your will and estate plan may never be perfect.

Where to Start

- Complete Worksheet 11, Your Net Worth
- Complete Worksheet 12, Your Will and Estate Plan
- Complete Worksheet 13, Personal Inventory
- Check with other parents to locate a lawyer who knows about your issues.
- Get a will!
- Keep going.
- Complete Worksheet 14, Your Will and Estate Plan: Summary Checklist

STEP SEVEN Securing your plan

Goal

To build a backup and resource to all the elements of a Personal Future Plan developed for your relative.

Your Challenges

- Staying hopeful amidst prophecies of gloom and doom.
- Finding other families who share your beliefs and are willing to act on them.
- Organizing a group to back up your plans.
- Staying clear of government money.

Where to Start

- Seek out other parents and families who would be willing to create an organization devoted exclusively to ensuring a good life for your relatives with disabilities.
- Complete Worksheet 15, Securing Your Plan: Summary Checklist.
- Rest before you start the cycle again.
- Celebrate!

resources

The following resources provide additional light on the topics in each chapter.

STEP ONE

Whole Child, Whole Parent (New York, Harper Collins, 1987) Polly Berends

An affectionate and practical look at the true nature and vocation of parenting.

PATH: Planning Alternate Tomorrows With Hope (Toronto, Inclusion Press, 1994) Marsha Forest, Jack Pearpoint, and John O'Brien

PATH is a valuable process often used by our facilitators to clarify the vision and identify next steps for Personal Networks described in Step Two. This is one of several references available from three of the most prominent leaders and thinkers in the disability field. Their catalogue of listings and newsmagazine can be obtained by contacting them at:
Inclusion Press
24 Thome Crescent
Toronto, Ontario M6H 2S5
tel (416) 658-5363

The Grim Reader: Writings on Death, Dying and Living On (New York, Doubleday, 1997) Maura Spiegel and Richard Tristman, editors

These enlightening and idiosyncratic pieces offer a fresh encounter with mortality and our fear of death.

Best Boy (Only Child Motion Pictures, New York) Directed by Ira Wohl

An Academy award-winning film and its sequel offer a great story and a great reason for developing a clear vision and sharing it. Ira Wohl is both the filmmaker and the cousin of 'best boy,' a middle aged man leaving home for the first time. Available at libraries and selected video stores.

STEP TWO

A Woman's Book of Life: The Biology, Psychology and Spirituality of the Feminine Life Cycle (New York, Riverhead Books, 1996) Joan Borysenko

A feminine perspective on the power of relationships.

Man's Search for Meaning (Boston, Beacon Press, 1992) Viktor Frankl

A classic book in which the author explores each individual's remarkable qualities and unique potential against the backdrop of his own remarkable life.

Mind Body Health: The Effects of Attitudes, Emotions and Relationships (Massachusetts, Allyn & Bacon, 1996) Brent Hafen, Keith Karren, Kathryn Frandsen and Lee Smith

Solid research that demonstrates the importance of friendship and strong stable relationships for protecting your health.

Clara and Me: The Story of an Unexpected Friendship (Vancouver/Toronto, Whitecap Books, 1996) Deanna Kawatski

A candid and compelling account of the flow of friendship between "two vastly different vessels."

Slow Dance: A Story of Love, Stroke and Disability (Toronto, Vintage Press; Berkeley: Wild Cat Canyon Press, 1998) Bonnie Sherr Klein

This is an amazing book from an award-winning filmmaker who could also be described as an award-winning human being. Her insights are also evident in Step Four.

The Healing Web: Social Networks and Human Survival
(Hanover, University Press of New England, 1986)
Mark Pilisuk and Susan Hillier Parks
   A key reference on social network theory providing an
   intellectual foundation to the work of network building.

Does She Know She's There? (Markam, Fitzhenry &
Whiteside, 1999) Nicola Schaefer
   A fully updated edition that traces a Winnipeg family's
   life-altering and remarkably life-affirming journey with
   their daughter Catherine, who has complex disabilities.
   First published in 1978, this updated edition carries the
   reader through to the fall of 1999 and presents
   Catherine's vibrant spirit and huge capacity for joy.

Yes She Knows She's Here (Toronto, Inclusion Press, 1997)
Nicola Schaefer
   The sequel to the bestseller *Does She Know She's There?*
   and every bit as powerful. Written with wit, love, and
   wisdom.

STEP THREE

Home: The Making of Sanctuary (audiotape, Boulder,
Colorado, Sounds True Audio,1995) Gunilla Norris
   The author is a psychotherapist and the author of several
   books on everyday spirituality and place. Her view of
   home resonates with insight.

The National Home of Your Own Alliance
Institute on Disability
University of New Hampshire
125 Technology Drive
Durham, New Hampshire
U.S.A. 3825
1-800-220-8770 http://alliance.unh.edu
   The alliance shares information and referral resources
   about programs and practices that support home owner-
   ship and person controlled supports for people with

disabilities. Information is available in a variety of formats including Braille, large print, captioned videos, and audiocassette tapes.

STEP FOUR

And Then Came John: The Story of John McGough (video, Telesis Productions, Mendocino, California)
A true story of one man's gifts and contributions and his impact on an entire community. This production honors John, not as an artist with Down syndrome, but as an artist.

The Soul's Code: In Search of Character and Calling (New York, Warner Books, 1996) James Hillman
This author continues to reshape, redefine, and deepen our understanding of the human character. His views on soul and destiny will provide you with a new view on matters formerly taken for granted. A hopeful new vision of the unique genius in everyone, including our relatives with disabilities.

What's Really Worth Doing and How to Do It: A Book for People Who Love Someone Labeled Disabled (Toronto, Inclusion Press, 1994) Judith Snow
Words of wisdom from one of the most influential thinkers in our field.

STEP FIVE

The Diving Bell and the Butterfly (London, Fourth Estate, 1997) Jean-Dominique Bauby
A provocative and deeply moving account of life after a massive stroke when a blinking left eyelid is your only means of communication.

Frames of Mind: The Theory of Multiple Intelligences (New York, Basic Books, 1993) Howard Gardner
Each of Gardner's books deepens our appreciation for the limitations and potential of that enigmatic and elusive term, "intelligence."

The Mismeasure of Man (New York, Norton & Company, 1981) Stephen Jay Gould

This book chronicles the ravages perpetrated on people with mental handicaps as a result of a pseudo-scientific study written in 1913 by Henry Goddard entitled The Kallikak Family. The study was later discovered to be completely fabricated, but not before scientific racism and hereditarian IQ theory had taken hold. The roots of the new unworthiness equation have their roots with Goddard, a self-confessed fraud, and Gould's social history reveals the prejudice at its base.

Crossing the River: Creating a Conceptual Revolution in Community and Disability (Cambridge, Mass., Brookline Books, 1992) David Schwartz

An eloquent description of the paradigm shift required to transform services for people with disabilities.

STEP SIX

Your Money or Your Life: Transforming Your Relationship with Money and Achieving Financial Independence (New York, Penguin Books, 1993) Joe Dominguez and Vicki Robin

A bestseller for years. Thinking about life, work, and money with a new attitude.

Lifelong Security for your Mentally Disabled Child (Toronto, Royal Trust, 1997)

In association with PLAN and the Canadian Special Olympics. Available from PLAN.

STEP SEVEN

The Four-Fold Way: Walking the Paths of the Warrior, Teacher, Healer and Visionary (Harper, San Francisco, 1993) Angeles Arrien

A treasury of practical wisdom for leaders of all persuasions interested in creating new organizations based on new ways of thinking.

*Building Community from the Inside Out: A Path Toward
Finding and Mobilizing a Community's Assets* (Chicago, ACTA
Publications, 1993) John McKnight and John Kretzman
  Practical advice on how to connect isolated and labeled
  people into their neighborhoods, associations, and
  communities.

The Careless Society: Community and Its Counterfeits
(New York, Basic Books, 1995) John McKnight
  Essays by John McKnight on the limitations of human
  services and professional practice and the role of
  community in appreciating and welcoming the gifts of
  everyone.

Who Cares: Rediscovering Community (Colorado, Westview
Press, 1997) David Schwartz
  Another book by a critical theorist and social analyst.
  This one is resplendent with examples of community-
  driven alternatives to the limitations many of us
  experience at the hands of the needs-based social
  service system.

*Making Money While Making a Difference: How to Profit
with a Nonprofit Partner* (Homewood, Illinois, High Tide
Press, 1999) Richard Steckel with Robin Simons, Jeffrey
Simons, and Norman Tanen
  Simply the best book available for non-profit groups
  wanting to develop strategic alliances with the for-profit
  sector. Richard Steckel is an international guru with
  the wit and wisdom to inspire all budding social
  entrepreneurs.

Comments on *A Good Life*

I think the next edition of *A Good Life* should include

_____

_____

_____

The following information needs to be changed in the
next edition:

_____

_____

_____

General comments

I liked

_____

_____

I disliked

_____

_____

For additional copies of *A Good Life* or more information regarding PLAN (Planned
Lifetime Advocacy Network), please visit our web site at:

Web site http://www.plan.ca   *E-mail* planned_lifetime@telus.net

or contact us at

PLAN – Planned Lifetime Advocacy Network
101B – 3790 Canada Way
Burnaby, BC V5G 1G4
Phone 604.439.9566   *Fax* 604.439.7001

Al Etmanski can also be contacted directly at aetmanski@PLAN.ca